# THE NEW FOLGER LIBRARY SHAKESPEARE

Designed to make Shakespeare's great plays available to all readers, the New Folger Library edition of Shakespeare's plays provides accurate texts in modern spelling and punctuation, as well as scene-by-scene action summaries, full explanatory notes, many pictures clarifying Shakespeare's language, and notes recording all significant departures from the early printed versions. Each play is prefaced by a brief introduction, by a guide to reading Shakespeare's language, and by accounts of his life and theater. Each play is followed by an annotated list of further readings and by a "Modern Perspective" written by an expert on that particular play.

Barbara A. Mowat is Director of Research *emerita* at the Folger Shakespeare Library, Consulting Editor of *Shakespeare Quarterly*, and author of *The Dramaturgy of Shakespeare's Romances* and of essays on Shakespeare's plays and their editing.

Paul Werstine is Professor of English in the Graduate School and at King's University College at Western University. He is a general editor of the New Variorum Shakespeare and author of *Early Modern Playhouse Manuscripts and the Editing of Shakespeare*, as well as many papers and essays on the printing and editing of Shakespeare's plays.

# Folger Shakespeare Library

The Folger Shakespeare Library in Washington, D.C., is a privately funded research library dedicated to Shakespeare and the civilization of early modern Europe. It was founded in 1932 by Henry Clay and Emily Jordan Folger, and incorporated as part of Amherst College in Amherst, Massachusetts, one of the nation's oldest liberal arts colleges, from which Henry Folger had graduated in 1879. In addition to its role as the world's preeminent Shakespeare collection and its emergence as a leading center for Renaissance studies, the Folger Shakespeare Library offers a wide array of cultural and educational programs and services for the general public.

EDITORS

**BARBARA A. MOWAT**
*Director of Research emerita*
*Folger Shakespeare Library*

**PAUL WERSTINE**
*Professor of English*
*King's University College at the University of*
*Western Ontario, Canada*

**FOLGER** Shakespeare Library

The Tragedy of

# Romeo and Juliet

By
WILLIAM SHAKESPEARE

Edited by Barbara A. Mowat
and Paul Werstine

An Updated Edition

Simon & Schuster Paperbacks
New York  London  Toronto  Sydney

Simon & Schuster Paperbacks
A Division of Simon & Schuster, Inc.
1230 Avenue of the Americas
New York, NY 10020

Washington Square Press New Folger Edition August 1992
This Simon & Schuster paperback edition December 2011

SIMON & SCHUSTER PAPERBACKS and colophon are registered
trademarks of Simon & Schuster, Inc.

For information about special discounts for bulk purchases,
please contact Simon & Schuster Special Sales at 1-866-506-1949
or business@simonandschuster.com.

The Simon & Schuster Speakers Bureau can bring authors
to your live event. For more information or to book an
event, contact the Simon & Schuster Speakers Bureau at
1-866-248-3049 or visit our website at www.simonspeakers.com.

Manufactured in the United States of America

35  34  33  32

ISBN 978-0-7434-7711-6

# From the Director of the Folger Shakespeare Library

It is hard to imagine a world without Shakespeare. Since their composition four hundred years ago, Shakespeare's plays and poems have traveled the globe, inviting those who see and read his works to make them their own.

Readers of the New Folger Editions are part of this ongoing process of "taking up Shakespeare," finding our own thoughts and feelings in language that strikes us as old or unusual and, for that very reason, new. We still struggle to keep up with a writer who could think a mile a minute, whose words paint pictures that shift like clouds. These expertly edited texts, presented here with accompanying explanatory notes and up-to-date critical essays, are distinctive because of what they do: they allow readers not simply to keep up, but to engage deeply with a writer whose works invite us to think, and think again.

These New Folger Editions of Shakespeare's plays are also special because of where they come from. The Folger Shakespeare Library in Washington, DC, where the Editions are produced, is the single greatest documentary source of Shakespeare's works. An unparalleled collection of early modern books, manuscripts, and artwork connected to Shakespeare, the Folger's holdings have been consulted extensively in the preparation of these texts. The Editions also reflect the expertise gained through the regular performance of Shakespeare's works in the Folger's Elizabethan Theater.

I want to express my deep thanks to editors Barbara Mowat and Paul Werstine for creating these indispensable editions of Shakespeare's works, which incorporate the best of textual scholarship with a richness of commentary that is both inspired and engaging. Readers who want to know more about Shakespeare and his plays can follow the paths these distinguished scholars have tread by visiting the Folger itself, where a range of physical and digital resources (available online) exist to supplement the material in these texts. I commend to you these words, and hope that they inspire.

*Michael Witmore*
Director, Folger Shakespeare Library

# Contents

# Editors' Preface

In recent years, ways of dealing with Shakespeare's texts and with the interpretation of his plays have been undergoing significant change. This edition, while retaining many of the features that have always made the Folger Shakespeare so attractive to the general reader, at the same time reflects these current ways of thinking about Shakespeare. For example, modern readers, actors, and teachers have become interested in the differences between, on the one hand, the early forms in which Shakespeare's plays were first published and, on the other hand, the forms in which editors through the centuries have presented them. In response to this interest, we have based our edition on what we consider the best early printed version of a particular play (explaining our rationale in a section called "An Introduction to This Text") and have marked our changes in the text—unobtrusively, we hope, but in such a way that the curious reader can be aware that a change has been made and can consult the "Textual Notes" to discover what appeared in the early printed version.

Current ways of looking at the plays are reflected in our brief introductions, in many of the commentary notes, in the annotated lists of "Further Reading," and especially in each play's "Modern Perspective," an essay written by an outstanding scholar who brings to the reader his or her fresh assessment of the play in the light of today's interests and concerns.

As in the Folger Library General Reader's Shakespeare, which this edition replaces, we include explanatory notes designed to help make Shakespeare's language clearer to a modern reader, and we place the notes on the page facing the text that they explain. We also follow the earlier edition in including illustrations—of objects, of clothing, of mythological figures—from books and manuscripts in the Folger Library collection. We provide fresh accounts of the life of Shakespeare, of the publishing of his plays, and of the theaters in which his plays were performed, as well as an introduction to the text itself. We also include a section called "Reading Shakespeare's Language," in which we try to help readers learn to "break the code" of Elizabethan poetic language.

For each section of each volume, we are indebted to a host of generous experts and fellow scholars. The "Reading Shakespeare's Language" sections, for example, could not have been written had not Arthur King, of Brigham Young University, and Randal Robinson, author of *Unlocking Shakespeare's Language*, led the way in untangling Shakespearean language puzzles and shared their insights and methodologies generously with us. "Shakespeare's Life" profited by the careful reading given it by S. Schoenbaum; "Shakespeare's Theater" was read and strengthened by Andrew Gurr, John Astington, and William Ingram; and "The Publication of Shakespeare's Plays" is indebted to the comments of Peter W. M. Blayney. We, as editors, take sole responsibility for any errors in our editions.

We are grateful to the authors of the "Modern Perspectives"; to Leeds Barroll and David Bevington for their generous encouragement; to the Huntington and Newberry Libraries for fellowship support; to King's University College for the grants it has provided to Paul Werstine; to the Social Sciences and Humanities Research Council of Canada, which has provided him with Research Time Stipends; to R. J. Shroyer of the University of Western Ontario for essential computer support; and to the Folger Institute's Center for

Shakespeare Studies for its sponsorship of a workshop on "Shakespeare's Texts for Students and Teachers" (funded by the National Endowment for the Humanities and led by Richard Knowles of the University of Wisconsin), a workshop from which we learned an enormous amount about what is wanted by college and high-school teachers of Shakespeare today.

In preparing this preface for the publication of *Romeo and Juliet* in 1992, we wrote: "Our biggest debt is to the Folger Shakespeare Library: to Werner Gundersheimer, Director of the Library, who has made possible our edition; to Jean Miller, the Library's Art Curator, who combed the Library holdings for illustrations, and to Julie Ainsworth, Head of the Photography Department, who carefully photographed them; to Peggy O'Brien, Director of Education, who gave us expert advice about the needs being expressed by Shakespeare teachers and students (and to Martha Christian and other 'master teachers' who used our texts in manuscript in their classrooms); to the staff of the Academic Programs Division, especially Paul Menzer (who drafted 'Further Reading' material), Mary Tonkinson, Lena Cowen Orlin, Molly Haws, and Jessica Hymowitz; and, finally, to the staff of the Library Reading Room, whose patience and support have been invaluable."

As we revise the play for publication in 2011, we add to the above our gratitude to Gail Kern Paster, Director of the Library since 2002, whose interest and support are unfailing (and whose scholarly expertise is an invaluable resource); to Stephen Llano, our production editor at Simon & Schuster, whose expertise, attention to detail, and wisdom are essential to this project; to Deborah Curren-Aquino, who provides extensive editorial and production support; to Alice Falk for her expert copyediting; to Mary Bloodworth and Michael

Poston for their unfailing computer support; and to the staff of the Library's Research Division, especially Christina Certo (whose help is crucial), David Schalkwyk (Director of Research), Mimi Godfrey, Jennifer Rahm, Kathleen Lynch, Carol Brobeck, Owen Williams, Sarah Werner, and Adrienne Schevchuk. Finally, we once again express our thanks to Jean Miller, who continues to unearth wonderful images, and to the ever-supportive staff of the Library Reading Room.

Barbara A. Mowat and Paul Werstine
2011

# Shakespeare's *Romeo and Juliet*

In *Romeo and Juliet*, Shakespeare creates a world of violence and generational conflict in which two young people fall in love and die because of that love. The story is rather extraordinary in that the normal problems faced by young lovers are here so very large. It is not simply that the families of Romeo and Juliet disapprove of the lovers' affection for each other; rather, the Montagues and the Capulets are on opposite sides in a blood feud and are trying to kill each other on the streets of Verona. Every time a member of one of the two families dies in the fight, his relatives demand the blood of his killer. Because of the feud, if Romeo is discovered with Juliet by her family, he will be killed. Once Romeo is banished, the only way that Juliet can avoid being married to someone else is to take a potion that apparently kills her, so that she is buried with the bodies of her slain relatives. In this violent, death-filled world, the movement of the story from love at first sight to the union of the lovers in death seems almost inevitable.

What is so striking about this play is that despite its extraordinary setting (one perhaps reflecting Elizabethan attitudes about hot-blooded Italians), it has become the quintessential story of young love. Because most young lovers feel that they have to overcome giant obstacles in order to be together, because they feel that they would rather die than be kept apart, and especially because the language that Shakespeare gives his young lovers is so exquisite, allowing them to say to each other just what we would all say to a lover if we only knew how, it is easy to respond to this play as if it were about all young lovers rather than about a particular couple in a very unusual world. (When the play was rewritten in

"Two households, both alike in dignity." (Prologue.1)

From Publius Terentius Afer, *Comœdiae* . . . (1496).

the seventeenth century as *The History and Fall of Caius Marius*, the violent setting became that of a particularly discordant period in classical Rome; when Leonard Bernstein and his collaborators [Arthur Laurents and Stephen Sondheim] rewrote the play as *West Side Story*, they chose the violent world of New York street gangs.)

After you have read the play, we invite you to read "A Modern Perspective" on *Romeo and Juliet*, written by Gail Kern Paster, Director of the Folger Shakespeare Library.

# Reading Shakespeare's Language

For many people today, reading Shakespeare's language can be a problem—but it is a problem that can be solved. Those who have studied Latin (or even French or German or Spanish) and those who are used to reading poetry will have little difficulty understanding the language of Shakespeare's poetic drama. Others, however, need to develop the skills of untangling unusual sentence structures and of recognizing and understanding poetic compressions, omissions, and wordplay. And even those skilled in reading unusual sentence structures may have occasional trouble with Shakespeare's words. Four hundred years of "static"—caused by changes in language and in life—intervene between his speaking and our hearing. Most of his immense vocabulary is still in use, but a few of his words are no longer used, and many of his words now have meanings quite different from those they had in the sixteenth century. In the theater, most of these difficulties are solved for us by actors who study the language and articulate it for us so that the essential meaning is heard—or, when combined with stage action, is at least *felt*. When reading on one's own, one must do what each actor does: go over the lines (often with a dictionary close at hand) until the puzzles are solved and the lines yield up their poetry and the characters speak in words and phrases that are, suddenly, rewarding and wonderfully memorable.

## Shakespeare's Words

As you begin to read the opening scenes of a play by Shakespeare, you may notice occasional unfamiliar words. Some are unfamiliar simply because we no longer use them. In the opening scenes of *Romeo and Juliet*, for example, you will find the words *misadventured* (i.e., unlucky), *an* (i.e., if), *marry* (an old oath "by the Virgin Mary," which had by Shakespeare's time become a mere interjection, like "indeed"), and *soft* (an interjection that means "hold," "enough," or "wait a minute"). Words of this kind are explained in notes to the text and will become familiar the more of Shakespeare's plays you read.

In *Romeo and Juliet*, as in all of Shakespeare's writing, more problematic are the words that we still use but that now have different meanings. In the opening scenes of *Romeo and Juliet*, for example, the word *heavy* has the meaning of "sorrowful," the word *envious* is used where we would say "malicious," *sadly* where we would use "gravely" or "seriously," *his* where we would use "its," *happy* where we would say "fortunate," *cousin* where we would say "kinsman," and *still* where we would say "always." Such words will be explained in the notes to the text, but they, too, will become familiar as you continue to read Shakespeare's language.

Some words are strange not because of the "static" introduced by changes in language over the past centuries but because these are words that Shakespeare uses to build a dramatic world that has its own space and time. *Romeo and Juliet*, for example, builds, in its opening scenes, a location that is characterized by specific customs and conflicts. The play creates this sense of place through references to "civil blood," to maskers, to Lammastide, to bucklers, clubs, bills, and partisans. Furthermore, *Romeo and Juliet* introduces us to a poetic language by means of which its characters shape their world. This is the language of love poetry (spread throughout Europe in the sonnets of the fourteenth-century Italian poet Petrarch), which we hear in references to "Dian's wit," to Aurora, to Petrarch himself, to "Cupid's arrow," and "love's weak childish bow." (Gail Kern Paster's essay, "A Modern Perspective," at the back of this edition of *Romeo and Juliet*, discusses the impact that the world of Petrarchan love poetry has on the life and death of the young lovers.) These "local" references create the Verona that Juliet, Romeo, Mercutio, and their fellows and guardians inhabit; it will become increasingly familiar to you as you get further into the play.

## Shakespeare's Sentences

In an English sentence, meaning is dependent on the place given each word. "The dog bit the boy" and "The boy bit the dog" mean very different things, even though the individual words are the same. Because English places such importance on the positions of words in sentences, on the way words are arranged, unusual arrangements can puzzle a reader. Shakespeare frequently shifts his sentences away from "normal" English arrangements—often in order to create the rhythm he seeks, sometimes in order to use a line's poetic rhythm to emphasize a particular word, sometimes to give a character his or her own speech patterns or to allow the character to speak in a special way. When we attend a good performance of the play, the actors will have worked out the sentence structures and will articulate the sentences so that the meaning is clear. When reading the play, we need to do as the actor does: that is, when puzzled by a character's speech, we check to see if words are being presented in an unusual sequence.

Shakespeare often places the verb before the subject

(e.g., instead of "He goes" we find "Goes he"). In the opening scene of *Romeo and Juliet*, when Montague says (1.1.140) "Away from light steals home my heavy son" (instead of "my son steals home"), he is using such a construction; Benvolio does so as well when, at 1.1.110–11, he says, "In the instant *came* / The fiery *Tybalt*," and at 1.2.89–90, when he says, "At this same ancient feast of Capulet's / *Sups* the fair *Rosaline*." Such inversions rarely cause much confusion. More problematic is Shakespeare's frequent placing of the object before the subject and verb (e.g., instead of "I hit him," we might find "Him I hit"). Sampson's line to Gregory (1.1.29), "Me they shall feel," is an example of such an inversion. Montague's "Black and portentous must this humor prove" (1.1.144) is a variant of such a construction, this time with the predicate adjectives "black and portentous" preceding the subject and verb. Paris uses a similar inversion when he says, at 1.2.4, "Of honorable reckoning are you both" (where the "normal" order would be "You are both of honorable reckoning"), as does Capulet at 1.2.26–30, when he says, "Such comfort as do lusty young men feel . . . shall you this night / Inherit at my house" (where the normal order would be "You shall inherit [i.e., receive] such comfort at my house as lusty young men do feel").

Inversions are not the only unusual sentence structures in Shakespeare's language. Often in his sentences words that would normally appear together are separated from each other. (Again, this is often done to create a particular rhythm or to stress a particular word.) Capulet's instruction to Paris to "like her most whose merit most shall be" (1.2.31) separates the subject ("merit") from its verb ("shall be"). Benvolio's lines that begin at 1.1.122—"A troubled mind drove me to walk abroad, / *Where* underneath the grove of sycamore / That westward rooteth from this city side, / So early walking *did I see your son*"—interrupt the normal construction "where I did see your son" by inserting a series of phrases and inverting the subject and part of the verb. The Nurse, in 1.3, interrupts the sequence "weaned upon that day" when she says, "And *she was weaned* (I never shall forget it) / Of all the days of the year, *upon that day*" (26–27). In order to create sentences that seem more like the English of everyday speech, one can rearrange the words, putting together the word clusters ("merit shall be," "where I did see," "she was weaned upon that day"), placing the remaining words in their more familiar order. The result will usually be an increase in clarity but a loss of rhythm or a shift in emphasis.

Locating and rearranging words that "belong together" is especially necessary in passages that separate subjects from verbs and verbs from objects by long delaying or expanding interruptions. When the Prince, at 1.1.91–93, says to the citizens of Verona,

> *Three civil brawls* bred of an airy word
> By thee, old Capulet, and Montague,
> *Have* thrice *disturbed* the quiet of *our streets,*

he uses such an interrupted construction. Romeo uses a similar construction when he says, at 1.4.113-16, "*my mind misgives* [i.e., fears that] / *Some consequence* yet hanging in the stars / *Shall* bitterly *begin* his fearful date [i.e., its dreadful term] / With this night's revels." In some plays (*Hamlet*, for instance), long interrupted sentences play an important part in the play's language. In *Romeo and Juliet*, such constructions are rare, since the sentences in this play tend to be shorter than in most of Shakespeare's plays.

Finally, in *Romeo and Juliet*, as in other of Shakespeare's plays, sentences are sometimes complicated not because of unusual structures or interruptions but because Shakespeare omits words and parts of words that English sentences normally require. (In conversation, we, too, often omit words. We say, "Heard from him yet?" and our hearer supplies the missing "Have you.") Frequent reading of Shakespeare—and of other poets—trains us to supply such missing words. In plays written ten years or so after *Romeo and Juliet*, Shakespeare uses omissions both of verbs and of nouns to great dramatic effect. In *Romeo and Juliet* omissions are few and seem to result from the poet's wish to create regular iambic pentameter lines. At 1.1.107, for instance, Montague asks "were you by?" instead of "were you nearby?" creating a rhythmically regular line. At 1.1.121 ("Peered forth the golden window of the east"), Benvolio, by omitting the word "from" in the phrase "forth from," again creates a regular rhythm. At 1.1.133 he omits the word "one" in the line "And gladly shunned [one] who gladly fled from me," and at 1.2.104 he omits the phrase "that of" from the lines "let there be weighed / Your lady's love against [that of] some other maid."

## Shakespearean Wordplay

Shakespeare plays with language so often and so variously that entire books are written on the topic. Here we will mention only two kinds of wordplay, puns and metaphors. A pun is a play on words that have more than one meaning. The opening scene of *Romeo and Juliet* begins with a whole series of puns: *move* is used to mean "provoke" and then in its more usual sense, and *stand* is used to mean "take a stand" and "stand still," building to Gregory's conclusion that "if thou art moved thou runnest away." In these examples, the dialogue openly reminds us that the words *move* and *stand* have more than one meaning. In other places in this scene, as throughout the play, words are used so that the second meaning is implied but not spelled out. When, to take one of hundreds of examples, at 1.4.17–18 Mercutio says to Romeo, "Borrow Cupid's wings / And soar with them above a common bound," the word *bound* has the primary meaning of "a leap," but the meaning of "a limit" is also suggested. (In the glosses to the text, puns of this sort are often indicated by numbered meanings—e.g., *bound* is glossed as "(1) leap; (2) limit.") Puns are so important in this play that a section of one very crucial scene (3.5) is built around very serious punning as Juliet, on the surface, expresses anger that Romeo has killed her cousin, while, with the same words, she expresses her grief at being separated from Romeo:

JULIET
    God pardon him. I do with all my heart,
    And yet no man like he doth grieve my heart.
LADY CAPULET
    That is because the traitor murderer lives.
JULIET
    Ay, madam, from the reach of these my hands.
    Would none but I might venge my cousin's death!
                         (3.5.87–91)

In these lines, the word *grieve*, for example, is heard by her mother as meaning "incense with anger," but it also means "afflict with longing"; the word *reach* is heard by her mother as meaning "grasp," but it also means "touch." In all of Shakespeare's plays, but especially in *Romeo and Juliet*, one must stay alert to the sounds of words and to the possibility of double meanings.

A metaphor is a play on words in which one object

or idea is expressed as if it were something else, something with which it is said to share common features. For instance, when Romeo meets Juliet at the dance, and says, as he touches her hand (1.5.104–05), "If I profane with my unworthiest hand / This holy shrine," and goes on to talk about their meeting as if he were a pilgrim at the shrine of a saint, he is using metaphoric language. When he sees Juliet through her window and asks, "what light through yonder window breaks?" (2.2.2), he begins a series of metaphors in which he tries to put into words how Juliet looks to him—like the sun, like stars, like a winged messenger of heaven. Metaphors are often used when the idea being conveyed is hard to express, and the speaker is thus given language that helps to carry the idea or the feeling to his or her listener—and to the audience. In Romeo's metaphors of Juliet-as-saint and Juliet-as-light, he uses metaphors from the poetic tradition that attempt to express the overpowering feelings that come with being in love.

## Implied Stage Action

Finally, in reading Shakespeare's plays we should always remember that what we are reading is a performance script. The dialogue is written to be spoken by actors who, at the same time, are moving, gesturing, picking up objects, weeping, shaking their fists. Some stage action is described in what are called "stage directions"; some is suggested within the dialogue itself. We must learn to be alert to such signals as we stage the play in our imaginations. When, in the first scene of *Romeo and Juliet*, Tybalt says, "What, art thou drawn among these heartless hinds? / Turn thee, Benvolio; look upon thy death," it is clear that Benvolio must earlier have drawn his sword, and Benvolio's response to Tybalt, "Put up thy sword," makes it just as clear that Tybalt has drawn his—probably just when he says "Turn thee, Benvolio." When Lady Capulet says, in 1.3, "Nurse, give leave awhile. / We must talk in secret.—Nurse, come back again" (8–9), we can be sure that the Nurse begins to leave; since she soon enters into the conversation, we can be equally sure that she returns as ordered. At several places in *Romeo and Juliet*, signals to the reader are not quite so clear. When Sampson says, at 1.1.34, "My naked weapon is out," one would assume that he has drawn his sword. The dialogue that follows, though, makes it improbable that he is standing there with his sword drawn. Here a director—and you as reader—must decide just what Sampson would do as he says these lines. Equally interesting challenges are offered by the fight scene in which Mercutio is killed, reportedly "under [Romeo's] arm." The text leaves open several possibilities for staging that killing.

It is immensely rewarding to work carefully with Shakespeare's language—with the words, the sentences, the wordplay, and the implied stage action—as readers for the past four centuries have discovered. It may be more pleasurable to attend a good performance of a play—though not everyone has thought so. But the joy of being able to stage a Shakespeare play in one's imagination, to return to passages that continue to yield further meanings (or further questions) the more one reads them—these are pleasures that, for many, rival (or at least augment) those of the performed text, and certainly make it worth considerable effort to "break the code" of Elizabethan poetic drama and let free the remarkable language that makes up a Shakespeare text.

# Shakespeare's Life

Surviving documents that give us glimpses into the life of William Shakespeare show us a playwright, poet, and actor who grew up in the market town of Stratford-upon-Avon, spent his professional life in London, and returned to Stratford a wealthy landowner. He was born in April 1564, died in April 1616, and is buried inside the chancel of Holy Trinity Church in Stratford.

We wish we could know more about the life of the world's greatest dramatist. His plays and poems are testaments to his wide reading—especially to his knowledge of Virgil, Ovid, Plutarch, Holinshed's *Chronicles*, and the Bible—and to his mastery of the English language, but we can only speculate about his education. We know that the King's New School in Stratford-upon-Avon was considered excellent. The school was one of the English "grammar schools" established to educate young men, primarily in Latin grammar and literature. As in other schools of the time, students began their studies at the age of four or five in the attached "petty school," and there learned to read and write in English, studying primarily the catechism from the Book of Common Prayer. After two years in the petty school, students entered the lower form (grade) of the grammar school, where they began the serious study of Latin grammar and Latin texts that would occupy most of the remainder of their school days. (Several Latin texts that Shakespeare used repeatedly in writing his plays and poems were texts that schoolboys memorized and recited.) Latin comedies were introduced early in the lower form; in the upper form, which the boys entered at age ten or eleven, students wrote their own Latin orations and declamations, studied Latin

Title page of a 1573 Latin and Greek catechism for children.
From Alexander Nowell, *Catechismus paruus pueris primum Latine* . . . (1573).

historians and rhetoricians, and began the study of Greek using the Greek New Testament.

Since the records of the Stratford "grammar school" do not survive, we cannot prove that William Shakespeare attended the school; however, every indication (his father's position as an alderman and bailiff of Stratford, the playwright's own knowledge of the Latin classics, scenes in the plays that recall grammar-school experiences—for example, *The Merry Wives of Windsor*, 4.1) suggests that he did. We also lack generally accepted documentation about Shakespeare's life after his schooling ended and his professional life in London began. His marriage in 1582 (at age eighteen) to Anne Hathaway and the subsequent births of his daughter Susanna (1583) and the twins Judith and Hamnet (1585) are recorded, but how he supported himself and where he lived are not known. Nor do we know when and why he left Stratford for the London theatrical world, nor how he rose to be the important figure in that world that he had become by the early 1590s.

We do know that by 1592 he had achieved some prominence in London as both an actor and a playwright. In that year was published a book by the playwright Robert Greene attacking an actor who had the audacity to write blank-verse drama and who was "in his own conceit [i.e., opinion] the only Shake-scene in a country." Since Greene's attack includes a parody of a line from one of Shakespeare's early plays, there is little doubt that it is Shakespeare to whom he refers, a "Shake-scene" who had aroused Greene's fury by successfully competing with university-educated dramatists like Greene himself. It was in 1593 that Shakespeare became a published poet. In that year he published his long narrative poem *Venus and Adonis*; in 1594, he followed it with *The Rape of Lucrece*. Both poems were dedicated to the young earl of South-

ampton (Henry Wriothesley), who may have become
Shakespeare's patron.

It seems no coincidence that Shakespeare wrote
these narrative poems at a time when the theaters were
closed because of the plague, a contagious epidemic disease that devastated the population of London. When
the theaters reopened in 1594, Shakespeare apparently
resumed his double career of actor and playwright and
began his long (and seemingly profitable) service as an
acting-company shareholder. Records for December of
1594 show him to be a leading member of the Lord
Chamberlain's Men. It was this company of actors,
later named the King's Men, for whom he would be a
principal actor, dramatist, and shareholder for the rest
of his career.

So far as we can tell, that career spanned about
twenty years. In the 1590s, he wrote his plays on
English history as well as several comedies and at least
two tragedies (*Titus Andronicus* and *Romeo and Juliet*).
These histories, comedies, and tragedies are the plays
credited to him in 1598 in a work, *Palladis Tamia*, that
in one chapter compares English writers with "Greek,
Latin, and Italian Poets." There the author, Francis
Meres, claims that Shakespeare is comparable to the
Latin dramatists Seneca for tragedy and Plautus for
comedy, and calls him "the most excellent in both kinds
for the stage." He also names him "Mellifluous and
honey-tongued Shakespeare": "I say," writes Meres,
"that the Muses would speak with Shakespeare's fine
filed phrase, if they would speak English." Since Meres
also mentions Shakespeare's "sugared sonnets among
his private friends," it is assumed that many of Shakespeare's sonnets (not published until 1609) were also
written in the 1590s.

In 1599, Shakespeare's company built a theater for
themselves across the river from London, naming it

the Globe. The plays that are considered by many to be Shakespeare's major tragedies (*Hamlet, Othello, King Lear*, and *Macbeth*) were written while the company was resident in this theater, as were such comedies as *Twelfth Night* and *Measure for Measure*. Many of Shakespeare's plays were performed at court (both for Queen Elizabeth I and, after her death in 1603, for King James I), some were presented at the Inns of Court (the residences of London's legal societies), and some were doubtless performed in other towns, at the universities, and at great houses when the King's Men went on tour; otherwise, his plays from 1599 to 1608 were, so far as we know, performed only at the Globe. Between 1608 and 1612, Shakespeare wrote several plays—among them *The Winter's Tale* and *The Tempest*—presumably for the company's new indoor Blackfriars theater, though the plays seem to have been performed also at the Globe and at court. Surviving documents describe a performance of *The Winter's Tale* in 1611 at the Globe, for example, and performances of *The Tempest* in 1611 and 1613 at the royal palace of Whitehall.

Shakespeare wrote very little after 1612, the year in which he probably wrote *King Henry VIII*. (It was at a performance of *Henry VIII* in 1613 that the Globe caught fire and burned to the ground.) Sometime between 1610 and 1613 he seems to have returned to live in Stratford-upon-Avon, where he owned a large house and considerable property, and where his wife and his two daughters and their husbands lived. (His son Hamnet had died in 1596.) During his professional years in London, Shakespeare had presumably derived income from the acting company's profits as well as from his own career as an actor, from the sale of his play manuscripts to the acting company, and, after 1599, from his shares as an owner of the Globe. It was presumably that income, carefully invested in land

Ptolemaic universe. (2.2.17)
From Marcus Manilius, *The sphere of . . .* (1675).

and other property, that made him the wealthy man that surviving documents show him to have become. It is also assumed that William Shakespeare's growing wealth and reputation played some part in inclining the crown, in 1596, to grant John Shakespeare, William's father, the coat of arms that he had so long sought. William Shakespeare died in Stratford on April 23, 1616 (according to the epitaph carved under his bust in Holy Trinity Church) and was buried on April 25. Seven years after his death, his collected plays were published as *Mr. William Shakespeares Comedies, Histories, & Tragedies* (the work now known as the First Folio).

The years in which Shakespeare wrote were among the most exciting in English history. Intellectually, the discovery, translation, and printing of Greek and Roman classics were making available a set of works and worldviews that interacted complexly with Christian texts and beliefs. The result was a questioning, a vital intellectual ferment, that provided energy for the period's amazing dramatic and literary output and that fed directly into Shakespeare's plays. The Ghost in *Hamlet*, for example, is wonderfully complicated in part because he is a figure from Roman tragedy— the spirit of the dead returning to seek revenge—who at the same time inhabits a Christian hell (or purgatory); Hamlet's description of humankind reflects at one moment the Neoplatonic wonderment at mankind ("What a piece of work is a man!") and, at the next, the Christian disparagement of human sinners ("And yet, to me, what is this quintessence of dust?").

As intellectual horizons expanded, so also did geographical and cosmological horizons. New worlds— both North and South America—were explored, and in them were found human beings who lived and worshipped in ways radically different from those of Renaissance Europeans and Englishmen. The universe during these years also seemed to shift and expand. Copernicus had earlier theorized that the earth was not the center of the cosmos but revolved as a planet around the sun. Galileo's telescope, created in 1609, allowed scientists to see that Copernicus had been correct: the universe was not organized with the earth at the center, nor was it so nicely circumscribed as people had, until that time, thought. In terms of expanding horizons, the impact of these discoveries on people's beliefs—religious, scientific, and philosophical—cannot be over-stated.

London, too, rapidly expanded and changed during the years (from the early 1590s to around 1610) that Shakespeare lived there. London—the center of England's government, its economy, its royal court, its overseas trade—was, during these years, becoming an exciting metropolis, drawing to it thousands of new citizens every year. Troubled by overcrowding, by poverty, by recurring epidemics of the plague, London was also a mecca for the wealthy and the aristocratic, and for those who sought advancement at court, or power in government or finance or trade. One hears in Shakespeare's plays the voices of London—the struggles for power, the fear of venereal disease, the language of buying and selling. One hears as well the voices of Stratford-upon-Avon—references to the nearby Forest of Arden, to sheepherding, to small-town gossip, to village fairs and markets. Part of the richness of Shakespeare's work is the influence felt there of the various worlds in which he lived: the world of metropolitan London, the world of small-town and rural England, the world of the theater, and the worlds of craftsmen and shepherds.

That Shakespeare inhabited such worlds we know from surviving London and Stratford documents, as well as from the evidence of the plays and poems themselves. From such records we can sketch the dramatist's life. We know from his works that he was a voracious reader. We know from legal and business documents that he was a multifaceted theater man who became a wealthy landowner. We know a bit about his family life and a fair amount about his legal and financial dealings. Most scholars today depend upon such evidence as they draw their picture of the world's greatest playwright. Such, however, has not always been the case. Until the late eighteenth century, the William Shakespeare who lived in most biographies was the creation of legend and tradition. This was the Shakespeare who was supposedly caught poaching deer at Charlecote, the estate of Sir Thomas Lucy close by Stratford; this was the Shakespeare who fled from Sir Thomas's vengeance and made his way in London by taking care of horses outside a playhouse; this was the Shakespeare who reportedly could barely read, but whose natural gifts were extraordinary, whose father was a butcher who allowed his gifted son sometimes to help in the butcher shop, where William supposedly killed calves "in a high style," making a speech for the occasion. It was this legendary William Shakespeare whose Falstaff (in *1* and *2 Henry IV*) so pleased Queen Elizabeth that she demanded a play about Falstaff in love, and demanded that it be written in fourteen days (hence the existence of *The Merry Wives of Windsor*). It was this legendary Shakespeare who reached the top of his acting career in the roles of the Ghost in *Hamlet* and old Adam in *As You Like It*—and who died of a fever contracted by drinking too hard at "a merry meeting" with the poets Michael Drayton and Ben Jonson. This legendary Shakespeare is a rambunctious, undisciplined man, as attractively "wild" as his plays were seen by earlier generations to be. Unfortunately, there is no trace of evidence to support these wonderful stories.

Perhaps in response to the disreputable Shakespeare of legend—or perhaps in response to the fragmentary and, for some, all-too-ordinary Shakespeare documented by surviving records—some people since the mid-nineteenth century have argued that William Shakespeare could not have written the plays that bear his name. These persons have put forward some dozen names as more likely authors, among them Queen Elizabeth, Sir Francis Bacon, Edward de Vere (earl of Oxford), and Christopher Marlowe. Such attempts to find what for these people is a more believable author of the plays is a tribute to the regard in which the plays are held. Unfortunately for their claims, the documents that exist that provide evidence for the facts of Shakespeare's life tie him inextricably to the body of plays and poems that bear his name. Unlikely as it seems to those who want the works to have been written by an aristocrat, a university graduate, or an "important" person, the plays and poems seem clearly to have been produced by a man from Stratford-upon-Avon with a very good "grammar-school" education and a life of experience in London and in the world of the London theater. How this particular man produced the works that dominate the cultures of much of the world four hundred years after his death is one of life's mysteries—and one that will continue to tease our imaginations as we continue to delight in his plays and poems.

# Shakespeare's Theater

The actors of Shakespeare's time are known to have performed plays in a great variety of locations. They played at court (that is, in the great halls of such royal residences as Whitehall, Hampton Court, and Greenwich); they played in halls at the universities of Oxford and Cambridge, and at the Inns of Court (the residences in London of the legal societies); and they also played in the private houses of great lords and civic officials. Sometimes acting companies went on tour from London into the provinces, often (but not only) when outbreaks of bubonic plague in the capital forced the closing of theaters to reduce the possibility of contagion in crowded audiences. In the provinces the actors usually staged their plays in churches (until around 1600) or in guildhalls. While surviving records show only a handful of occasions when actors played at inns while on tour, London inns were important playing places up until the 1590s.

The building of theaters in London had begun only shortly before Shakespeare wrote his first plays in the 1590s. These theaters were of two kinds: outdoor or public playhouses that could accommodate large numbers of playgoers, and indoor or private theaters for much smaller audiences. What is usually regarded as the first London outdoor public playhouse was called simply the Theatre. James Burbage—the father of Richard Burbage, who was perhaps the most famous actor in Shakespeare's company—built it in 1576 in an area north of the city of London called Shoreditch. Among the more famous of the other public playhouses that capitalized on the new fashion were the Curtain and the Fortune (both also built north of the city), the Rose,

The Globe

A stylized representation of the Globe theater.
From Claes Jansz Visscher, *Londinum florentissima
Britanniae urbs* . . . [c. 1625].

the Swan, the Globe, and the Hope (all located on the Bankside, a region just across the Thames south of the city of London). All these playhouses had to be built outside the jurisdiction of the city of London because many civic officials were hostile to the performance of drama and repeatedly petitioned the royal council to abolish it.

The theaters erected on the Bankside (a region under the authority of the Church of England, whose head was the monarch) shared the neighborhood with houses of prostitution and with the Paris Garden, where the blood sports of bearbaiting and bullbaiting were carried on. There may have been no clear distinction between playhouses and buildings for such sports, for we know that the Hope was used for both plays and baiting and that Philip Henslowe, owner of the Rose and, later, partner in the ownership of the Fortune, was also a partner in a monopoly on baiting. All these forms of entertainment were easily accessible to Londoners by boat across the Thames or over London Bridge.

Evidently Shakespeare's company prospered on the Bankside. They moved there in 1599. Threatened by difficulties in renewing the lease on the land where their first theater (the Theatre) had been built, Shakespeare's company took advantage of the Christmas holiday in 1598 to dismantle the Theatre and transport its timbers across the Thames to the Bankside, where, in 1599, these timbers were used in the building of the Globe. The weather in late December 1598 is recorded as having been especially harsh. It was so cold that the Thames was "nigh [nearly] frozen," and there was heavy snow. Perhaps the weather aided Shakespeare's company in eluding their landlord, the snow hiding their activity and the freezing of the Thames allowing them to slide the timbers across to the Bankside without paying tolls for repeated trips over London

Bridge. Attractive as this narrative is, it remains just
as likely that the heavy snow hampered transport of
the timbers in wagons through the London streets to
the river. It also must be remembered that the Thames
was, according to report, only "nigh frozen" and therefore as impassable as it ever was. Whatever the precise
circumstances of this fascinating event in English theater history, Shakespeare's company was able to begin
playing at their new Globe theater on the Bankside
in 1599. After this theater burned down in 1613 during the staging of Shakespeare's *Henry VIII* (its thatch
roof was set alight by cannon fire called for in performance), Shakespeare's company immediately rebuilt
on the same location. The second Globe seems to
have been a grander structure than its predecessor. It
remained in use until the beginning of the English Civil
War in 1642, when Parliament officially closed the theaters. Soon thereafter it was pulled down.

The public theaters of Shakespeare's time were very
different buildings from our theaters today. First of all,
they were open-air playhouses. As recent excavations of
the Rose and the Globe confirm, some were polygonal
or roughly circular in shape; the Fortune, however, was
square. The most recent estimates of their size put the
diameter of these buildings at 72 feet (the Rose) to 100
feet (the Globe), but we know that they held vast audiences of two or three thousand, who must have been
squeezed together quite tightly. Some of these spectators paid extra to sit or stand in the two or three levels
of roofed galleries that extended, on the upper levels,
all the way around the theater and surrounded an open
space. In this space were the stage and, perhaps, the
tiring house (what we would call dressing rooms), as
well as the so-called yard. In the yard stood the spectators who chose to pay less, the ones whom Hamlet
contemptuously called "groundlings." For a roof they

had only the sky, and so they were exposed to all kinds of weather. They stood on a floor that was sometimes made of mortar and sometimes of ash mixed with the shells of hazelnuts, which, it has recently been discovered, were standard flooring material in the period.

Unlike the yard, the stage itself was covered by a roof. Its ceiling, called "the heavens," is thought to have been elaborately painted to depict the sun, moon, stars, and planets. The exact size of the stage remains hard to determine. We have a single sketch of part of the interior of the Swan. A Dutchman named Johannes de Witt visited this theater around 1596 and sent a sketch of it back to his friend, Arend van Buchel. Because van Buchel found de Witt's letter and sketch of interest, he copied both into a book. It is van Buchel's copy, adapted, it seems, to the shape and size of the page in his book, that survives. In this sketch, the stage appears to be a large rectangular platform that thrusts far out into the yard, perhaps even as far as the center of the circle formed by the surrounding galleries. This drawing, combined with the specifications for the size of the stage in the building contract for the Fortune, has led scholars to conjecture that the stage on which Shakespeare's plays were performed must have measured approximately 43 feet in width and 27 feet in depth, a vast acting area. But the digging up of a large part of the Rose by late-twentieth-century archaeologists has provided evidence of a quite different stage design. The Rose stage was a platform tapered at the corners and much shallower than what seems to be depicted in the van Buchel sketch. Indeed, its measurements seem to be about 37.5 feet across at its widest point and only 15.5 feet deep. Because the surviving indications of stage size and design differ from each other so much, it is possible that the stages in other theaters, like the Theatre, the Curtain, and the Globe

Audience at a play.
From William Alabaster, *Roxana tragaedia* . . . [1632].

(the outdoor playhouses where we know that Shakespeare's plays were performed), were different from those at both the Swan and the Rose.

After about 1608 Shakespeare's plays were staged not only at the Globe but also at an indoor or private playhouse in Blackfriars. This theater had been constructed in 1596 by James Burbage in an upper hall of a former Dominican priory or monastic house. Although Henry VIII had dissolved all English monasteries in the 1530s (shortly after he had founded the Church of England), the area remained under church, rather than hostile civic, control. The hall that Burbage had purchased and renovated was a large one in which Parliament had once met. In the private theater that he constructed, the stage, lit by candles, was built across the narrow end of the hall, with boxes flanking it. The rest of the hall offered seating room only. Because there was no provision for standing room, the largest audience it could hold was less than a thousand, or about a quarter of what the Globe could accommodate. Admission to Blackfriars was correspondingly more expensive. Instead of a penny to stand in the yard at the Globe, it cost a minimum of sixpence to get into Blackfriars. The best seats at the Globe (in the Lords' Room in the gallery above and behind the stage) cost sixpence; but the boxes flanking the stage at Blackfriars were half a crown, or five times sixpence. Some spectators who were particularly interested in displaying themselves paid even more to sit on stools on the Blackfriars stage.

Whether in the outdoor or indoor playhouses, the stages of Shakespeare's time were different from ours. They were not separated from the audience by the dropping of a curtain between acts and scenes. Therefore the playwrights of the time had to find other ways of signaling to the audience that one scene (to be imagined as occurring in one location at a given time) had ended and the next (to be imagined at perhaps a different location at a later time) had begun. The customary way used by Shakespeare and many of his contemporaries was to have everyone on stage exit at the end of one scene and have one or more different characters enter to begin the next. In a few cases, where characters remain onstage from one scene to another, the dialogue or stage action makes the change of location clear, and the characters are generally to be imagined as having moved from one place to another. For example, in *Romeo and Juliet*, Romeo and his friends remain onstage in Act 1 from scene 4 to scene 5, but they are represented as having moved between scenes from the street that leads to Capulet's house into Capulet's house itself. The new location is signaled in part by the appearance onstage of Capulet's servingmen carrying napkins, something they would not take into the streets. Playwrights had to be quite resourceful in the use of hand properties, like the napkin, or in the use of dialogue to specify where the action was taking place in their plays because, in contrast to most of today's theaters, the playhouses of Shakespeare's time did not fill the stage with scenery to make the setting precise. A consequence of this difference was that the playwrights of Shakespeare's time did not have to specify exactly where the action of their plays was set when they did not choose to do so, and much of the action of their plays is tied to no specific place.

Usually Shakespeare's stage is referred to as a "bare stage," to distinguish it from the stages of the last two or three centuries with their elaborate sets. But the stage in Shakespeare's time was not completely bare. Philip Henslowe, owner of the Rose, lists in his inventory of stage properties a rock, three tombs, and two mossy banks. Stage directions in plays of the time also call for such things as thrones (or "states"), banquets (presumably tables with plaster replicas of food on them), and beds and tombs to be pushed onto the stage. Thus the stage often held more than the actors.

The actors did not limit their performing to the stage alone. Occasionally they went beneath the stage, as the Ghost appears to do in the first act of *Hamlet*. From there they could emerge onto the stage through a trapdoor. They could retire behind the hangings across the back of the stage, as, for example, the actor playing Polonius does when he hides behind the arras. Sometimes the hangings could be drawn back during a performance to "discover" one or more actors behind them. When performance required that an actor appear "above," as when Juliet is imagined to stand at the window of her chamber in the famous and misnamed "balcony scene," then the actor probably climbed the stairs to the gallery over the back of the stage and temporarily shared it with some of the spectators. The stage was also provided with ropes and winches so that actors could descend from, and reascend to, the "heavens."

Perhaps the greatest difference between dramatic performances in Shakespeare's time and ours was that in Shakespeare's England the roles of women were played by boys. (Some of these boys grew up to take male roles in their maturity.) There were no women in the acting companies. It had not always been so in the history of the English stage. There are records of women on English stages in the thirteenth and fourteenth centuries, two hundred years before Shakespeare's plays were performed. After the accession of James I in 1603, the queen of England and her ladies took part in entertainments at court called masques, and with the reopening of the theaters in 1660 at the restoration of Charles II, women again took their place on the public stage.

The chief competitors of such acting companies as the one to which Shakespeare belonged and for which he wrote were companies of exclusively boy actors. The competition was most intense in the early 1600s. There were then two principal children's companies: the Children of Paul's (the choirboys from St. Paul's Cathedral, whose private playhouse was near the cathedral); and the Children of the Chapel Royal (the choirboys from the monarch's private chapel, who performed at the Blackfriars theater built by Burbage in 1596). In *Hamlet* Shakespeare writes of "an aerie [nest] of children, little eyases [hawks], that cry out on the top of question and are most tyrannically clapped for 't. These are now the fashion and . . . berattle the common stages [attack the public theaters]." In the long run, the adult actors prevailed. The Children of Paul's dissolved around 1606. By about 1608 the Children of the Chapel Royal had been forced to stop playing at the Blackfriars theater, which was then taken over by the King's Men, Shakespeare's own troupe.

Acting companies and theaters of Shakespeare's time seem to have been organized in various ways. For example, with the building of the Globe, Shakespeare's company apparently managed itself, with the principal actors, Shakespeare among them, having the status of "sharers" and the right to a share in the takings, as well as the responsibility for a part of the expenses. Five of the sharers, including Shakespeare, owned the Globe. As actor, as sharer in an acting company and in ownership of theaters, and as playwright, Shakespeare was about as involved in the theatrical industry as one could imagine. Although Shakespeare and his fellows prospered, their status under the law was conditional upon the protection of powerful patrons. "Common players"—those who did not have patrons or masters—were classed in the language of the law with "vagabonds and sturdy beggars." So the actors had to secure for themselves the official rank of servants of patrons. Among the patrons under whose protection Shakespeare's company worked were the lord chamberlain and, after the accession of King James in 1603, the king himself.

In the early 1990s we seemed on the verge of learning a great deal more about the theaters in which Shakespeare and his contemporaries performed—or, at least, of opening up new questions about them. At that time about 70 percent of the Rose had been excavated, as had about 10 percent of the second Globe, the one built in 1614. It was then hoped that more would become available for study. However, excavation was halted at that point, and while it is not known if or when it will resume at these sites, archaeological discoveries in Shoreditch in 2008 in the vicinity of the Theatre may yield new information about the playhouses of Shakespeare's London.

# The Publication of Shakespeare's Plays

Eighteen of Shakespeare's plays found their way into print during the playwright's lifetime, but there is nothing to suggest that he took any interest in their publication. These eighteen appeared separately in editions in quarto, or, in the case of *Henry VI, Part 3*, octavo format. The quarto pages are not much larger than a modern mass-market paperback book, and the octavo pages are even smaller; these little books were sold unbound for a few pence. The earliest of the quartos that still survive were printed in 1594, the year that both *Titus Andronicus* and a version of the play now called *Henry VI, Part 2* became available. While almost every one of these early quartos displays on its title page the name of the acting company that performed the play, only about half provide the name of the playwright, Shakespeare. The first quarto edition to bear the name Shakespeare on its title page is *Love's Labor's Lost* of 1598. A few of the quartos were popular with the book-buying public of Shakespeare's lifetime; for example, quarto *Richard II* went through five editions between 1597 and 1615. But most of the quartos were far from best sellers; *Love's Labor's Lost* (1598), for instance, was not reprinted in quarto until 1631. After Shakespeare's death, two more of his plays appeared in quarto format: *Othello* in 1622 and *The Two Noble Kinsmen,* coauthored with John Fletcher, in 1634.

In 1623, seven years after Shakespeare's death, *Mr. William Shakespeares Comedies, Histories, & Tragedies* was published. This printing offered readers in a single book thirty-six of the thirty-eight plays now thought

to have been written by Shakespeare, including eighteen that had never been printed before. And it offered
them in a style that was then reserved for serious literature and scholarship. The plays were arranged in
double columns on pages nearly a foot high. This large
page size is called "folio," as opposed to the smaller
"quarto," and the 1623 volume is usually called the
Shakespeare First Folio. It is reputed to have sold for
the lordly price of a pound. (One copy at the Folger
Shakespeare Library is marked fifteen shillings—that
is, three-quarters of a pound.)

In a preface to the First Folio entitled "To the great
Variety of Readers," two of Shakespeare's former fellow actors in the King's Men, John Heminge and Henry
Condell, wrote that they themselves had collected their
dead companion's plays. They suggested that they had
seen his own papers: "we have scarce received from
him a blot in his papers." The title page of the Folio
declared that the plays within it had been printed
"according to the True Original Copies." Comparing the
Folio to the quartos, Heminge and Condell disparaged
the quartos, advising their readers that "before you
were abused with divers stolen and surreptitious copies, maimed, and deformed by the frauds and stealths
of injurious impostors." Many Shakespeareans of the
eighteenth and nineteenth centuries believed Heminge
and Condell and regarded the Folio plays as superior to
anything in the quartos.

Once we begin to examine the Folio plays in detail,
it becomes less easy to take at face value the word
of Heminge and Condell about the superiority of the
Folio texts. For example, of the first nine plays in the
Folio (one-quarter of the entire collection), four were
essentially reprinted from earlier quarto printings that
Heminge and Condell had disparaged, and four have
now been identified as printed from copies written in

the hand of a professional scribe of the 1620s named Ralph Crane; the ninth, *The Comedy of Errors*, was apparently also printed from a manuscript, but one whose origin cannot be readily identified. Evidently, then, eight of the first nine plays in the First Folio were not printed, in spite of what the Folio title page announces, "according to the True Original Copies," or Shakespeare's own papers, and the source of the ninth is unknown. Since today's editors have been forced to treat Heminge and Condell's pronouncements with skepticism, they must choose whether to base their own editions upon quartos or the Folio on grounds other than Heminge and Condell's story of where the quarto and Folio versions originated.

Editors have often fashioned their own narratives to explain what lies behind the quartos and Folio. They have said that Heminge and Condell meant to criticize only a few of the early quartos, the ones that offer much shorter and sometimes quite different, often garbled, versions of plays. Among the examples of these are the 1600 quarto of *Henry V* (the Folio offers a much fuller version) or the 1603 *Hamlet* quarto. (In 1604 a different, much longer form of the play got into print as a quarto.) Early twentieth-century editors speculated that these questionable texts were produced when someone in the audience took notes from the plays' dialogue during performances and then employed "hack poets" to fill out the notes. The poor results were then sold to a publisher and presented in print as Shakespeare's plays. More recently this story has given way to another in which the shorter versions are said to be re-creations from memory of Shakespeare's plays by actors who wanted to stage them in the provinces but lacked manuscript copies. Most of the quartos offer much better texts than these so-called bad quartos. Indeed, in most of the quartos we find texts that are at least equal to or better than what is printed in the Folio. Many Shakespeare enthusiasts persuaded themselves that most of the quartos were set into type directly from Shakespeare's own papers, although there is nothing on which to base this conclusion except the desire for it to be true. Thus speculation continues about how the Shakespeare plays got to be printed. All that we have are the printed texts.

The book collector who was most successful in bringing together copies of the quartos and the First Folio was Henry Clay Folger, founder of the Folger Shakespeare Library in Washington, D.C. While it is estimated that there survive around the world only about 230 copies of the First Folio, Mr. Folger was able to acquire more than seventy-five copies, as well as a large number of fragments, for the library that bears his name. He also amassed a substantial number of quartos. For example, only fourteen copies of the First Quarto of *Love's Labor's Lost* are known to exist, and three are at the Folger Shakespeare Library. As a consequence of Mr. Folger's labors, scholars visiting the Folger Shakespeare Library have been able to learn a great deal about sixteenth- and seventeenth-century printing and, particularly, about the printing of Shakespeare's plays. And Mr. Folger did not stop at the First Folio, but collected many copies of later editions of Shakespeare, beginning with the Second Folio (1632), the Third (1663–64), and the Fourth (1685). Each of these later folios was based on its immediate predecessor and was edited anonymously. The first editor of Shakespeare whose name we know was Nicholas Rowe, whose first edition came out in 1709. Mr. Folger collected this edition and many, many more by Rowe's successors, and the collecting continues.

# An Introduction to This Text

*Romeo and Juliet* was printed in a variety of forms between its earliest appearance in 1597 and its inclusion in the first collection of Shakespeare's plays, the First Folio of 1623.

In 1597 appeared *An Excellent conceited Tragedie of Romeo and Iuliet*, a quarto or pocket-size book that offers a version of the play markedly different from subsequent printings and from the play that most readers know. This version is only about two-thirds the length of later versions. It anticipates the language of these later versions quite closely (except for some apparent cuts) until near the end of Act 2. Then it offers a wedding scene that is radically different from the one in later texts. For the last three acts, the language of the First Quarto varies widely from that of later texts. While the plot is essentially the same, there sometimes is no sign at all of speeches found in later versions; and sometimes speeches appear in much abbreviated forms, which seem to most readers quite awkward in comparison to the fuller versions printed in 1599 and thereafter. This First Quarto has therefore been dubbed a "bad quarto."

In 1599 the Second Quarto, often called the "good quarto," was published. It was entitled *The Most Excellent and lamentable Tragedie, of Romeo and Iuliet. Newly corrected, augmented, and amended.* For the most part, this Second Quarto seems to have been printed from a manuscript containing the fuller version of the play that most readers know. Yet there are also undeniable signs that the printer of the Second Quarto consulted the First Quarto.

# *AN*
# EXCELLENT
## conceited Tragedie
### OF
# Romeo and Iuliet.

As it hath been often (with great applause)
plaid publiquely, by the right Honourable the L. of *Hunsdon*
his Seruants.

### LONDON,
Printed by Iohn Danter.
### 1597

Title page of a 1597 First Quarto of *Romeo and Juliet.*
From the Folger Shakespeare Library collection.

# THE
# MOST EX=
## cellent and lamentable
## Tragedie, of Romeo
### and *Iuliet.*

*Newly corrected, augmented, and*
*amended :*

As it hath bene sundry times publiquely acted, by the
right Honourable the Lord Chamberlaine
his Seruants.

# LONDON
Printed by Thomas Creede, for Cuthbert Burby, and are to
be sold at his shop neare the Exchange.
**1599.**

Title page of a 1599 Second Quarto of *Romeo and Juliet.*
From the Folger Shakespeare Library collection.

Nor arme nor face, ô be some other name
Belonging to a man.
Whats in a name that which we call a rose,
By any other word would smell as sweete,
So *Romeo* would wene he not *Romeo* cald,
Retaine that deare perfection which he owes,
Without that tytle, *Romeo* doffe thy name,
And for thy name which is no part of thee,
Take all my selfe.

  *Ro.* I take thee at thy word:
Call me but loue, and Ile be new baptizde,
Henceforth I neuer will be *Romeo.*

  *Iuli.* What man art thou, that thus beschreend in
So stumblest on my counsell?    (night

  *Ro.* By a name, I know not how to tell thee who I
My name deare saint, is hatefull to my selfe,  ( am:
Becaufe it is an enemie to thee,
Had I it written, I would teare the word.

  *Iuli.* My eares haue yet not drunk a hundred words
Of thy tongus vttering, yet I know the sound.
Art thou not *Romeo*, and a *Mountague?*

  *Ro.* Neither faire maide, if either thee diflike:

  *Iuli.* How camest thou hither, tel me, and wherfore?
The Orchard walls are high and hard to climbe,
And the place death, confidering who thou art,
If any of my kifmen find thee here.

  *Ro.* With loues light wings did I orepearch these
For stonie limits cannot hold loue out,     (walls,
And what loue can do, that dares loue attempt :
Therefore thy kinfmen are no stop to me.

  *Iu.* If they do see thee, they will murther thee.

  *Ro.* Alack there lies more perill in thine eye,
Then twentie of their swords, looke thou but sweete,
And I am proofe against their enmitie.

  *Iuli.* I would not for the world they saw thee here.

*Ro.* I

From the 1599 Second Quarto of *Romeo and Juliet.*
From the Folger Shakespeare Library collection.

# THE TRAGEDIE OF
## ROMEO and IVLIET.

### Actus Primus. Scœna Prima.

*Enter Sampson and Gregory, with Swords and Bucklers, of the House of Capulet.*

**Sampson.**

Gregory : A my word wee'l not carry coales.

*Greg.* No, for then we should be Colliars.

*Samp.* I mean, if we be in choller, wee'l draw.

*Greg.* I, While you liue, draw your necke out o'th Collar.

*Samp.* I strike quickly, being mou'd.

*Greg.* But thou art not quickly mou'd to strike.

*Samp.* A dog of the house of *Mountague*, moues me.

*Greg.* To moue, is to stir: and to be valiant, is to stand: Therefore, if thou art mou'd, thou runst away.

*Samp.* A dogge of that house shall moue me to stand: I will take the wall of any Man or Maid of *Mountagues*.

*Greg.* That shewes thee a weake slaue, for the weakest goes to the wall.

*Samp.* True, and therefore women being the weaker Vessels, are euer thrust to the wall: therefore I will push *Mountagues* men from the wall, and thrust his Maides to the wall. (their men.

*Greg.* The Quarrell is betweene our Masters, and vs their men.

*Samp.* 'Tis all one, I will shew my selfe a tyrant: when I haue fought with the men, I will bee ciuill with the Maids, and cut off their heads.

*Greg.* The heads of the Maids?

*Sam.* I, the heads of the Maids, or their Maiden-heads, Take it in what sense thou wilt.

*Greg.* They must take it in sence, that feele it.

*Samp.* Me they shall feele while I am able to stand: And 'tis knowne I am a pretty peece of flesh.

*Greg.* 'Tis well thou art not Fish : If thou had'st, thou had'st beene poore Iohn. Draw thy Toole, here comes of the House of the *Mountagues*.

*Enter two other Seruingmen.*

*Sam.* My naked weapon is out: quarrell, I wil back thee

*Gre.* How? Turne thy backe, and run.

*Sam.* Feare me not.

*Gre.* No marry : I feare thee.

*Sam.* Let vs take the Law of our sides: let them begin.

*Gr.* I will frowne as I passe by, & let them take it as they list

*Sam.* Nay, as they dare. I wil bite my Thumb at them, which is a disgrace to them, if they beare it.

*Abra.* Do you bite your Thumbe at vs sir?

*Samp.* I do bite my Thumbe, sir.

*Abra.* Do you bite your Thumb at vs, sir?

*Sam.* Is the Law of our side, if I say I?

*Gre.* No.

*Sam.* No sir, I do not bite my Thumbe at you sir: but I bite my Thumbe sir.

*Greg.* Do you quarrell sir?

*Abra.* Quarrell sir? no sir.

*Sam.* If you do sir, I am for you, I serue as good a man (as you

*Abra.* No better?

*Samp.* Well sir.

*Enter Bennolio.*

*Gr.* Say better: here comes one of my masters kinsmen.

*Samp.* Yes, better.

*Abra.* You Lye.

*Samp.* Draw if you be men. *Gregory,* remember thy washing blow.

*They Fight.*

*Ben.* Part Fooles, put vp your Swords, you know not what you do.

*Enter Tibalt.*

*Tyb.* What art thou drawne, among these heartlesse Hindes? Turne thee *Bennolio*, looke vpon thy death.

*Ben.* I do but keepe the peace, put vp thy Sword, Or manage it to part these men with me.

*Tyb.* What draw, and talke of peace? I hate the word As I hate hell, all *Mountagues*, and thee: Haue at thee Coward.

*Fight.*

*Enter three or foure Citizens with Clubs.*

*Offi.* Clubs, Bils, and Partisons, strike, beat them downe Downe with the *Capulets*, downe with the *Mountagues*.

*Enter old Capulet in his Gowne, and his wife.*

*Cap.* What noise is this? Giue me my long Sword ho.

*Wife.* A crutch, a crutch: why call you for a Sword?

*Cap.* My Sword I say : Old *Mountague* is come, And flourishes his Blade in spight of me.

*Enter old Mountague, & his wife.*

*Moun.* Thou villaine *Capulet*. Hold me not, let me go

*2 Wife.* Thou shalt not stir a foote to seeke a Foe.

*Enter Prince Eskales, with his Traine.*

*Prince.* Rebellious Subiects, Enemies to peace, Prophaners of this Neighbor-stained Steele, Will they not heare? What hoe, you Men, you Beasts, That quench the fire of your pernitious Rage, With purple Fountaines issuing from your Veines : On paine of Torture, from those bloody hands Throw your mistemper'd Weapons to the ground, And heare the Sentence of your moued Prince, Three ciuill Broyles, bred of an Ayery word, By thee old *Capulet* and *Mountague*, Haue thrice disturb'd the quiet of our streets, And made *Verona's* ancient Citizens Cast by their Graue beseeming Ornaments, To wield old Partizans, in hands as old,

Cankred

ee 3

For a short stretch (1.2.55–1.3.37), the Second Quarto seems to be no more than a reprint of the First Quarto. In 1609 a Third Quarto was reprinted from the Second.

A Fourth Quarto, undated, was reprinted from the Third. This Fourth Quarto has been dated by Carter Hailey as having been printed in 1623. Its printer appears to have consulted the First Quarto for some corrections and word choices.

The First Folio version appeared in 1623. It reprinted the Third Quarto, but its printer's copy must have been annotated by someone, because the Folio departs from the Third Quarto in ways that seem beyond the capacities of mere typesetters.

Recent editors have been virtually unanimous in their selection of the Second Quarto as the basis for their editions. In the latter half of the twentieth century it was widely assumed that (except for occasional consultation of the First Quarto) the Second Quarto was printed from Shakespeare's own manuscript. In contrast, the First Quarto has been said to reproduce an abridged version put together from memory by actors who had roles in the play as it was performed outside London. Some editors have become so convinced of the truth of such stories about the First Quarto as to depend on it as a record of what was acted. Nevertheless, as today's scholars reexamine the narratives about the origins of the printed texts, we discover that these narratives are based either on questionable evidence or sometimes on none at all, and we become more skeptical about ever identifying how the play assumed the forms in which it came to be printed.

The present edition is based on a fresh examination of the early printed texts rather than upon any modern edition.* It offers readers the text as it was printed in the Second Quarto (except for the passage reprinted in the Second Quarto from the First; there this edition follows the First Quarto). But the present edition offers an *edition* of the Second Quarto because it prints such editorial changes and such readings from other early printed versions as are, in the editors' judgment, needed to repair errors and deficiencies in the Second Quarto. Except for occasional readings and except for the single reprinted passage, this edition ignores the First Quarto because the First Quarto is, for the most part, so widely different from the Second.

For the convenience of the reader, we have modernized the punctuation and the spelling of the Second Quarto. Sometimes we go so far as to modernize certain old forms of words; for example, when *a* means "he," we change it to *he*; we change *mo* to *more*, and *ye* to *you*. It is not our practice in editing any of the plays to modernize words that sound distinctly different from modern forms. For example, when the early printed texts read *sith* or *apricocks* or *porpentine*, we have not modernized to *since, apricots, porcupine.* When the forms *an, and,* or *and if* appear instead of the modern form *if*, we have reduced *and* to *an* but have not changed any of these forms to their modern equivalent, *if.* We also modernize and, where necessary, correct passages in foreign languages, unless an error in the early printed text can be reasonably explained as a joke.

Whenever we change the wording of the Second Quarto or add anything to its stage directions, we mark

---

*We have also consulted the computerized text of the Second Quarto provided by the Text Archive of the Oxford University Computing Centre, to which we are grateful.

the change by enclosing it in superior half-brackets
($\ulcorner$ $\urcorner$). We want our readers to be immediately aware
when we have intervened. (Only when we correct an
obvious typographical error in the Second Quarto does
the change not get marked.) Whenever we change the
Second Quarto's wording or its punctuation so that
meaning changes, we list the change in the textual
notes at the back of the book, even if all we have done
is fix an obvious error.

We correct or regularize a number of the proper
names, as is the usual practice in editions of the play.
"Mountague" becomes "Montague," for example, and
the Prince's name, "Eskales," is printed as "Escalus."
Although neither Lady Montague nor Lady Capulet
receives the honorific title "Lady" in the early printed
versions of the play, the title is traditional in editions
and is consistent with the social relations of the families as these are depicted both in the play and in its
source. Therefore we refer to these characters as "Lady
Montague" and "Lady Capulet."

This edition differs from many earlier ones in its
efforts to aid the reader in imagining the play as a performance. Thus stage directions are written with reference to the stage. For example, we do not describe
Romeo and Juliet at their parting in Act 3 as being
"at the window" (the First Quarto's stage direction)
because there is unlikely to have been an actual window above Shakespeare's stage. Instead, we follow the
Second Quarto and describe them simply as "aloft,"
i.e., in the gallery above the stage.

Whenever it is reasonably certain, in our view, that
a speech is accompanied by a particular action, we
provide a stage direction describing the action. (Occasional exceptions to this rule occur when the action is
so obvious that to add a stage direction would insult
the reader.) Stage directions for the entrance of char-

acters in mid-scene are, with rare exceptions, placed so that they immediately precede the characters' participation in the scene, even though these entrances may appear somewhat earlier in the early printed texts. Whenever we move a stage direction, we record this change in the textual notes. Latin stage directions (e.g., *Exeunt*) are translated into English (e.g., *They exit*).

We expand the often severely abbreviated forms of names used as speech headings in early printed texts into the full names of the characters. We also regularize the speakers' names in speech headings, using only a single designation for each character, even though the early printed texts sometimes use a variety of designations. Variations in the speech headings of the early printed texts are recorded in the textual notes.

In the present edition, as well, we mark with a dash any change of address within a speech, unless a stage direction intervenes. When the *-ed* ending of a word is to be pronounced, we mark it with an accent. Like editors for the last two hundred years and more, we print metrically linked lines in the following way:

BENVOLIO
  Good morrow, cousin.
ROMEO                    Is the day so young?
                                (1.1.163–64)

However, when there are a number of short verse-lines that can be linked in more than one way, we do not, with rare exceptions, indent any of them.

## The Explanatory Notes

The notes that appear on the pages facing the text are designed to provide readers with the help they may need to enjoy the play. Whenever the meaning of a word in the text is not readily accessible in a good contemporary dictionary, we offer the meaning in a note. Sometimes we provide a note even when the relevant meaning is to be found in the dictionary but when the word has acquired since Shakespeare's time other potentially confusing meanings. In our notes, we try to offer modern synonyms for Shakespeare's words. We also try to indicate to the reader the connection between the word in the play and the modern synonym. For example, Shakespeare sometimes uses the word *head* to mean "source," but, for modern readers, there may be no connection evident between these two words. We provide the connection by explaining Shakespeare's usage as follows: "**head:** fountainhead, source." On some occasions, a whole phrase or clause needs explanation. Then we rephrase in our own words the difficult passage, and add at the end synonyms for individual words in the passage. When scholars have been unable to determine the meaning of a word or phrase, we acknowledge the uncertainty. Biblical quotations are from the Geneva Bible (1560), with spelling modernized.

*The Tragedy of*

# ROMEO

### AND

# JULIET

# Characters in the Pl

ROMEO
MONTAGUE, his father
LADY MONTAGUE, his mother
BENVOLIO, their kinsman
ABRAM, a Montague servingman
BALTHASAR, Romeo's servingman

JULIET
CAPULET, her father
LADY CAPULET, her mother
NURSE to Juliet
TYBALT, kinsman to the Capulets
PETRUCHIO, Tybalt's companion
Capulet's Cousin
SAMPSON ⎫
GREGORY ⎬ *servingmen*
PETER ⎭
Other Servingmen

ESCALUS, Prince of Verona
PARIS, the Prince's kinsman and Juliet's suitor
MERCUTIO, the Prince's kinsman and Romeo's friend
Paris' Page

FRIAR LAWRENCE
FRIAR JOHN
APOTHECARY
Three or four Citizens
Three Musicians
Three Watchmen

CHORUS

Attendants, Maskers, Torchbearers, a Boy with a drum,
Gentlemen, Gentlewomen, Tybalt's Page, Servingmen.

*The Tragedy of*

# ROMEO

## AND

# JULIET

ACT 1

0 SD. **Chorus:** a character who addresses the audience, commenting on the action (Here this commentary is in the form of a sonnet.)

1. **dignity:** social position

3. **mutiny:** riot

4. **civil:** of citizens; also (ironically here) civilized

5–6. **From . . . life:** i.e., **from these** warring families were born two ill-fated **lovers   fatal:** fateful; deadly   **star-crossed:** thwarted by fate through the malign influence of the stars

7. **misadventured:** unlucky

11. **but:** except for

12. **two . . . stage:** i.e., the subject of our two-hour performance

"Two households, both alike in dignity." (Prologue.1)
From Publius Terentius Afer, *Comœdiae . . .* (1496).

# THE PROLOGUE

*⌐Enter⌐ Chorus.*

Two households, both alike in dignity
(In fair Verona, where we lay our scene),
From ancient grudge break to new mutiny,
Where civil blood makes civil hands unclean.
From forth the fatal loins of these two foes                    5
A pair of star-crossed lovers take their life;
Whose misadventured piteous overthrows
Doth with their death bury their parents' strife.
The fearful passage of their death-marked love
And the continuance of their parents' rage,                      10
Which, but their children's end, naught could remove,
Is now the two hours' traffic of our stage;
The which, if you with patient ears attend,
What here shall miss, our toil shall strive to mend.
                                        *⌐Chorus exits.⌐*

**1.1**   A street fight breaks out between the Montagues and the Capulets, which is broken up by the ruler of Verona, Prince Escalus. He threatens the Montagues and Capulets with death if they fight again.

A melancholy Romeo enters and is questioned by his cousin Benvolio, who learns that the cause of Romeo's sadness is unrequited love.

---

0 SD. **bucklers:** small shields (See picture, page 10.)

1. **carry coals:** i.e., suffer humiliation patiently

2. **colliers:** carriers of coal

3. **an . . . draw:** if we are angry, we will **draw** our swords

5. **collar:** i.e., the hangman's noose

6. **moved:** provoked

8. **A dog:** i.e., even **a dog**

10. **stand:** i.e., **stand** one's ground

13. **take the wall:** i.e., walk close to **the wall** (forcing others into the middle of the street)

15. **goes to the wall:** proverbial for "is shoved aside"

16–17. **women . . . vessels:** biblical: 1 Peter 3.7 (Here begins a series of sexual puns on **thrust, heads,** and **stand** [lines 17–30].)

20–21. **The quarrel . . . men:** i.e., the maids are not involved

22. **one:** the same

23. **civil:** gentle, humane

# ⌈ACT 1⌉

## ⌈Scene 1⌉

*Enter Sampson and Gregory, with swords and bucklers,*
*of the house of Capulet.*

SAMPSON  Gregory, on my word we'll not carry coals.
GREGORY  No, for then we should be colliers.
SAMPSON  I mean, an we be in choler, we'll draw.
GREGORY  Ay, while you live, draw your neck out of
    collar.                                                                  5
SAMPSON  I strike quickly, being moved.
GREGORY  But thou art not quickly moved to strike.
SAMPSON  A dog of the house of Montague moves me.
GREGORY  To move is to stir, and to be valiant is to
    stand. Therefore if thou art moved thou runn'st      10
    away.
SAMPSON  A dog of that house shall move me to stand. I
    will take the wall of any man or maid of Montague's.
GREGORY  That shows thee a weak slave, for the weak-
    est goes to the wall.                                              15
SAMPSON  'Tis true, and therefore women, being the
    weaker vessels, are ever thrust to the wall. There-
    fore I will push Montague's men from the wall and
    thrust his maids to the wall.
GREGORY  The quarrel is between our masters and us      20
    their men.
SAMPSON  'Tis all one. I will show myself a tyrant.
    When I have fought with the men, I will be civil
    with the maids; I will cut off their heads.

9

27. **what sense:** whatever meaning
28. **take it in sense:** wordplay on **sense** as physical sensation
32. **poor-john:** dried, salted fish, of poor quality; **tool:** sword; **comes:** i.e., come men
37. **Fear:** mistrust
38. **marry:** i.e., indeed; **fear:** am afraid of
39. **take . . . sides:** have the law on our side
42. **list:** please
43. **bite my thumb:** a gesture of defiance

A gentleman with sword and buckler. (1.1.0 SD)
From Cesare Vecellio, *Habiti antichi et moderni* . . . [1598].

IF THEY SAY

GREGORY  The heads of the maids?                                    25

SAMPSON  Ay, the heads of the maids, or their maiden-
heads. Take it in what sense thou wilt.

GREGORY  They must take it ⌜in⌝ sense that feel it.

SAMPSON  Me they shall feel while I am able to stand,
and 'tis known I am a pretty piece of flesh.          30

GREGORY  'Tis well thou art not fish; if thou hadst, thou
hadst been poor-john. Draw thy tool. Here comes
of the house of Montagues.

*Enter ⌜Abram with another Servingman.⌝*

SAMPSON  My naked weapon is out. Quarrel, I will back
thee.                                                            35

GREGORY  How? Turn thy back and run?

SAMPSON  Fear me not.

GREGORY  No, marry. I fear thee!

SAMPSON  Let us take the law of our sides; let them
begin.                                                           40

GREGORY  I will frown as I pass by, and let them take it
as they list.

SAMPSON  Nay, as they dare. I will bite my thumb at
them, which is disgrace to them if they bear it.
⌜*He bites his thumb.*⌝

ABRAM  Do you bite your thumb at us, sir?                           45

SAMPSON  I do bite my thumb, sir.

ABRAM  Do you bite your thumb at us, sir?

SAMPSON, ⌜*aside to Gregory*⌝ Is the law of our side if I
say "Ay"?

GREGORY, ⌜*aside to Sampson*⌝ No.                                   50

SAMPSON  No, sir, I do not bite my thumb at you, sir,
but I bite my thumb, sir.

GREGORY  Do you quarrel, sir?

ABRAM  Quarrel, sir? No, sir.

SAMPSON  But if you do, sir, I am for you. I serve as        55
good a man as you.

ABRAM  No better.

64. **washing:** slashing with great force
67. **heartless hinds:** cowardly servants
70. **manage:** use
73. **Have at thee:** i.e., on guard!
73 SD. **partisans:** long-handled bladed weapons (See picture, page 14.)
74. **Clubs, bills:** a rallying cry to apprentices, who carried heavy staffs or **clubs,** and watchmen, who carried long-handled weapons or **bills**
76. **long sword:** heavy, old-fashioned weapon

Italian citizen in long gown. (1.1.75 SD)
From Cesare Vecellio, *Degli habiti antichi et moderni . . .* (1590).

SAMPSON  Well, sir.

*Enter Benvolio.*

GREGORY, ⌜*aside to Sampson*⌝ Say "better"; here comes
   one of my master's kinsmen.                          60
SAMPSON  Yes, better, sir.
ABRAM  You lie.
SAMPSON  Draw if you be men.—Gregory, remember
   thy washing blow.                    *They fight.*
BENVOLIO  Part, fools!          ⌜*Drawing his sword.*⌝  65
   Put up your swords. You know not what you do.

*Enter Tybalt,* ⌜*drawing his sword.*⌝

TYBALT
   What, art thou drawn among these heartless hinds?
   Turn thee, Benvolio; look upon thy death.
BENVOLIO
   I do but keep the peace. Put up thy sword,
   Or manage it to part these men with me.              70
TYBALT
   What, drawn and talk of peace? I hate the word
   As I hate hell, all Montagues, and thee.
   Have at thee, coward!              ⌜*They fight.*⌝

*Enter three or four Citizens with clubs or partisans.*

⌜CITIZENS⌝
   Clubs, bills, and partisans! Strike! Beat them down!
   Down with the Capulets! Down with the Montagues!  75

*Enter old Capulet in his gown, and his Wife.*

CAPULET
   What noise is this? Give me my long sword, ho!
LADY CAPULET  A crutch, a crutch! Why call you for a
   sword?

*Enter old Montague and his Wife.*

80. **spite:** defiance

84. **Profaners . . . steel:** i.e., you who put weapons to degrading use by shedding your neighbors' blood

87. **purple:** crimson

89. **mistempered:** (1) tempered (hardened) for bad purposes; (2) ill-tempered, angry

90. **movèd:** angry

95. **grave-beseeming:** appropriately sober

97. **Cankered . . . cankered:** rusted . . . virulent

99. **forfeit of the peace:** penalty for disturbing the peace

103. **our:** The prince uses the royal "we."

104. **common:** public

Partisans and other weapons. (1.1.73 SD)
From Louis de Gaya, *A treatise of the arms . . .* (1678).

CAPULET
  My sword, I say. Old Montague is come
  And flourishes his blade in spite of me.                    80

MONTAGUE
  Thou villain Capulet!—Hold me not; let me go.

*Unexpected Rhyme*

LADY MONTAGUE
  Thou shalt not stir one foot to seek a foe.

*Enter Prince Escalus with his train.*

PRINCE
  Rebellious subjects, enemies to peace,
  Profaners of this neighbor-stainèd steel—
  Will they not hear?—What ho! You men, you beasts,          85
  That quench the fire of your pernicious rage
  With purple fountains issuing from your veins:
  On pain of torture, from those bloody hands
  Throw your mistempered weapons to the ground,
  And hear the sentence of your movèd prince.                90
  Three civil brawls bred of an airy word
  By thee, old Capulet, and Montague,
  Have thrice disturbed the quiet of our streets
  And made Verona's ancient citizens
  Cast by their grave-beseeming ornaments                    95
  To wield old partisans in hands as old,
  Cankered with peace, to part your cankered hate.
  If ever you disturb our streets again,
  Your lives shall pay the forfeit of the peace.
  For this time all the rest depart away.                   100
  You, Capulet, shall go along with me,
  And, Montague, come you this afternoon
  To know our farther pleasure in this case,
  To old Free-town, our common judgment-place.
  Once more, on pain of death, all men depart.              105

⌜*All but Montague, Lady Montague,*
*and Benvolio*⌝ *exit.*

*Did they ever know why they are fighting?*

106. **set . . . new abroach:** i.e., stirred up the old **quarrel** anew (literally, started it flowing again)

114. **Who:** i.e., which; **withal:** with it, i.e., with the **sword** (line 111)

116. **on . . . part:** on one side and on the other

117. **either part:** both sides

122. **abroad:** out of doors

124. **That . . . side: that** grows on the west **side** of the **city**

126. **made:** went; **'ware:** aware

128. **affections:** desires

129–30. **Which . . . found:** i.e., **which** wanted **most** to find a place to be alone

132. **Pursued . . . his:** followed **my** own inclination by **not** questioning him about **his**

133. **who:** one **who**

MONTAGUE, ⌜*to Benvolio*⌝
  Who set this ancient quarrel new abroach?
  Speak, nephew, were you by when it began?

BENVOLIO
  Here were the servants of your adversary,
  And yours, close fighting ere I did approach.
  I drew to part them. In the instant came      110
  The fiery Tybalt with his sword prepared,
  Which, as he breathed defiance to my ears,
  He swung about his head and cut the winds,
  Who, nothing hurt withal, hissed him in scorn.
  While we were interchanging thrusts and blows    115
  Came more and more and fought on part and part,
  Till the Prince came, who parted either part.

LADY MONTAGUE
  O, where is Romeo? Saw you him today?
  Right glad I am he was not at this fray.

BENVOLIO
  Madam, an hour before the worshiped sun      120
  Peered forth the golden window of the east,
  A troubled mind ⌜drove⌝ me to walk abroad,
  Where underneath the grove of sycamore
  That westward rooteth from this city side,
  So early walking did I see your son.      125
  Towards him I made, but he was 'ware of me
  And stole into the covert of the wood.
  I, measuring his affections by my own
  (Which then most sought where most might not be
     found,      130
  Being one too many by my weary self),
  Pursued my humor, not pursuing his,
  And gladly shunned who gladly fled from me.

MONTAGUE
  Many a morning hath he there been seen,
  With tears augmenting the fresh morning's dew,    135
  Adding to clouds more clouds with his deep sighs.

137. **all so soon:** just as **soon**
139. **Aurora's:** Aurora is goddess of the dawn.
140. **heavy:** sorrowful
144. **humor:** state of mind
148. **importuned:** questioned (accent on second syllable)
151. **Is . . . true:** i.e., **is** perhaps **not** being **true** or faithful **to himself**
152. **close:** synonymous with **secret**
153. **sounding:** being sounded or searched into
154. **envious:** malicious; **worm:** cankerworm, a caterpillar that destroys buds (See picture, below.)
155. **he:** i.e., it; **his:** its; **leaves:** petals
160. **his grievance:** the cause of his distress
161. **happy:** fortunate
162. **shrift:** confession

A cankerworm. (1.1.154; 2.3.31)
From John Johnstone, *Opera aliquot . . .* (1650–62).

But all so soon as the all-cheering sun
Should in the farthest east begin to draw
The shady curtains from Aurora's bed,
Away from light steals home my heavy son          140
And private in his chamber pens himself,
Shuts up his windows, locks fair daylight out,          *Relate to*
And makes himself an artificial night.          *love issue?*
Black and portentous must this humor prove,
Unless good counsel may the cause remove.          145

BENVOLIO
My noble uncle, do you know the cause?

MONTAGUE
I neither know it nor can learn of him.

BENVOLIO
Have you importuned him by any means?

MONTAGUE
Both by myself and many other friends.
But he, ⌜his⌝ own affections' counselor,          150
Is to himself—I will not say how true,
But to himself so secret and so close,
So far from sounding and discovery,
As is the bud bit with an envious worm
Ere he can spread his sweet leaves to the air          155
Or dedicate his beauty to the same.
Could we but learn from whence his sorrows grow,          *Rhyme*
We would as willingly give cure as know.

*Enter Romeo.*

BENVOLIO
See where he comes. So please you, step aside.
I'll know his grievance or be much denied.          160

MONTAGUE
I would thou wert so happy by thy stay
To hear true shrift.—Come, madam, let's away.
                    ⌜*Montague and Lady Montague*⌝ *exit.*

163. **morrow:** morning
174. **view:** appearance
175. **in proof:** in our experience of it
176. **love . . . still:** Cupid, god of **love,** is often pictured with his eyes blindfolded. (See picture, below.) **view:** ability to see **still:** always
177. **his will:** his purposes
182. **create:** created
183. **vanity:** foolishness
184. **well-seeming:** attractive in appearance
186. **Still-waking:** always wakeful
189. **coz:** cousin

A blindfolded Cupid. (1.1.176; 1.4.4)
From Henry Peacham, *Minerua Britanna* . . . [1612].

**BENVOLIO**
 Good morrow, cousin.

**ROMEO**      Is the day so young?

**BENVOLIO**
 But new struck nine.         165

**ROMEO**     Ay me, sad hours seem long.
 Was that my father that went hence so fast?

**BENVOLIO**
 It was. What sadness lengthens Romeo's hours?

**ROMEO**
 Not having that which, having, makes them short.

**BENVOLIO** In love?          170

**ROMEO** Out—

**BENVOLIO** Of love?

**ROMEO**
 Out of her favor where I am in love.

**BENVOLIO**
 Alas that love, so gentle in his view,
 Should be so tyrannous and rough in proof!  175

**ROMEO**
 Alas that love, whose view is muffled still,
 Should without eyes see pathways to his will!
 Where shall we dine?—O me! What fray was here?
 Yet tell me not, for I have heard it all.
 Here's much to do with hate, but more with love. 180
 Why then, O brawling love, O loving hate,
 O anything of nothing first ⌈create!⌉
 O heavy lightness, serious vanity,
 Misshapen chaos of ⌈well-seeming⌉ forms,
 Feather of lead, bright smoke, cold fire, sick health, 185
 Still-waking sleep that is not what it is!
 This love feel I, that feel no love in this.
 Dost thou not laugh?

**BENVOLIO**    No, coz, I rather weep.

**ROMEO**
 Good heart, at what?         190

**193–95. Griefs ... thine:** i.e., you increase the weight of grief **in my breast** by adding your own **griefs** to it (The words **propagate, breast,** and **pressed** lend Romeo's words a sexual implication, as if the new **griefs** are bred upon his existing **griefs.**)

**198. Being purged:** i.e., **love, being purged,** is (The image is of the **smoke** of **love being** cleansed of impurities.)

**200. discreet:** judicious

**203. Soft:** i.e., wait

**204. An if:** if

**207. in sadness:** seriously (Romeo responds [line 208] as if **in sadness** meant "sadly" or "mournfully." The wordplay continues in lines 209–12.)

**211. ill urged to:** unkindly pressed upon

**215. fair mark:** target plainly in sight

**217. Cupid's arrow:** See picture, below. **Dian's wit:** the wisdom of Diana, goddess of chastity, who was opposed to love and marriage

**218. proof:** i.e., well-tested armor

Cupid shooting an arrow. (1.1.217)
From Francesco Petrarca, *Opera* ... [1508].

BENVOLIO                    At thy good heart's oppression.
ROMEO  Why, such is love's transgression.
  Griefs of mine own lie heavy in my breast,
  Which thou wilt propagate to have it pressed
  With more of thine. This love that thou hast shown        195
  Doth add more grief to too much of mine own.
  Love is a smoke made with the fume of sighs;
  Being purged, a fire sparkling in lovers' eyes;
  Being vexed, a sea nourished with loving tears.
  What is it else? A madness most discreet,                 200
  A choking gall, and a preserving sweet.
  Farewell, my coz.
BENVOLIO              Soft, I will go along.
  An if you leave me so, you do me wrong.
ROMEO
  Tut, I have lost myself. I am not here.                   205
  This is not Romeo. He's some other where.
BENVOLIO
  Tell me in sadness, who is that you love?
ROMEO  What, shall I groan and tell thee?
BENVOLIO
  Groan? Why, no. But sadly tell me who.
ROMEO
  A sick man in sadness makes his will—                     210
  A word ill urged to one that is so ill.
  In sadness, cousin, I do love a woman.
BENVOLIO
  I aimed so near when I supposed you loved.
ROMEO
  A right good markman! And she's fair I love.
BENVOLIO
  A right fair mark, fair coz, is soonest hit.              215
ROMEO
  Well in that hit you miss. She'll not be hit
  With Cupid's arrow. She hath Dian's wit,
  And, in strong proof of chastity well armed,

219. **uncharmed:** i.e., not subject to (**love's**) spell

224. **with . . . store: Beauty dies when she** does, and so does beauty's **store**, the reserve of **beauty** that has been deposited with her so that she may bestow it upon her offspring.

225. **still:** always

226. **sparing:** refusal to marry

229. **fair . . . fair:** beautiful . . . just

231. **forsworn to:** sworn not to

238. **To . . . more:** i.e., **to** force me to dwell even **more** upon her **exquisite** beauty

243. **a mistress:** any woman; **passing:** surpassingly

244. **but as a note:** except **as a** marginal **note**

245. **who:** i.e., the one **who; passed:** surpassed

247. **I'll . . . debt:** i.e., I will **teach** you **to forget** or **die** in the attempt

Italian lady in a mask. (1.1.239)
From Cesare Vecellio, *Degli habiti antichi et moderni . . .* (1590).

From love's weak childish bow she lives uncharmed.
She will not stay the siege of loving terms,          220
Nor bide th' encounter of assailing eyes,
Nor ope her lap to saint-seducing gold.
O, she is rich in beauty, only poor
That, when she dies, with beauty dies her store.

BENVOLIO
Then she hath sworn that she will still live chaste?   225

ROMEO
She hath, and in that sparing ⌜makes⌝ huge waste;
For beauty, starved with her severity,
Cuts beauty off from all posterity.
She is too fair, too wise, wisely too fair,
To merit bliss by making me despair.                  230
She hath forsworn to love, and in that vow
Do I live dead, that live to tell it now.

BENVOLIO
Be ruled by me. Forget to think of her.

ROMEO
O, teach me how I should forget to think!

BENVOLIO
By giving liberty unto thine eyes.                    235
Examine other beauties.

ROMEO                        'Tis the way
To call hers, exquisite, in question more.
These happy masks that kiss fair ladies' brows,
Being black, puts us in mind they hide the fair.      240
He that is strucken blind cannot forget
The precious treasure of his eyesight lost.
Show me a mistress that is passing fair;
What doth her beauty serve but as a note
Where I may read who passed that passing fair?        245
Farewell. Thou canst not teach me to forget.

BENVOLIO
I'll pay that doctrine or else die in debt.

                                        *They exit.*

**1.2** In conversation with Capulet, Count Paris declares his wish to marry Juliet. Capulet invites him to a party that night.

Capulet gives a servant the guest list for the party and orders him off to issue invitations. The servant cannot read the list and asks for help from Romeo and Benvolio. When they find out that Rosaline, on whom Romeo dotes, is invited to the party, they decide to go too.

———————

0 SD. **County:** Count

1. **bound:** under bond to keep the peace

4. **reckoning:** reputation

7. **o'er:** over again

15. **hopeful lady of my earth:** perhaps, the only surviving child of my body, and thus my only heir **earth:** body; or, land and possessions

18. **agreed:** i.e., consenting

18–19. **within . . . voice:** i.e., I will consent to her marrying only someone she has chosen herself **fair:** favorable **according:** assenting

20. **accustomed:** customary

22–23. **and . . . number more:** Capulet invites and welcomes Paris to be **one more** guest among the great many already invited. **store:** abundance

26. **lusty:** vigorous

⌜Scene 2⌝

*Enter Capulet, County Paris, and* ⌜*a Servingman.*⌝

CAPULET
But Montague is bound as well as I,
In penalty alike, and 'tis not hard, I think,
For men so old as we to keep the peace.

PARIS
Of honorable reckoning are you both,
And pity 'tis you lived at odds so long.            5
But now, my lord, what say you to my suit?

CAPULET
But saying o'er what I have said before.
My child is yet a stranger in the world.
She hath not seen the change of fourteen years.
Let two more summers wither in their pride        10
Ere we may think her ripe to be a bride.

PARIS
Younger than she are happy mothers made.

CAPULET
And too soon marred are those so early made.
Earth hath swallowed all my hopes but she;
She's the hopeful lady of my earth.               15
But woo her, gentle Paris, get her heart;
My will to her consent is but a part.
And, she agreed, within her scope of choice
Lies my consent and fair according voice.
This night I hold an old accustomed feast,        20
Whereto I have invited many a guest
Such as I love; and you among the store,
One more, most welcome, makes my number more.
At my poor house look to behold this night
Earth-treading stars that make dark heaven light. 25
Such comfort as do lusty young men feel
When well-appareled April on the heel
Of limping winter treads, even such delight

29. **fennel:** herb believed to inspire passion (See picture, page 30.)

30. **Inherit:** receive

32–33. **Which . . . none:** i.e., when you gaze upon the women present, you may find my daughter to be merely one of the crowd   **reck'ning:** reckoning, distinction, estimation

35. **sirrah:** term of address to a social inferior

41. **meddle:** busy himself; **yard:** yardstick; **last:** model of the foot

42. **pencil:** artist's paintbrush

46. **In good time:** at just the right moment

48. **another's anguish:** another pain's **anguish**

50. **another's:** i.e., another grief's

52. **rank:** virulent

53. **Your plantain leaf:** a **leaf** used to staunch bleeding (**Your** is impersonal, meaning "the" or "a.") See picture, below.

55. **your broken shin:** a cut **shin**

57. **bound:** in bonds, imprisoned

Plantain. (1.2.53)
From John Gerard, *The herball . . .* (1597).

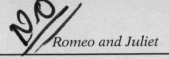
Among fresh fennel buds shall you this night
Inherit at my house. Hear all, all see,                                    30
And like her most whose merit most shall be;
Which, on more view of many, mine, being one,
May stand in number, though in reck'ning none.
Come go with me. ⌜*To Servingman, giving him a list.*⌝
            Go, sirrah, trudge about                    35
Through fair Verona, find those persons out
Whose names are written there, and to them say
My house and welcome on their pleasure stay.
              ⌜*Capulet and Paris*⌝ *exit.*

SERVINGMAN  Find them out whose names are written
    here! It is written that the shoemaker should           40
    meddle with his yard and the tailor with his last, the
    fisher with his pencil and the painter with his nets.
    But I am sent to find those persons whose names
    are here writ, and can never find what names the
    writing person hath here writ. I must to the learned.  45
    In good time!

           *Enter Benvolio and Romeo.*

BENVOLIO, ⌜*to Romeo*⌝
Tut, man, one fire burns out another's burning;
One pain is lessened by another's anguish.
Turn giddy, and be helped by backward turning.
One desperate grief cures with another's languish.      50
Take thou some new infection to thy eye,
And the rank poison of the old will die.

ROMEO
Your plantain leaf is excellent for that.

BENVOLIO
For what, I pray thee?

ROMEO            For your broken shin.               55

BENVOLIO  Why Romeo, art thou mad?

ROMEO
Not mad, but bound more than a madman is,

59. **e'en:** evening (i.e., afternoon)
61. **God . . . e'en: God** give you **good** afternoon
64–65. **without book:** by memory, by rote
67. **Rest you merry:** i.e., good-bye
87. **crush:** i.e., drink
89. **ancient:** traditional

Fennel. (1.2.29)
From John Gerard, *The herball* . . . (1597).

Shut up in prison, kept without my food,
Whipped and tormented, and—good e'en, good
  fellow.                                                    60
SERVINGMAN  God gi' good e'en. I pray, sir, can you
  read?
ROMEO
  Ay, mine own fortune in my misery.
SERVINGMAN  Perhaps you have learned it without
  book. But I pray, can you read anything you see?          65
ROMEO
  Ay, if I know the letters and the language.
SERVINGMAN  You say honestly. Rest you merry.
ROMEO  Stay, fellow. I can read.     *(He reads the letter.)*
  *Signior Martino and his wife and daughters,*
  *County Anselme and his beauteous sisters,*               70
  *The lady widow of Vitruvio,*
  *Signior Placentio and his lovely nieces,*
  *Mercutio and his brother Valentine,*
  *Mine Uncle Capulet, his wife and daughters,*
  *My fair niece Rosaline and Livia,*                       75
  *Signior Valentio and his cousin Tybalt,*
  *Lucio and the lively Helena.*
  A fair assembly. Whither should they come?
SERVINGMAN  Up.
ROMEO  Whither? To supper?                                  80
SERVINGMAN  To our house.
ROMEO  Whose house?
SERVINGMAN  My master's.
ROMEO
  Indeed I should have asked thee that before.
SERVINGMAN  Now I'll tell you without asking. My          85
  master is the great rich Capulet, and, if you be not
  of the house of Montagues, I pray come and crush a
  cup of wine. Rest you merry.          ⌐*He exits.*⌐
BENVOLIO
  At this same ancient feast of Capulet's

92. **unattainted:** impartial
97. **these who:** i.e., **these** eyes which
101. **fair:** i.e., to be beautiful
102. **poised:** weighed
103. **scales:** i.e., Romeo's eyes (**Scales** is treated as a singular noun.) See picture, below.
104. **maid:** maiden
106. **scant:** scarcely
108. **mine own:** i.e., the **sight of** my love, Rosaline

**1.3** Lady Capulet informs Juliet of Paris's marriage proposal and praises him extravagantly. Juliet says that she has not even dreamed of marrying, but that she will consider Paris as a possible husband if her parents wish her to.

———————

3. **What:** an interjection, here perhaps suggesting impatience; **ladybird:** sweetheart

Scales. (1.2.103)
From Silvestro Pietrasanta, . . . *Symbola heroica* . . . (1682).

Sups the fair Rosaline whom thou so loves,                    90
With all the admired beauties of Verona.
Go thither, and with unattainted eye
Compare her face with some that I shall show,
And I will make thee think thy swan a crow.

ROMEO
When the devout religion of mine eye                          95
Maintains such falsehood, then turn tears to fire;
And these who, often drowned, could never die,
Transparent heretics, be burnt for liars.
One fairer than my love? The all-seeing sun
Ne'er saw her match since first the world begun.             100

BENVOLIO
Tut, you saw her fair, none else being by,
Herself poised with herself in either eye;
But in that crystal scales let there be weighed
Your lady's love against some other maid
That I will show you shining at this feast,                  105
And she shall scant show well that now seems best.

ROMEO
I'll go along, no such sight to be shown,
But to rejoice in splendor of mine own.

⌜*They exit.*⌝

⌜Scene 3⌝

*Enter* ⌜*Lady Capulet*⌝ *and Nurse.*

LADY CAPULET
Nurse, where's my daughter? Call her forth to me.

NURSE
Now, by my maidenhead at twelve year old,
I bade her come.—What, lamb! What, ladybird!
God forbid. Where's this girl? What, Juliet!

*Enter Juliet.*

5. **How now:** an exclamation, here expressing, perhaps, surprise

8. **give leave:** i.e., excuse us

10. **thou's:** thou shalt

14. **teen:** suffering

16. **Lammastide:** August 1 is Lammas Day. **Lammastide** (i.e., Lammas time) may refer either to that day or to the time around it. **Lammas Eve** [line 19] is July 31.

17. **odd:** a few

24. **Marry:** a mild interjection (originally, an oath "by the Virgin Mary")

28. **wormwood:** a bitter-tasting plant; **dug:** breast

33. **fool:** term of endearment

34. **fall out with:** become irritated with

35. **"Shake" . . . dovehouse:** i.e., **the dovehouse** shook with the earthquake **quoth:** said

35–36. **I trow:** an exclamation meaning "I'm sure" or "I believe"

JULIET  How now, who calls?        5

NURSE  Your mother.

JULIET
  Madam, I am here. What is your will?

LADY CAPULET
  This is the matter.—Nurse, give leave awhile.
  We must talk in secret.—Nurse, come back again.
  I have remembered me, thou's hear our counsel.    10
  Thou knowest my daughter's of a pretty age.

NURSE
  Faith, I can tell her age unto ⌜an⌝ hour.

LADY CAPULET  She's not fourteen.

NURSE  I'll lay fourteen of my teeth (and yet, to my teen
    be it spoken, I have but four) she's not fourteen.  15
    How long is it now to Lammastide?

LADY CAPULET  A fortnight and odd days.

NURSE
  Even or odd, of all days in the year,
  Come Lammas Eve at night shall she be fourteen.
  Susan and she (God rest all Christian souls!)    20
  Were of an age. Well, Susan is with God;
  She was too good for me. But, as I said,
  On Lammas Eve at night shall she be fourteen.
  That shall she. Marry, I remember it well.
  'Tis since the earthquake now eleven years,    25
  And she was weaned (I never shall forget it)
  Of all the days of the year, upon that day.
  For I had then laid wormwood to my dug,
  Sitting in the sun under the dovehouse wall.
  My lord and you were then at Mantua.    30
  Nay, I do bear a brain. But, as I said,
  When it did taste the wormwood on the nipple
  Of my dug and felt it bitter, pretty fool,
  To see it tetchy and fall out with ⌜the⌝ dug.
  "Shake," quoth the dovehouse. 'Twas no need, I    35
    trow,

39. **high-lone:** i.e., by herself
39–40. **by th' rood:** a mild oath   **rood:** cross
42. **even:** just; **broke her brow:** cut her forehead
47. **by my holidam:** a mild oath   **holidam:** presumably "holy dame" (Mary)
50. **an:** if
53. **stinted:** quit (crying)
58. **stone:** testicle
66. **once:** one day

To bid me trudge.
And since that time it is eleven years.
For then she could stand high-lone. Nay, by th'
 rood,            40
She could have run and waddled all about,
For even the day before, she broke her brow,
And then my husband (God be with his soul,
He was a merry man) took up the child.
"Yea," quoth he, "Dost thou fall upon thy face? 45
Thou wilt fall backward when thou hast more wit,
Wilt thou not, Jule?" And, by my holidam,
The pretty wretch left crying and said "Ay."
To see now how a jest shall come about!
I warrant, an I should live a thousand years, 50
I never should forget it. "Wilt thou not, Jule?"
 quoth he.
And, pretty fool, it stinted and said "Ay."

**LADY CAPULET**
Enough of this. I pray thee, hold thy peace.

**NURSE**
Yes, madam, yet I cannot choose but laugh 55
To think it should leave crying and say "Ay."
And yet, I warrant, it had upon its brow
A bump as big as a young cock'rel's stone,
A perilous knock, and it cried bitterly.
"Yea," quoth my husband. "Fall'st upon thy face? 60
Thou wilt fall backward when thou comest to age,
Wilt thou not, Jule?" It stinted and said "Ay."

**JULIET**
And stint thou, too, I pray thee, nurse, say I.

**NURSE**
Peace. I have done. God mark thee to his grace,
Thou wast the prettiest babe that e'er I nursed. 65
An I might live to see thee married once,
I have my wish.

70. **disposition:** liking

73–74. **thy teat:** the nipple at which you nursed

78. **much . . . years:** i.e., at about the same age

79. **maid:** maiden, virgin

82. **man of wax:** the ideal form **of** a **man** such as an artist might fashion in **wax**

87. **Read o'er the volume:** Here begins a very affected description of Paris as if he were a beautiful but unbound book in need of **a cover** (line 94). See picture, below.

89. **married lineament:** perfectly matched feature

90. **content:** (1) pleasure (for the viewer); (2) substance (as in the contents of a book)

92. **margent:** margin, where obscure passages are explained

93. **unbound:** (1) not within a binding; (2) unmarried

95. **pride:** glory, magnificence

A bound book with clasps. (1.3.87; 3.2.89–90)
From *Notitia vtraque cum Orientis tum Occidentis . . .* (1552).

LADY CAPULET
  Marry, that "marry" is the very theme
  I came to talk of.—Tell me, daughter Juliet,
  How stands your ⌜disposition⌝ to be married?　　70

JULIET
  It is an ⌜honor⌝ that I dream not of.　OOF.

NURSE
  An ⌜honor?⌝ Were not I thine only nurse,
  I would say thou hadst sucked wisdom from thy
    teat.

LADY CAPULET
  Well, think of marriage now. Younger than you　75
  Here in Verona, ladies of esteem,
  Are made already mothers. By my count
  I was your mother much upon these years
  That you are now a maid. Thus, then, in brief:
  The valiant Paris seeks you for his love.　　80

NURSE
  A man, young lady—lady, such a man
  As all the world—why, he's a man of wax.

LADY CAPULET
  Verona's summer hath not such a flower.

NURSE
  Nay, he's a flower, in faith, a very flower.

LADY CAPULET
  What say you? Can you love the gentleman?　85
  This night you shall behold him at our feast.
  Read o'er the volume of young Paris' face,
  And find delight writ there with beauty's pen.
  Examine every married lineament
  And see how one another lends content,　　90
  And what obscured in this fair volume lies
  Find written in the margent of his eyes.
  This precious book of love, this unbound lover,
  To beautify him only lacks a cover.
  The fish lives in the sea, and 'tis much pride　95

96. **fair without ... within:** a beautiful outside **to hide** the beauty **within**

97–98. **That book ... story:** In the opinion of many, a beautifully bound **book** shares **the glory** of **the story** printed on its pages.

103. **move:** evokes, prompts

104. **endart:** throw or cast (as if it were a dart)

108–9. **in extremity:** is urgent

109. **wait:** be in attendance, do service

110. **straight:** immediately

**1.4** Romeo and Benvolio approach the Capulets' party with their friend Mercutio and others, wearing the disguises customarily donned by "maskers." Romeo is anxious because of an ominous dream. Mercutio mocks him with a speech about a dream-giving queen of fairies.

————————

0 SD. **Maskers:** participants in an impromptu masquerade of their own devising (They wear masks and fancy clothes, and offer to dance.)

1. **What:** an interjection that here introduces a question; **this speech:** i.e., an apology to their host for intruding

2. **on:** i.e., go forward with our masquerade

3. **The ... prolixity: such** wordiness **is** out-of-date

For fair without the fair within to hide.
That book in many's eyes doth share the glory
That in gold clasps locks in the golden story.
So shall you share all that he doth possess
By having him, making yourself no less.                    100

NURSE
No less? Nay, bigger. Women grow by men.

LADY CAPULET
Speak briefly. Can you like of Paris' love?

JULIET
I'll look to like, if looking liking move.
But no more deep will I endart mine eye
Than your consent gives strength to make ⌜it⌝ fly.        105

*Enter ⌜Servingman.⌝*

SERVINGMAN Madam, the guests are come, supper
served up, you called, my young lady asked for, the
Nurse cursed in the pantry, and everything in
extremity. I must hence to wait. I beseech you,
follow straight.                                           110

LADY CAPULET
We follow thee.                          ⌜*Servingman exits.*⌝
                    Juliet, the County stays.

NURSE  Go, girl, seek happy nights to happy days.
                                             *They exit.*


⌜Scene 4⌝

*Enter Romeo, Mercutio, Benvolio, with five or six other*
*Maskers, Torchbearers, ⌜and a Boy with a drum.⌝*

ROMEO
What, shall this speech be spoke for our excuse?
Or shall we on without apology?

BENVOLIO
The date is out of such prolixity.

4–8. **We'll . . . entrance:** i.e., we will not preface our dancing with speeches given by someone dressed up as **Cupid** or with a timidly spoken **prologue    hoodwinked:** blindfolded (See picture, page 20.)    **Tartar's . . . bow:** an Oriental lip-shaped bow (See picture, page 48.)    **of lath:** made from a thin strip of wood like a stage prop **crowkeeper:** scarecrow    **without-book:** memorized

10. **measure . . . measure:** i.e., give **them** a dance

11. **ambling:** i.e., dancing

12. **heavy:** sad (Romeo goes on to pun on **light,** sole/**soul, soar/sore,** and **bound.**)

13. **gentle:** a complimentary epithet

16. **So:** i.e., that **so**

18. **bound:** (1) leap; (2) limit

19. **sore:** sorely, painfully

21. **bound a pitch:** i.e., leap to any height

23. **should you:** you would

28. **Prick . . . down:** i.e., wound **love for** wounding you **and you** thus defeat it (with a suggestion that "**pricking**" may satisfy desire and thus deflate it)

30. **for a visor: for a** face that is itself a mask

31. **cote:** observe

We'll have no Cupid hoodwinked with a scarf,
Bearing a Tartar's painted bow of lath,
Scaring the ladies like a crowkeeper,                                    5
⌐Nor no without-book prologue, faintly spoke
After the prompter, for our entrance.⌐
But let them measure us by what they will.
We'll measure them a measure and be gone.                          10

ROMEO
Give me a torch. I am not for this ambling.
Being but heavy I will bear the light.

MERCUTIO
Nay, gentle Romeo, we must have you dance.

ROMEO
Not I, believe me. You have dancing shoes
With nimble soles. I have a soul of lead                               15
So stakes me to the ground I cannot move.

MERCUTIO
You are a lover. Borrow Cupid's wings
And soar with them above a common bound.

ROMEO
I am too sore enpiercèd with his shaft
To soar with his light feathers, and so bound                        20
I cannot bound a pitch above dull woe.
Under love's heavy burden do I sink.

⌐MERCUTIO⌐
And to sink in it should you burden love—
Too great oppression for a tender thing.

ROMEO
Is love a tender thing? It is too rough,                               25
Too rude, too boist'rous, and it pricks like thorn.

MERCUTIO
If love be rough with you, be rough with love.
Prick love for pricking, and you beat love down.—
Give me a case to put my visage in.—
A visor for a visor. What care I                                      30
What curious eye doth cote deformities?
Here are the beetle brows shall blush for me.

34. **betake . . . legs:** i.e., dance

35. **wantons:** playful persons

37. **I . . . phrase:** i.e., **I am** the subject of the following old sayings

38. **I'll . . . on:** Proverbial: "He that worst may must hold the **candle**."

39. **The . . . done:** Proverbial: "When **game** is best it is time to leave."

40. **dun's . . . word:** Proverbial: "**Dun's the mouse**" (i.e., "Be still"), a fitting motto for a constable on night watch **dun's:** gray-brown is

41. **dun:** a play on **done** (line 39, with a reference to the game called "**Dun** the horse is in **the mire**")

42. **save your reverence:** a request to be excused for mentioning an indecent word, in this case **love,** which, for Mercutio, is equivalent to **mire**

44. **we burn daylight:** i.e., we waste time (Romeo takes him literally and objects, presumably because it is evening. In lines 46–47 Mercutio explains his sense: using up torchlight **in delay** is as wasteful as using **lights** in daytime.)

48. **good:** proper

49. **in that:** i.e., **in our meaning** (line 48); **wits:** senses

51. **wit:** wisdom

53. **tonight:** last night

BENVOLIO
  Come, knock and enter, and no sooner in
  But every man betake him to his legs.

ROMEO
  A torch for me. Let wantons light of heart        35
  Tickle the senseless rushes with their heels,
  For I am proverbed with a grandsire phrase:
  I'll be a candle holder and look on;
  The game was ne'er so fair, and I am ⌜done.⌝

*let's see*
*about the*

MERCUTIO
  Tut, dun's the mouse, the constable's own word.        40
  If thou art dun, we'll draw thee from the mire—
  Or, save ⌜your⌝ reverence, love—wherein thou
    stickest
  Up to the ears. Come, we burn daylight, ho!

ROMEO
  Nay, that's not so.        45
MERCUTIO                    I mean, sir, in delay
  We waste our lights; in vain, ⌜light⌝ lights by day.
  Take our good meaning, for our judgment sits
  Five times in that ere once in our ⌜five⌝ wits.

ROMEO
  And we mean well in going to this masque,        50
  But 'tis no wit to go.
MERCUTIO                    Why, may one ask?
ROMEO
  I dreamt a dream tonight.
MERCUTIO                        And so did I.
ROMEO
  Well, what was yours?        55
MERCUTIO                    That dreamers often lie.
ROMEO
  In bed asleep while they do dream things true.
MERCUTIO
  O, then I see Queen Mab hath been with you.

60. **agate stone:** quartz crystal set in a ring

62. **Drawn with:** pulled by; **atomi:** minute creatures, atoms

64. **spinners':** spiders'

65. **cover of: cover** made **of**

66. **traces:** harness straps

67. **collars:** neck-rolls of the harnesses

68. **film:** fine thread, filament

69. **wagoner:** driver

72–74. These lines are printed by many editors between lines 63 and 64.

73. **joiner:** cabinetmaker; **grub:** grubworm

75. **in this state: in this** ceremonial splendor

77. **on cur'sies:** of curtsies (**On** means "of" in lines 78 and 79 as well.); **straight:** immediately

81. **sweetmeats:** candies or candied fruit

83. **smelling out a suit:** i.e., finding someone who will pay him to present a petition to the king

84. **tithe-pig's tail: tail** of a pig due to the church as part of one's tithe

89. **breaches:** gaps in fortifications; **ambuscadoes:** ambushes; **Spanish blades:** swords of Toledo steel

90. **healths:** toasts; **anon:** straightaway

91. **Drums:** i.e., he dreams of **drums**

94. **plats:** plaits, braids

She is the fairies' midwife, and she comes
In shape no bigger than an agate stone          60
On the forefinger of an alderman,
Drawn with a team of little ⌈atomi⌉
Over men's noses as they lie asleep.
Her wagon spokes made of long spinners' legs,
The cover of the wings of grasshoppers,          65
Her traces of the smallest spider web,
Her collars of the moonshine's wat'ry beams,
Her whip of cricket's bone, the lash of film,
Her wagoner a small gray-coated gnat,
Not half so big as a round little worm          70
Pricked from the lazy finger of a ⌈maid.⌉
Her chariot is an empty hazelnut,
Made by the joiner squirrel or old grub,
Time out o' mind the fairies' coachmakers.
And in this state she gallops night by night          75
Through lovers' brains, and then they dream of love;
On courtiers' knees, that dream on cur'sies straight;
O'er lawyers' fingers, who straight dream on fees;
O'er ladies' lips, who straight on kisses dream,
Which oft the angry Mab with blisters plagues          80
Because their ⌈breaths⌉ with sweetmeats tainted are.
Sometime she gallops o'er a courtier's nose,
And then dreams he of smelling out a suit.
And sometime comes she with a tithe-pig's tail,
Tickling a parson's nose as he lies asleep;          85
Then he dreams of another benefice.
Sometime she driveth o'er a soldier's neck,
And then dreams he of cutting foreign throats,
Of breaches, ambuscadoes, Spanish blades,
Of healths five fathom deep, and then anon          90
Drums in his ear, at which he starts and wakes
And, being thus frighted, swears a prayer or two
And sleeps again. This is that very Mab
That plats the manes of horses in the night

95. **bakes the elflocks in:** i.e., mats, tangles
98. **learns:** teaches
105. **vain fantasy:** insubstantial imagination
107. **who:** which
110. **his:** its
113. **misgives:** is apprehensive that
115. **his fearful date:** its dreadful term
116. **expire:** cause to end
118. **forfeit:** penalty paid by the debtor at the end of **the term of a** loan he cannot pay; **untimely:** premature
120. **lusty:** lively
121. **drum:** drummer
121 SD. Even though the Maskers seem not to exit, the entrance of the Servingmen indicates that the scene changes to a room in Capulet's house.

A Tartar's bow. (1.4.5)
From Balthasar Küchler,
*Repraesentatio der fürstlichen Auffzug . . .* [1611].

And bakes the ⌜elflocks⌝ in foul sluttish hairs, 95
Which once untangled much misfortune bodes.
This is the hag, when maids lie on their backs,
That presses them and learns them first to bear,
Making them women of good carriage.
This is she— 100

ROMEO         Peace, peace, Mercutio, peace.
Thou talk'st of nothing.

MERCUTIO                    True, I talk of dreams,
Which are the children of an idle brain,
Begot of nothing but vain fantasy, 105
Which is as thin of substance as the air
And more inconstant than the wind, who woos
Even now the frozen bosom of the north
And, being angered, puffs away from thence,
Turning his side to the dew-dropping south. 110

BENVOLIO
This wind you talk of blows us from ourselves.
Supper is done, and we shall come too late.

ROMEO
I fear too early, for my mind misgives
Some consequence yet hanging in the stars
Shall bitterly begin his fearful date 115
With this night's revels, and expire the term
Of a despisèd life closed in my breast
By some vile forfeit of untimely death.
But he that hath the steerage of my course
Direct my ⌜sail.⌝ On, lusty gentlemen. 120

BENVOLIO   Strike, drum.

*They march about the stage
and ⌜then withdraw to the side.⌝*

**1.5** Capulet welcomes the disguised Romeo and his friends. Romeo, watching the dance, is caught by the beauty of Juliet. Overhearing Romeo ask about her, Tybalt recognizes his voice and is enraged at the intrusion.

Romeo then meets Juliet, and they fall in love. Not until they are separated do they discover that they belong to enemy houses.

———————

2. **take away:** i.e., **take away** the dirty dishes

7. **joint stools: stools** made of joined parts

8. **court cupboard:** sideboard; **plate:** utensils

9. **marchpane:** marzipan

16. **longer liver:** survivor (proverbial)

17. SD. **Enter . . . to . . . Maskers:** direction to those entering to approach others already onstage—here, **the Maskers**

19. **walk a bout:** i.e., dance a round

22. **makes dainty:** coyly refuses (to dance)

23–24. **Am . . . now?:** i.e., have I hit close to home?

⌈Scene 5⌉

*Servingmen come forth with napkins.*

⌈FIRST⌉ SERVINGMAN    Where's Potpan that he helps not
to take away? He shift a trencher? He scrape a
trencher?

⌈SECOND⌉ SERVINGMAN    When good manners shall lie
all in one or two men's hands, and they unwashed        5
too, 'tis a foul thing.

⌈FIRST⌉ SERVINGMAN    Away with the joint stools, remove the court cupboard, look to the plate.—
Good thou, save me a piece of marchpane, and, as
thou loves me, let the porter let in Susan Grind       10
stone and Nell.—Anthony and Potpan!

⌈THIRD⌉ SERVINGMAN    Ay, boy, ready.

⌈FIRST⌉ SERVINGMAN    You are looked for and called for,
asked for and sought for, in the great chamber.

⌈THIRD⌉ SERVINGMAN    We cannot be here and there too.      15
Cheerly, boys! Be brisk awhile, and the longer liver
take all.                              ⌈*They move aside.*⌉

*Enter* ⌈*Capulet and his household,*⌉ *all the guests and
gentlewomen to* ⌈*Romeo, Mercutio, Benvolio, and*⌉ *the
*⌈*other*⌉ *Maskers.*

CAPULET
Welcome, gentlemen. Ladies that have their toes
Unplagued with corns will walk ⌈a bout⌉ with
you.—                                                    20
Ah, my mistresses, which of you all
Will now deny to dance? She that makes dainty,
She, I'll swear, hath corns. Am I come near you
now?—
Welcome, gentlemen. I have seen the day                  25
That I have worn a visor and could tell
A whispering tale in a fair lady's ear,
Such as would please. 'Tis gone, 'tis gone, 'tis gone.

31. **A hall:** i.e., clear the **hall** for dancing
32. **turn . . . up:** i.e., remove the boards and trestles
39. **By 'r Lady:** an oath, "**by** our **Lady**"
47. **ward:** one under the care of a guardian
54. **dear:** precious
57. **measure done:** dance ended; **her . . . stand:** where she stands
58. **rude:** roughly formed

Masked gentlemen and ladies. (1.5.38)
From Giacomo Franco,
*Habiti d'huomeni et donne venetiane . . .* (1609).

You are welcome, gentlemen.—Come, musicians,
  play.                  *Music plays and they dance.*   30
A hall, a hall, give room!—And foot it, girls.—
More light, you knaves, and turn the tables up,
And quench the fire; the room is grown too hot.—
Ah, sirrah, this unlooked-for sport comes well.—
Nay, sit, nay, sit, good cousin Capulet,   35
For you and I are past our dancing days.
How long is 't now since last yourself and I
Were in a mask?

CAPULET'S COUSIN   By 'r Lady, thirty years.

CAPULET
What, man, 'tis not so much, 'tis not so much.   40
'Tis since the nuptial of ⌜Lucentio,⌝
Come Pentecost as quickly as it will,
Some five and twenty years, and then we masked.

CAPULET'S COUSIN
'Tis more, 'tis more. His son is elder, sir.
His son is thirty.   45

CAPULET          Will you tell me that?
His son was but a ward two years ago.

ROMEO, ⌜*to a Servingman*⌝
What lady's that which doth enrich the hand
Of yonder knight?

SERVINGMAN   I know not, sir.   50

ROMEO
O, she doth teach the torches to burn bright!
It seems she hangs upon the cheek of night
As a rich jewel in an Ethiop's ear—
Beauty too rich for use, for Earth too dear.
So shows a snowy dove trooping with crows   55
As yonder lady o'er her fellows shows.
The measure done, I'll watch her place of stand
And, touching hers, make blessèd my rude hand.
Did my heart love till now? Forswear it, sight,
For I ne'er saw true beauty till this night.   60

61. **should be:** must **be**
64. **antic face:** grotesque or fantastic mask
65. **fleer:** sneer; **solemnity:** festivity
66. **stock:** line of descent
70. **in spite:** out of malice
75. **bears . . . portly:** comports himself **like a** dignified or handsome
80. **patient:** calm
82. **fair presence:** attractive, pleasing manner
83. **ill-beseeming semblance:** unsuitable way to appear
87. **goodman:** a man below the rank of gentleman; **Go to:** an expression of anger
89. **God . . . soul:** i.e., **God** save me

TYBALT
  This, by his voice, should be a Montague.—
  Fetch me my rapier, boy.               ⌜*Page exits.*⌝
                     What, dares the slave
  Come hither covered with an antic face
  To fleer and scorn at our solemnity?                    65
  Now, by the stock and honor of my kin,
  To strike him dead I hold it not a sin.

CAPULET
  Why, how now, kinsman? Wherefore storm you so?

TYBALT
  Uncle, this is a Montague, our foe,
  A villain that is hither come in spite                  70
  To scorn at our solemnity this night.

CAPULET
  Young Romeo is it?

TYBALT                    'Tis he, that villain Romeo.

CAPULET
  Content thee, gentle coz. Let him alone.
  He bears him like a portly gentleman,                   75
  And, to say truth, Verona brags of him
  To be a virtuous and well-governed youth.
  I would not for the wealth of all this town
  Here in my house do him disparagement.
  Therefore be patient. Take no note of him.              80
  It is my will, the which if thou respect,
  Show a fair presence and put off these frowns,
  An ill-beseeming semblance for a feast.

TYBALT
  It fits when such a villain is a guest.
  I'll not endure him.                                    85

CAPULET                    He shall be endured.
  What, goodman boy? I say he shall. Go to.
  Am I the master here or you? Go to.
  You'll not endure him! God shall mend my soul,

91. **You . . . cock-a-hoop:** i.e., **you will** be reckless; **you'll . . . man:** i.e., you will take charge

92. **shame:** disgrace, loss of esteem

94. **saucy:** insolent

97. Capulet begins to intersperse his rebuke of Tybalt with comments to his guests (**my hearts**) and servants. **princox:** insolent boy

100. **Patience perforce:** i.e., enforced calmness; **willful choler:** obstinate anger

104. **If . . . hand:** The fourteen lines of dialogue that begin with this line have the structure and rhyme scheme of a sonnet. In its central metaphor, Romeo is a **pilgrim** (line 108) visiting a **holy shrine** (line 105). See picture, below.

109. **Which . . . this:** i.e., **your hand** shows seemly (**mannerly**) **devotion** in touching mine

111. **palmers':** Palmers were pilgrims returning with palm branches from the Holy Land.

116. **move:** initiate (blessings or favors)

A pilgrim. (1.5.104–18)
From Henry Peacham, *Minerua Britanna . . .* [1612].

HOMEWORK !!! !!!

You'll make a mutiny among my guests,     90
You will set cock-a-hoop, you'll be the man!

**TYBALT**
Why, uncle, 'tis a shame.

**CAPULET**          Go to, go to.
You are a saucy boy. Is 't so indeed?
This trick may chance to scathe you. I know what.     95
You must contrary me. Marry, 'tis time—
Well said, my hearts.—You are a princox, go.
Be quiet, or—More light, more light!—for shame,
I'll make you quiet.—What, cheerly, my hearts!

**TYBALT**
Patience perforce with willful choler meeting     100
Makes my flesh tremble in their diff'rent greeting.
I will withdraw, but this intrusion shall,
Now seeming sweet, convert to bitt'rest gall.

                          *He exits.*

Here we go.

**ROMEO,** ⌜*taking Juliet's hand*⌝
If I profane with my unworthiest hand
This holy shrine, the gentle sin is this:     105
My lips, two blushing pilgrims, ready stand
To smooth that rough touch with a tender kiss.

**JULIET**
Good pilgrim, you do wrong your hand too much,
Which mannerly devotion shows in this;
For saints have hands that pilgrims' hands do touch,     110
And palm to palm is holy palmers' kiss.

**ROMEO**
Have not saints lips, and holy palmers too?

**JULIET**
Ay, pilgrim, lips that they must use in prayer.

**ROMEO**
O then, dear saint, let lips do what hands do.
They pray: grant thou, lest faith turn to despair.     115

**JULIET**
Saints do not move, though grant for prayers' sake.

117. **move not:** keep still

122. **by th' book:** i.e., according to rule

124. **What is:** who is

128. **I nursed:** i.e., I was wet nurse to; **withal:** with

130. **the chinks:** plenty of coin (money)

132. **dear:** costly; **my foe's debt:** owed to a foe, i.e., Juliet

133. **The . . . best:** alluding to the proverb Romeo cited at 1.4.39: "When game is **best** it is time to leave."

136. **banquet:** a light meal; or, dessert: **towards:** i.e., about to be served

137. **Is it e'en so:** i.e., must you go

140. **by my fay:** a mild oath, "**by my** faith"

ROMEO
Then move not while my prayer's effect I take.

                           ⌜*He kisses her.*⌝

Thus from my lips, by thine, my sin is purged.
JULIET
Then have my lips the sin that they have took.
ROMEO
Sin from my lips? O trespass sweetly urged!     120
Give me my sin again.          ⌜*He kisses her.*⌝
JULIET              You kiss by th' book.
NURSE
Madam, your mother craves a word with you.
            ⌜*Juliet moves toward her mother.*⌝
ROMEO
What is her mother?
NURSE             Marry, bachelor,     125
Her mother is the lady of the house,
And a good lady, and a wise and virtuous.
I nursed her daughter that you talked withal.
I tell you, he that can lay hold of her
Shall have the chinks.     ⌜*Nurse moves away.*⌝  130
ROMEO, ⌜*aside*⌝          Is she a Capulet?
O dear account! My life is my foe's debt.
BENVOLIO
Away, begone. The sport is at the best.
ROMEO
Ay, so I fear. The more is my unrest.
CAPULET
Nay, gentlemen, prepare not to be gone.     135
We have a trifling foolish banquet towards.—
Is it e'en so? Why then, I thank you all.
I thank you, honest gentlemen. Good night.—
More torches here.—Come on then, let's to bed.—
Ah, sirrah, by my fay, it waxes late.     140
I'll to my rest.
        ⌜*All but Juliet and the Nurse begin to exit.*⌝

149. **like:** likely
154. **Prodigious:** monstrous, unnatural

A melancholy lover.
From Robert Burton, *The anatomy of melancholy . . .* (1638).

JULIET
  Come hither, nurse. What is yond gentleman?
NURSE
  The son and heir of old Tiberio.
JULIET
  What's he that now is going out of door?
NURSE
  Marry, that, I think, be young Petruchio.          145
JULIET
  What's he that follows here, that would not dance?
NURSE   I know not.
JULIET
  Go ask his name. ⌜*The Nurse goes.*⌝ If he be marrièd,
  My grave is like to be my wedding bed.          Dramatic
NURSE, ⌜*returning*⌝                                 Irony
  His name is Romeo, and a Montague,          150
  The only son of your great enemy.          Foreshadowing
JULIET
  My only love sprung from my only hate!          Quote 8
  Too early seen unknown, and known too late!
  Prodigious birth of love it is to me
  That I must love a loathèd enemy.          155
NURSE
  What's this? What's this?
JULIET                    A rhyme I learned even now
  Of one I danced withal.
                    *One calls within "Juliet."*
NURSE                    Anon, anon.
  Come, let's away. The strangers all are gone.          160
                              *They exit.*

*The Tragedy of*

# ROMEO

## AND

# JULIET

ACT 2

0 SD.  **Chorus:** Again the Chorus's speech is in the form of a sonnet.

2.  **gapes:** desires eagerly

3.  **fair:** i.e., fair one (Rosaline)

4.  **matched:** compared

5.  **again:** in return

6.  **Alike bewitchèd:** just as **bewitched** as Juliet is

7.  **complain:** plead for favor

8.  **fearful:** frightening

9.  **held:** considered; **access:** i.e., **access** to Juliet

10.  **use:** are accustomed

13.  **time means:** time (lends them) means

14.  **Temp'ring . . . sweet:** mixing great difficulties (**extremities**) with great pleasure (**extreme sweet**)

**2.1**  Romeo finds himself so in love with Juliet that he cannot leave her. He scales a wall and enters Capulet's garden. Meanwhile Benvolio and Mercutio look for him in vain.

———————

2.  **earth:** body (which is **dull** [i.e., slow] because it is moving away from what attracts it, its **center**)

⌜*ACT 2*⌝

*Another Sonet ?????...?*

⌜*Enter*⌝ *Chorus.*

Now old desire doth in his deathbed lie,
And young affection gapes to be his heir.
That fair for which love groaned for and would die,
With tender Juliet ⌜matched,⌝ is now not fair.
Now Romeo is beloved and loves again,                               5
Alike bewitchèd by the charm of looks,
But to his foe supposed he must complain,
And she steal love's sweet bait from fearful hooks.
Being held a foe, he may not have access
To breathe such vows as lovers use to swear,                       10
And she as much in love, her means much less
To meet her new belovèd anywhere.
But passion lends them power, time means, to meet,
Temp'ring extremities with extreme sweet.

⌜*Chorus exits.*⌝


⌜*Scene 1*⌝

*Enter Romeo alone.*

ROMEO
Can I go forward when my heart is here?
Turn back, dull earth, and find thy center out.

⌜*He withdraws.*⌝

*Enter Benvolio with Mercutio.*

65

6. **orchard:** garden (See picture, page 72.)

8. **conjure:** raise up a spirit by invoking its proper name (In line 9 Mercutio tries out a variety of names for Romeo.)

10. **likeness:** form (Sighs and rhyming were traditionally associated with lovers.)

14. **gossip:** familiar acquaintance; **fair:** flattering

16. **Abraham:** i.e., old (as the biblical **Abraham**) **Cupid,** though **young,** was an ancient god. **trim:** accurately

17. **King . . . maid:** alluding to a ballad

19. **ape:** fool; **conjure him:** raise his ghost (See picture, below.)

23. **demesnes:** regions

27. **raise:** conjure up in a magic **circle** (Mercutio's rather explicit sexual meaning is carried in the words **raise, mistress' circle, stand,** and **laid.**)

30. **were some spite:** would be **some** injury

A conjurer. (2.1.19)
From Laurentius Wolffgang Woyt,
. . . *Emblematischer Parnassus* . . . (1728–30).

BENVOLIO
  Romeo, my cousin Romeo, Romeo!
MERCUTIO   He is wise
  And, on my life, hath stol'n him home to bed.                 5
BENVOLIO
  He ran this way and leapt this orchard wall.
  Call, good Mercutio.
⌜MERCUTIO⌝            Nay, I'll conjure too.
  Romeo! Humors! Madman! Passion! Lover!
  Appear thou in the likeness of a sigh.                        10
  Speak but one rhyme and I am satisfied.
  Cry but "Ay me," ⌜pronounce⌝ but "love" and
  ⌜"dove."⌝
  Speak to my gossip Venus one fair word,
  One nickname for her purblind son and ⌜heir,⌝                 15
  Young Abraham Cupid, he that shot so ⌜trim⌝
  When King Cophetua loved the beggar maid.—
  He heareth not, he stirreth not, he moveth not.
  The ape is dead, and I must conjure him.—
  I conjure thee by Rosaline's bright eyes,                     20
  By her high forehead, and her scarlet lip,
  By her fine foot, straight leg, and quivering thigh,
  And the demesnes that there adjacent lie,
  That in thy likeness thou appear to us.
BENVOLIO
  An if he hear thee, thou wilt anger him.                      25
MERCUTIO
  This cannot anger him. 'Twould anger him
  To raise a spirit in his mistress' circle
  Of some strange nature, letting it there stand
  Till she had laid it and conjured it down.
  That were some spite. My invocation                           30
  Is fair and honest. In his mistress' name,
  I conjure only but to raise up him.
BENVOLIO
  Come, he hath hid himself among these trees

34. **consorted:** in league; **humorous:** moody
36. **mark:** target
37. **medlar:** a fruit, also called **open-arse** (line 41) See picture, page 96.
41. **pop'rin pear: a pear** from Poperinghe, in Flanders
42. **truckle bed:** i.e., trundle **bed**

**2.2** From Capulet's garden Romeo overhears Juliet express her love for him. When he answers her, they acknowledge their love and their desire to be married.

———————

0 SD. The scene now moves into Capulet's garden. Though the action is continuous, editors mark a new scene because of the change in location.
1 SD. **above:** in the gallery over the stage, as at a window
2–9. **what light . . . wear it:** In this elaborate comparison, Romeo plays first with the idea of **the sun** (Juliet) in a contest with **the moon** (equated with Diana, goddess of the moon). As **the sun** rises, **the moon** begins to look **pale.** The image then shifts toward Diana's role as goddess of chastity. Juliet is the **maid** of Diana as long as Juliet is a virgin. **vestal livery:** clothing worn by Diana's maidens **sick and green:** perhaps a reference to greensickness, a form of anemia thought to afflict girls in puberty, making them pale

To be consorted with the humorous night.
Blind is his love and best befits the dark.                    35

MERCUTIO
If love be blind, love cannot hit the mark.
Now will he sit under a medlar tree
And wish his mistress were that kind of fruit
As maids call medlars when they laugh alone.—
O Romeo, that she were, O, that she were                       40
An ⌐open-arse,⌐ thou a pop'rin pear.
Romeo, good night. I'll to my truckle bed;
This field-bed is too cold for me to sleep.—
Come, shall we go?

BENVOLIO                    Go, then, for 'tis in vain          45
To seek him here that means not to be found.
                                            ⌐They⌐ exit.


                        ⌐Scene 2⌐

                ⌐Romeo comes forward.⌐


ROMEO
He jests at scars that never felt a wound.

                ⌐Enter Juliet above.⌐

But soft, what light through yonder window breaks?
It is the East, and Juliet is the sun.
Arise, fair sun, and kill the envious moon,
Who is already sick and pale with grief
That thou, her maid, art far more fair than she.              5
Be not her maid since she is envious.
Her vestal livery is but sick and green,
And none but fools do wear it. Cast it off.
It is my lady. O, it is my love!
O, that she knew she were!                                    10
She speaks, yet she says nothing. What of that?
Her eye discourses; I will answer it.

17. **spheres:** In Ptolemaic astronomy, the heavenly bodies were carried in their orbits around the Earth **in** crystalline **spheres.**

22. **stream:** issue a stream of light

33. **him:** the **messenger of heaven** (line 31)

36. **wherefore:** why

38. **be but:** only **be**

42. **Thou . . . Montague:** i.e., you would still be yourself even if you were **not** called **Montague**

43. **nor . . . nor:** neither . . . **nor**

44–45. **O . . . man:** See longer note, page 245.

Ptolemaic universe. (2.2.17)
From Marcus Manilius, *The sphere of . . .* (1675).

I am too bold. 'Tis not to me she speaks.
Two of the fairest stars in all the heaven,        15
Having some business, ⌜do⌝ entreat her eyes
To twinkle in their spheres till they return.
What if her eyes were there, they in her head?
The brightness of her cheek would shame those
   stars        20
As daylight doth a lamp; her eye in heaven
Would through the airy region stream so bright
That birds would sing and think it were not night.
See how she leans her cheek upon her hand.
O, that I were a glove upon that hand,        25
That I might touch that cheek!
JULIET                         Ay me.
ROMEO, ⌜*aside*⌝                         She speaks.
O, speak again, bright angel, for thou art
As glorious to this night, being o'er my head,        30
As is a wingèd messenger of heaven
Unto the white-upturnèd wond'ring eyes
Of mortals that fall back to gaze on him
When he bestrides the lazy puffing clouds
And sails upon the bosom of the air.        35
JULIET
O Romeo, Romeo, wherefore art thou Romeo?
Deny thy father and refuse thy name,
Or, if thou wilt not, be but sworn my love,
And I'll no longer be a Capulet.
ROMEO, ⌜*aside*⌝
Shall I hear more, or shall I speak at this?        40
JULIET
'Tis but thy name that is my enemy.
Thou art thyself, though not a Montague.
What's Montague? It is nor hand, nor foot,
Nor arm, nor face. O, be some other name
Belonging to a man.        45
What's in a name? That which we call a rose

49. **owes:** owns
51. **for thy name:** in return **for thy name**
54. **Call me but:** only **call me; new baptized:** given a new Christian name
56. **bescreened:** i.e., concealed
57. **counsel:** secrets
66. **thee dislike:** displeases you
69. **death:** i.e., mortally dangerous
71. **o'erperch:** fly over
73. **And . . . attempt: love dares** to **attempt** whatever it is possible for **love** to **do**
74. **stop:** obstacle

An orchard. (2.1.6)
From Octavio Boldoni, *Theatrum temporaneum* . . . (1636).

By any other word would smell as sweet.
So Romeo would, were he not Romeo called,
Retain that dear perfection which he owes
Without that title. Romeo, doff thy name,                    50
And, for thy name, which is no part of thee,
Take all myself.

ROMEO                    I take thee at thy word.
Call me but love, and I'll be new baptized.
Henceforth I never will be Romeo.                            55

JULIET
What man art thou that, thus bescreened in night,
So stumblest on my counsel?

ROMEO                              By a name
I know not how to tell thee who I am.
My name, dear saint, is hateful to myself                    60
Because it is an enemy to thee.
Had I it written, I would tear the word.

JULIET
My ears have yet not drunk a hundred words
Of thy tongue's uttering, yet I know the sound.
Art thou not Romeo, and a Montague?                          65

ROMEO
Neither, fair maid, if either thee dislike.

JULIET
How camest thou hither, tell me, and wherefore?
The orchard walls are high and hard to climb,
And the place death, considering who thou art,
If any of my kinsmen find thee here.                         70

ROMEO
With love's light wings did I o'erperch these walls,
For stony limits cannot hold love out,
And what love can do, that dares love attempt.
Therefore thy kinsmen are no stop to me.

JULIET
If they do see thee, they will murder thee.                  75

78. **proof:** invulnerably armed
81. **but:** unless
83. **proroguèd:** deferred; **wanting of:** lacking
92. **For that:** because of **that**
93. **Fain . . . form:** I would gladly follow the proper formalities
94. **compliment:** observance of ceremony
97–98. **At lovers' . . . laughs:** a classical commonplace   **Jove:** king of the Roman gods (See picture, below.)
102. **So:** so that; **else:** otherwise
103. **too fond:** too much in love
104. **havior light:** behavior immodest
105. **true:** faithful, constant

Jove. (2.2.98)
From Vincenzo Cartari, *Le vere e noue imagini . . .* (1615).

ROMEO
  Alack, there lies more peril in thine eye
  Than twenty of their swords. Look thou but sweet,
  And I am proof against their enmity.

JULIET
  I would not for the world they saw thee here.

ROMEO
  I have night's cloak to hide me from their eyes,          80
  And, but thou love me, let them find me here.
  My life were better ended by their hate
  Than death prorogued, wanting of thy love.

JULIET
  By whose direction found'st thou out this place?

ROMEO
  By love, that first did prompt me to inquire.          85
  He lent me counsel, and I lent him eyes.
  I am no pilot; yet, wert thou as far
  As that vast shore ⌈washed⌉ with the farthest sea,
  I should adventure for such merchandise.

JULIET
  Thou knowest the mask of night is on my face,          90
  Else would a maiden blush bepaint my cheek
  For that which thou hast heard me speak tonight.
  Fain would I dwell on form; fain, fain deny
  What I have spoke. But farewell compliment.
  Dost thou love me? I know thou wilt say "Ay,"          95
  And I will take thy word. Yet, if thou swear'st,
  Thou mayst prove false. At lovers' perjuries,
  They say, Jove laughs. O gentle Romeo,
  If thou dost love, pronounce it faithfully.
  Or, if thou thinkest I am too quickly won,          100
  I'll frown and be perverse and say thee nay,
  So thou wilt woo, but else not for the world.
  In truth, fair Montague, I am too fond,
  And therefore thou mayst think my ⌈havior⌉ light.
  But trust me, gentleman, I'll prove more true          105

106. **coying:** affectation of shyness; **strange:** distant, apparently reluctant

107. **should:** i,e., would

110. **light:** unchaste or frivolous

111. **discoverèd:** revealed

115. **orb:** sphere (See note to line 17, above.)

125. **unadvised:** ill-considered

Than those that have ⌐more⌐ coying to be strange.
I should have been more strange, I must confess,
But that thou overheard'st ere I was ware
My true-love passion. Therefore pardon me,
And not impute this yielding to light love,                    110
Which the dark night hath so discoverèd.

ROMEO
Lady, by yonder blessèd moon I vow,
That tips with silver all these fruit-tree tops—

JULIET
O, swear not by the moon, th' inconstant moon,
That monthly changes in her ⌐circled⌐ orb,                    115
Lest that thy love prove likewise variable.

ROMEO
What shall I swear by?

JULIET                         Do not swear at all.
Or, if thou wilt, swear by thy gracious self,
Which is the god of my idolatry,                              120
And I'll believe thee.

ROMEO                          If my heart's dear love—

JULIET
Well, do not swear. Although I joy in thee,
I have no joy of this contract tonight.
It is too rash, too unadvised, too sudden,                    125
Too like the lightning, which doth cease to be
Ere one can say "It lightens." Sweet, good night.
This bud of love, by summer's ripening breath,
May prove a beauteous flower when next we meet.
Good night, good night. As sweet repose and rest              130
Come to thy heart as that within my breast.

ROMEO
O, wilt thou leave me so unsatisfied? *Bruh*

JULIET
What satisfaction canst thou have tonight?

ROMEO
Th' exchange of thy love's faithful vow for mine.

136. **would it were:** i.e., wish **it were** in my possession
138. **frank:** lavish
139. **but:** only
148. **substantial:** real, not dreamed
150. **thy bent of love:** the intention **of** your **love**
155. **thee my lord:** i.e., you as **my lord**
160. **By and by:** immediately
161. **strife:** striving, efforts

JULIET

  I gave thee mine before thou didst request it,       135

  And yet I would it were to give again.

ROMEO

  Wouldst thou withdraw it? For what purpose, love?

JULIET

  But to be frank and give it thee again.

  And yet I wish but for the thing I have.

  My bounty is as boundless as the sea,       140

  My love as deep. The more I give to thee,

  The more I have, for both are infinite.

                   ⌜*Nurse calls from within.*⌝

  I hear some noise within. Dear love, adieu.—

  Anon, good nurse.—Sweet Montague, be true.

  Stay but a little; I will come again.       ⌜*She exits.*⌝   145

ROMEO

  O blessèd, blessèd night! I am afeard,

  Being in night, all this is but a dream,

  Too flattering sweet to be substantial.

         ⌜*Reenter Juliet above.*⌝

JULIET

  Three words, dear Romeo, and good night indeed.

  If that thy bent of love be honorable,       150

  Thy purpose marriage, send me word tomorrow,

  By one that I'll procure to come to thee,

  Where and what time thou wilt perform the rite,

  And all my fortunes at thy foot I'll lay

  And follow thee my ⌜lord⌝ throughout the world.    155

⌜NURSE *within*⌝    Madam.

JULIET

  I come anon.—But if thou meanest not well,

  I do beseech thee—

⌜NURSE *within*⌝    Madam.

JULIET   By and by, I come.—       160

  To cease thy strife and leave me to my grief.

  Tomorrow will I send.

165. **want:** lack

166. **from:** i.e., go away from

168. **But . . . school:** i.e., **but love** goes away **from love** as **schoolboys** go **toward school; heavy:** gloomy

170. **tassel-gentle:** tercel-gentle, a male falcon

171. **Bondage is hoarse:** i.e., those bound by, for example, their fathers' rules can only hoarsely whisper their desires

172. **Echo:** Shunned by her lover, Narcissus, the mythological **Echo** dwindled to a mere voice and lived in caves, condemned to repeat what others spoke.

177. **attending:** listening (French *attendre*)

179. **My dear:** For this reading, see longer note, page 246.

183. **year:** i.e., years

ROMEO   So thrive my soul—
JULIET   A thousand times good night.          ⌜*She exits.*⌝
ROMEO
  A thousand times the worse to want thy light.          165
  Love goes toward love as schoolboys from their
    books,
  But love from love, toward school with heavy looks.
                                             ⌜*Going.*⌝

      *Enter Juliet* ⌜*above*⌝ *again.*

JULIET
  Hist, Romeo, hist! O, for a falc'ner's voice
  To lure this tassel-gentle back again!          170
  Bondage is hoarse and may not speak aloud,
  Else would I tear the cave where Echo lies
  And make her airy tongue more hoarse than ⌜mine⌝
  With repetition of "My Romeo!"
ROMEO
  It is my soul that calls upon my name.          175
  How silver-sweet sound lovers' tongues by night,
  Like softest music to attending ears.
JULIET
  Romeo.
ROMEO          My ⌜dear.⌝
JULIET                    What o'clock tomorrow          180
  Shall I send to thee?
ROMEO                    By the hour of nine.
JULIET
  I will not fail. 'Tis twenty year till then.
  I have forgot why I did call thee back.
ROMEO
  Let me stand here till thou remember it.          185
JULIET
  I shall forget, to have thee still stand there,
  Rememb'ring how I love thy company.

191. **a wanton's:** a spoiled child's
193. **gyves:** leg chains (See picture, below.)
195. **his:** its
196. **would:** wish
201. **morrow:** morning
204. **ghostly:** spiritual; **close:** secluded
205. **dear:** precious; **hap:** good fortune

**2.3** Determined to marry Juliet, Romeo hurries to Friar Lawrence. The Friar agrees to marry them, expressing the hope that the marriage may end the feud between their families.

———

1–4. **The gray-eyed . . . wheels:** For textual questions associated with these lines, see longer note, page 246.
3. **fleckled:** light-splotched
4. **From forth:** away from; **Titan's:** Titan is a poetic name for the sun god, whose chariot is the sun. (See picture, page 86.)

A prisoner in gyves. (2.2.193)
From Cesare Vecellio, *Degli habiti antichi et moderni* . . . (1590).

ROMEO
And I'll still stay, to have thee still forget,
Forgetting any other home but this.

JULIET
'Tis almost morning. I would have thee gone, 190
And yet no farther than a wanton's bird,
That lets it hop a little from his hand,
Like a poor prisoner in his twisted gyves,
And with a silken thread plucks it back again,
So loving-jealous of his liberty. 195

ROMEO
I would I were thy bird.

JULIET                            Sweet, so would I.
Yet I should kill thee with much cherishing.
Good night, good night. Parting is such sweet
  sorrow 200
That I shall say "Good night" till it be morrow.
                                        ⌜*She exits.*⌝

⌜ROMEO⌝
Sleep dwell upon thine eyes, peace in thy breast.
Would I were sleep and peace so sweet to rest.
Hence will I to my ghostly friar's close cell,
His help to crave, and my dear hap to tell. 205
                                    *He exits.*


⌜Scene 3⌝

*Enter Friar ⌜Lawrence⌝ alone with a basket.*

FRIAR LAWRENCE
The gray-eyed morn smiles on the frowning night,
⌜Check'ring⌝ the eastern clouds with streaks of light,
And fleckled darkness like a drunkard reels
From forth day's path and Titan's ⌜fiery⌝ wheels.
Now, ere the sun advance his burning eye, 5
The day to cheer and night's dank dew to dry,

7. **osier cage:** i.e., basket made of willow twigs
10. **What . . . womb:** i.e., the **grave** in which she buries her dead **is** also **her womb**
11. **divers kind:** various kinds
13. **virtues:** powers
14. **None . . . some:** i.e., **none** is totally lacking in **some** powers (This idea is expanded in lines 17–18 below.)
15. **mickle:** great; **grace:** capacity to heal
18. **to the Earth:** i.e., to humankind
19. **but:** i.e., **but** that; **strained:** perverted
20. **Revolts . . . birth:** i.e., it **revolts from** its nature
22. **by action dignified:** i.e., acquires worth through a good **action**
24. **medicine power:** healing remedy has **power**
25–26. **with . . . each part:** i.e., with the sense of smell enlivens every **part** of the body
27. **stays:** stops
29. **grace:** virtue; **rude will:** violent inclinations, desires
31. **canker:** cankerworm (See note to **worm** at 1.1.154.)
33. **Benedicite:** bless you (This five-syllable word is accented on the first, third, and fifth syllables.)
35. **argues:** indicates; **distempered:** disturbed
37. **his:** its

I must upfill this osier cage of ours
With baleful weeds and precious-juicèd flowers.
The Earth that's nature's mother is her tomb;
What is her burying grave, that is her womb;                    10
And from her womb children of divers kind
We sucking on her natural bosom find,
Many for many virtues excellent,
None but for some, and yet all different.
O, mickle is the powerful grace that lies                      15
In plants, herbs, stones, and their true qualities.
For naught so vile that on the Earth doth live
But to the Earth some special good doth give;
Nor aught so good but, strained from that fair use,
Revolts from true birth, stumbling on abuse.                   20
Virtue itself turns vice, being misapplied,
And vice sometime by action dignified.

*Enter Romeo.*

Within the infant rind of this weak flower
Poison hath residence and medicine power:
For this, being smelt, with that part cheers each              25
   part;
Being tasted, stays all senses with the heart.
Two such opposèd kings encamp them still
In man as well as herbs—grace and rude will;
And where the worser is predominant,                           30
Full soon the canker death eats up that plant.

ROMEO
   Good morrow, father.

FRIAR LAWRENCE          Benedicite.
   What early tongue so sweet saluteth me?
   Young son, it argues a distempered head                     35
   So soon to bid "Good morrow" to thy bed.
   Care keeps his watch in every old man's eye,
   And, where care lodges, sleep will never lie;
   But where unbruisèd youth with unstuffed brain

43. **distemp'rature:** disturbance of the mind
55. **Both our remedies:** the cure for both of us
56. **physic:** medicine
58. **My intercession . . . foe:** my petition is in aid of my enemy (Juliet) as well as of myself
59. **homely in thy drift:** straightforward in your meaning
60. **shrift:** absolution
64. **save:** except
67. **pass:** move along

The sun god in his chariot. (2.3.4; 3.2.1–2)
From Vincenzo Cartari, *Le vere e noue imagini . . .* (1615).

Doth couch his limbs, there golden sleep doth            40
    reign.
Therefore thy earliness doth me assure
Thou art uproused with some distemp'rature,
Or, if not so, then here I hit it right:
Our Romeo hath not been in bed tonight.            45

ROMEO
That last is true. The sweeter rest was mine.

FRIAR LAWRENCE
God pardon sin! Wast thou with Rosaline?

ROMEO
With Rosaline, my ghostly father? No.
I have forgot that name and that name's woe.

*[margin handwritten: romeo doesn't love rosaline]*

FRIAR LAWRENCE
That's my good son. But where hast thou been            50
    then?

ROMEO
I'll tell thee ere thou ask it me again.
I have been feasting with mine enemy,
Where on a sudden one hath wounded me
That's by me wounded. Both our remedies            55
Within thy help and holy physic lies.
I bear no hatred, blessèd man, for, lo,
My intercession likewise steads my foe.

FRIAR LAWRENCE
Be plain, good son, and homely in thy drift.
Riddling confession finds but riddling shrift.            60

ROMEO
Then plainly know my heart's dear love is set
On the fair daughter of rich Capulet.
As mine on hers, so hers is set on mine,
And all combined, save what thou must combine
By holy marriage. When and where and how            65
We met, we wooed, and made exchange of vow
I'll tell thee as we pass, but this I pray,
That thou consent to marry us today.

73. **deal of brine:** quantity of salt water (tears)

76. **season:** preserve; flavor

77. **The . . . clears:** i.e., the clouds of your **sighs** have **not yet** been dispersed by (this morning's) **sun**

83. **sentence:** truism, cliché

85. **may fall:** i.e., **may** be excused for acting immorally (This cliché assumes that men are morally stronger than women.)

86. **chid'st:** chided, scolded

88. **bad'st me:** bade me, told me to

91. **Her I love now:** i.e., she whom **I now love**

95. **read by rote:** recite from memory; **spell:** i.e., understand the meaning (literally, **read** letter by letter)

97. **In one respect:** i.e., because of **one** consideration

**FRIAR LAWRENCE**
Holy Saint Francis, what a change is here!
Is Rosaline, that thou didst love so dear,     70
So soon forsaken? Young men's love then lies
Not truly in their hearts, but in their eyes.
Jesu Maria, what a deal of brine
Hath washed thy sallow cheeks for Rosaline!
How much salt water thrown away in waste     75
To season love, that of it doth not taste!
The sun not yet thy sighs from heaven clears,
Thy old groans yet ringing in mine ancient ears.
Lo, here upon thy cheek the stain doth sit
Of an old tear that is not washed off yet.     80
If e'er thou wast thyself, and these woes thine,
Thou and these woes were all for Rosaline.
And art thou changed? Pronounce this sentence then:
Women may fall when there's no strength in men.     85

**ROMEO**
Thou chid'st me oft for loving Rosaline.

**FRIAR LAWRENCE**
For doting, not for loving, pupil mine.

**ROMEO**
And bad'st me bury love.

**FRIAR LAWRENCE**        Not in a grave
To lay one in, another out to have.     90

**ROMEO**
I pray thee, chide me not. Her I love now
Doth grace for grace and love for love allow.
The other did not so.

**FRIAR LAWRENCE**        O, she knew well
Thy love did read by rote, that could not spell.     95
But come, young waverer, come, go with me.
In one respect I'll thy assistant be,
For this alliance may so happy prove
To turn your households' rancor to pure love.

100. **stand on:** i.e., insist on

**2.4** Mercutio and Benvolio meet the newly enthusiastic Romeo in the street. Romeo defeats Mercutio in a battle of wits. The Nurse finds Romeo, and he gives her a message for Juliet: meet me at Friar Lawrence's cell this afternoon, and we will there be married.

---

1. **should:** can
2. **tonight:** last night
3. **his man:** Romeo's servant
8. **his father's:** Romeo's **father's**
10. **answer it:** accept the challenge
12. **how:** i.e., by saying **how**
16. **pin:** bull's-eye
17. **blind . . . butt shaft:** Cupid's unbarbed arrow
20. **prince of cats:** Tybalt is the name of the Cat in the popular series of stories about Reynard the Fox.
21. **compliments:** i.e., fencing etiquette
22. **prick-song:** a written counterpoint to a simple melody

**ROMEO**
  O, let us hence. I stand on sudden haste. 100
**FRIAR LAWRENCE**
  Wisely and slow. They stumble that run fast.
                                    *They exit.*


⌜Scene 4⌝

*Enter Benvolio and Mercutio.*

**MERCUTIO**
  Where the devil should this Romeo be?
  Came he not home tonight?
**BENVOLIO**
  Not to his father's. I spoke with his man.
**MERCUTIO**
  Why, that same pale hard-hearted wench, that
    Rosaline, 5
  Torments him so that he will sure run mad.
**BENVOLIO**
  Tybalt, the kinsman to old Capulet,
  Hath sent a letter to his father's house.
**MERCUTIO**  A challenge, on my life.
**BENVOLIO**  Romeo will answer it. 10
**MERCUTIO**  Any man that can write may answer a letter.
**BENVOLIO**  Nay, he will answer the letter's master, how
    he dares, being dared.
**MERCUTIO**  Alas, poor Romeo, he is already dead,
    stabbed with a white wench's black eye, run 15
    through the ear with a love-song, the very pin of his
    heart cleft with the blind bow-boy's butt shaft. And
    is he a man to encounter Tybalt?
⌜**BENVOLIO**⌝  Why, what is Tybalt?
**MERCUTIO**  More than prince of cats. O, he's the coura- 20
    geous captain of compliments. He fights as you sing
    prick-song, keeps time, distance, and proportion.

23. **rests:** pauses (in music and fencing); **minim:** a musical note, in ancient music the shortest

25. **first house:** i.e., best fencing school

26. **first . . . cause:** causes demanding satisfaction according to the code of dueling

27. **passado:** a step forward with a thrust; **punto reverso:** backhanded thrust; **hay:** successful thrust (*ai*, Italian for "thou hast [it]")

29. **The pox of:** i.e., curses on

29–30. **affecting phantasimes:** pretentious fops

30. **new tuners of accent:** fashionable phrasemakers

31. **tall:** brave

35. **stand . . . on:** insist **so much** upon; **form:** fashion (but the word also means **bench** [line 36])

39. **Without his roe:** (1) without the first syllable of his name (so that nothing is left of him but a lover's sigh: "O me"); (2) without his "dear" (A **roe** is a small deer.); (3) sexually spent

41. **numbers:** verses; **Petrarch:** fourteenth-century Italian poet, who wrote sonnets to an idealized lady, **Laura; to:** in comparison to

43–44. **Dido . . . Cleopatra . . . Helen . . . Hero . . . Thisbe:** legendary and fictional romantic heroines (See pictures, pages 94, 100, and 106.) **hildings:** good-for-nothings

46–47. **French slop:** baggy trousers

50. **slip:** wordplay on a **slip** as a **counterfeit** coin (line 47); **conceive:** understand

52. **strain:** act in violation of

He rests his minim rests, one, two, and the third in
your bosom—the very butcher of a silk button, a
duelist, a duelist, a gentleman of the very first house    25
of the first and second cause. Ah, the immortal
*passado*, the *punto reverso*, the *hay!*

BENVOLIO  The what?

MERCUTIO  The pox of such antic, lisping, affecting
⌜phantasimes,⌝ these new tuners of accent: "By    30
Jesu, a very good blade! A very tall man! A very good
whore!" Why, is not this a lamentable thing, grandsire, that we should be thus afflicted with these
strange flies, these fashion-mongers, these ⌜"pardon-me" 's,⌝ who stand so much on the new form    35
that they cannot sit at ease on the old bench? O their
bones, their bones!

*Enter Romeo.*

BENVOLIO  Here comes Romeo, here comes Romeo.

MERCUTIO  Without his roe, like a dried herring. O
flesh, flesh, how art thou fishified! Now is he for the    40
numbers that Petrarch flowed in. Laura to his lady
was a kitchen wench (marry, she had a better love
to berhyme her), Dido a dowdy, Cleopatra a gypsy,
Helen and Hero hildings and harlots, Thisbe a gray
eye or so, but not to the purpose.—Signior Romeo,    45
*bonjour.* There's a French salutation to your French
slop. You gave us the counterfeit fairly last night.

ROMEO  Good morrow to you both. What counterfeit
did I give you?

MERCUTIO  The slip, sir, the slip. Can you not conceive?    50

ROMEO  Pardon, good Mercutio, my business was
great, and in such a case as mine a man may strain
courtesy.

MERCUTIO  That's as much as to say such a case as
yours constrains a man to bow in the hams.    55

ROMEO  Meaning, to curtsy.

59. **pink:** (1) perfect example; (2) a flower; (3) a decorative eyelet on a shoe

62. **pump:** shoe; **flowered:** pinked, decorated

67–68. **O . . . singleness:** i.e., **O** feeble joke, unique in its weakness **solely singular:** unique (the only **sole** left)

71. **Switch and spurs:** Romeo calls on Mercutio to urge on his wit as if it were a horse.

71–72. **cry a match:** declare myself the winner

73. **wild-goose chase:** a race in which the rider in the lead chooses the course

76. **Was . . . goose?:** i.e., have **I** scored a victory over **you** by talking of **the goose?**

78. **for the goose:** as a fool

81. **sweeting:** a sweet-flavored apple

85. **cheveril:** kid leather, which **stretches** easily

86. **ell:** about 45 inches

Dido. (2.4.43)
From [Guillaume Rouillé,] . . . *Promptuarii iconum* . . . (1553).

MERCUTIO  Thou hast most kindly hit it.

ROMEO  A most courteous exposition.

MERCUTIO  Nay, I am the very pink of courtesy.

ROMEO  "Pink" for flower. 60

MERCUTIO  Right.

ROMEO  Why, then is my pump well flowered.

MERCUTIO  Sure wit, follow me this jest now till thou hast worn out thy pump, that when the single sole of it is worn, the jest may remain, after the wearing, 65 solely singular.

ROMEO  O single-soled jest, solely singular for the singlencss.

MERCUTIO  Come between us, good Benvolio. My wits faints. 70

ROMEO  Switch and spurs, switch and spurs, or I'll cry a match.

MERCUTIO  Nay, if our wits run the wild-goose chase, I am done, for thou hast more of the wild goose in one of thy wits than, I am sure, I have in my whole 75 five. Was I with you there for the goose?

ROMEO  Thou wast never with me for anything when thou wast not there for the goose.

MERCUTIO  I will bite thee by the ear for that jest.

ROMEO  Nay, good goose, bite not. 80

MERCUTIO  Thy wit is a very bitter sweeting; it is a most sharp sauce.

ROMEO  And is it not, then, well served into a sweet goose?

MERCUTIO  O, here's a wit of cheveril that stretches 85 from an inch narrow to an ell broad.

ROMEO  I stretch it out for that word "broad," which added to the goose, proves thee far and wide a broad goose.

MERCUTIO  Why, is not this better now than groaning 90 for love? Now art thou sociable, now art thou Romeo, now art thou what thou art, by art as well as

94. **natural:** idiot

95. **bauble:** (1) jester's baton; (2) penis (Possible sexual puns continue in lines 95–102 with the words **hole, tale, hair, large, short, whole, depth,** and **occupy.**)

97–98. **against the hair:** i.e., against my wishes

104. **goodly gear:** attractive stuff

105. **a shirt and a smock:** i.e., a man and a woman (**A shirt** was a man's undergarment, **a smock** a woman's.)

112. **e'en:** i.e., afternoon

115. **dial:** clock; **prick:** point; penis

116. **Out upon you:** expression of annoyance; **What: what** sort of

119. **By my troth:** truly (a mild oath)

125. **fault:** lack

Medlars, or open-arses. (2.1.37, 39, 41)
From *The grete herball* . . . (1529).

by nature. For this driveling love is like a great
natural that runs lolling up and down to hide his
bauble in a hole.                                                    95

BENVOLIO  Stop there, stop there.

MERCUTIO  Thou desirest me to stop in my tale against
the hair.

BENVOLIO  Thou wouldst else have made thy tale large.

MERCUTIO  O, thou art deceived. I would have made it  100
short, for I was come to the whole depth of my tale
and meant indeed to occupy the argument no
longer.

*Enter Nurse and her man ⌜Peter.⌝*

ROMEO  Here's goodly gear. A sail, a sail!

MERCUTIO  Two, two—a shirt and a smock.               105

NURSE  Peter.

PETER  Anon.

NURSE  My fan, Peter.

MERCUTIO  Good Peter, to hide her face, for her fan's
the fairer face.                                                    110

NURSE  God you good morrow, gentlemen.

MERCUTIO  God you good e'en, fair gentlewoman.

NURSE  Is it good e'en?

MERCUTIO  'Tis no less, I tell you, for the bawdy hand of
the dial is now upon the prick of noon.             115

NURSE  Out upon you! What a man are you?

ROMEO  One, gentlewoman, that God hath made, himself to mar.

NURSE  By my troth, it is well said: "for himself to
mar," quoth he? Gentlemen, can any of you tell me  120
where I may find the young Romeo?

ROMEO  I can tell you, but young Romeo will be older
when you have found him than he was when you
sought him. I am the youngest of that name, for
fault of a worse.                                                   125

NURSE  You say well.

127. **took:** understood

129. **confidence:** Nurse's mistake for "conference"

131. **indite:** a deliberate "mistake" for "invite"

132. **bawd:** procuress (The word also had the dialect meaning **hare** [line 134].) **So ho:** hunter's cry

134–35. **Lenten pie:** one that should contain no meat

135. **something:** somewhat; **hoar:** musty (with a pun on "whore"); **ere it be spent:** before it's used up

140. **for a score:** i.e., to pay for

141. **hoars:** turns moldy, hoary

147. **saucy merchant:** insolent fellow

148. **ropery:** perhaps, indecent talk; or, perhaps, roguery

151. **stand to:** i.e., defend

152. **An:** if

153. **lustier:** more vigorous

154. **jacks:** rascals

155. **flirt-gills:** flirting women

156. **skains-mates:** meaning unknown

157. **suffer:** allow

MERCUTIO  Yea, is the worst well? Very well took, i'
  faith, wisely, wisely.

NURSE  If you be he, sir, I desire some confidence with
  you.                                                    130

BENVOLIO  She will indite him to some supper.

MERCUTIO  A bawd, a bawd, a bawd. So ho!

ROMEO  What hast thou found?

MERCUTIO  No hare, sir, unless a hare, sir, in a Lenten
  pie that is something stale and hoar ere it be spent.  135
  ⌜*Singing.*⌝      *An old hare hoar,*
              *And an old hare hoar,*
                *Is very good meat in Lent.*
              *But a hare that is hoar*
              *Is too much for a score*                    140
                *When it hoars ere it be spent.*

  Romeo, will you come to your father's? We'll to
  dinner thither.

ROMEO  I will follow you.

MERCUTIO  Farewell, ancient lady. Farewell, lady, lady,  145
  lady.                        ⌜*Mercutio and Benvolio*⌝ *exit.*

NURSE  I pray you, sir, what saucy merchant was this
  that was so full of his ropery?

ROMEO  A gentleman, nurse, that loves to hear himself
  talk and will speak more in a minute than he will     150
  stand to in a month.

NURSE  An he speak anything against me, I'll take him
  down, an he were lustier than he is, and twenty
  such jacks. An if I cannot, I'll find those that shall.
  Scurvy knave, I am none of his flirt-gills; I am none  155
  of his skains-mates. ⌜*To Peter.*⌝ And thou must stand
  by too and suffer every knave to use me at his
  pleasure.

PETER  I saw no man use you at his pleasure. If I had,
  my weapon should quickly have been out. I war-        160
  rant you, I dare draw as soon as another man, if I
  see occasion in a good quarrel, and the law on my
  side.

167. **inquire you out:** find you
169. **in:** i.e., into
174. **weak:** despicable
175. **commend me:** offer my greetings
180. **mark me:** listen to me
184. **shrift:** confession
192. **tackled stair:** rope ladder
193. **topgallant:** summit (literally, the platform atop a mast on a ship)
194. **convoy:** means of conveyance
195. **quit:** reward

Cleopatra. (2.4.43)
From Jacobus de Strada,
*Epitome thesauri antiquitatum . . .* (1557).

NURSE  Now, afore God, I am so vexed that every part
about me quivers. Scurvy knave! ⌜*To Romeo.*⌝ Pray  165
you, sir, a word. And, as I told you, my young lady
bid me inquire you out. What she bid me say, I will
keep to myself. But first let me tell you, if you
should lead her in a fool's paradise, as they say, it
were a very gross kind of behavior, as they say. For  170
the gentlewoman is young; and therefore, if you
should deal double with her, truly it were an ill
thing to be offered to any gentlewoman, and very
weak dealing.

ROMEO  Nurse, commend me to thy lady and mistress.  175
I protest unto thee—

NURSE  Good heart, and i' faith I will tell her as much.
Lord, Lord, she will be a joyful woman.

ROMEO  What wilt thou tell her, nurse? Thou dost not
mark me.  180

NURSE  I will tell her, sir, that you do protest, which, as
I take it, is a gentlemanlike offer.

ROMEO  Bid her devise
Some means to come to shrift this afternoon,
And there she shall at Friar Lawrence' cell  185
Be shrived and married. Here is for thy pains.
⌜*Offering her money.*⌝

NURSE  No, truly, sir, not a penny.

ROMEO  Go to, I say you shall.

NURSE
This afternoon, sir? Well, she shall be there.

ROMEO
And stay, good nurse, behind the abbey wall.  190
Within this hour my man shall be with thee
And bring thee cords made like a tackled stair,
Which to the high topgallant of my joy
Must be my convoy in the secret night.
Farewell. Be trusty, and I'll quit thy pains.  195
Farewell. Commend me to thy mistress.

200. **counsel:** i.e., a secret

203. **prating:** chattering

204–5. **would . . . aboard:** i.e., is eager to claim her

205. **had as lief:** i.e., would just as happily

209. **clout:** rag; **versal:** i.e., universal

210. **a letter:** i.e., the same **letter**

212. **that's the dog's name:** because the letter *R* may be sounded as a growl

214. **sententious:** the Nurse's mistake for "sentence," i.e., clever saying; **of it:** about it

219. **apace:** quickly

**2.5** Juliet waits impatiently for the Nurse to return. Her impatience grows when the Nurse, having returned, is slow to deliver Romeo's message. Finally Juliet learns that if she wants to marry Romeo, she need only go to Friar Lawrence's cell that afternoon.

———————————

**NURSE**
Now, God in heaven bless thee! Hark you, sir.

**ROMEO** What sayst thou, my dear nurse?

**NURSE**
Is your man secret? Did you ne'er hear say
"Two may keep counsel, putting one away"?      200

**ROMEO**
Warrant thee, my man's as true as steel.

**NURSE** Well, sir, my mistress is the sweetest lady. Lord,
Lord, when 'twas a little prating thing—O, there is
a nobleman in town, one Paris, that would fain lay
knife aboard, but she, good soul, had as lief see a    205
toad, a very toad, as see him. I anger her sometimes
and tell her that Paris is the properer man, but I'll
warrant you, when I say so, she looks as pale as any
clout in the versal world. Doth not rosemary and
Romeo begin both with a letter?      210

**ROMEO** Ay, nurse, what of that? Both with an *R*.

**NURSE** Ah, mocker, that's the ⌜dog's⌝ name. *R* is for
the—No, I know it begins with some other letter,
and she hath the prettiest sententious of it, of you
and rosemary, that it would do you good to hear it.    215

**ROMEO** Commend me to thy lady.

**NURSE** Ay, a thousand times.—Peter.

**PETER** Anon.

**NURSE** Before and apace.

                                  ⌜*They*⌝ *exit.*


⌜Scene 5⌝

*Enter Juliet.*

**JULIET**
The clock struck nine when I did send the Nurse.
In half an hour she promised to return.
Perchance she cannot meet him. That's not so.
O, she is lame! Love's heralds should be thoughts,
Which ten times faster glides than the sun's beams,    5

6. **louring:** darkly threatening

7. **Therefore . . . Love:** i.e., this is why **Love** (i.e., Venus, goddess of love) is often represented in a chariot drawn by quick-winged **doves** (See picture, below.)

12. **affections:** feelings, emotions

16. **feign as:** act as if

23. **them:** i.e., **news** (often used in the plural)

26. **Give me leave:** i.e., leave me alone

27. **jaunt:** tiring journey

31. **stay:** wait

35. **in:** i.e., with respect to

Venus and Cupid. (2.5.7–8)
From Joannes ab Indagine, *The book of palmestry . . .* (1666).

Driving back shadows over louring hills.
Therefore do nimble-pinioned doves draw Love,
And therefore hath the wind-swift Cupid wings.
Now is the sun upon the highmost hill
Of this day's journey, and from nine till twelve          10
Is ⌜three⌝ long hours, yet she is not come.
Had she affections and warm youthful blood,
She would be as swift in motion as a ball;
My words would bandy her to my sweet love,
And his to me.                                            15
But old folks, many feign as they were dead,
Unwieldy, slow, heavy, and pale as lead.

　　　　　*Enter Nurse* ⌜*and Peter.*⌝

O God, she comes!—O, honey nurse, what news?
Hast thou met with him? Send thy man away.
NURSE  Peter, stay at the gate.          ⌜*Peter exits.*⌝  20
JULIET
　Now, good sweet nurse—O Lord, why lookest thou
　　sad?
　Though news be sad, yet tell them merrily.
　If good, thou shamest the music of sweet news
　By playing it to me with so sour a face.               25
NURSE
　I am aweary. Give me leave awhile.
　Fie, how my bones ache! What a jaunt have I!
JULIET
　I would thou hadst my bones, and I thy news.
　Nay, come, I pray thee, speak. Good, good nurse,
　　speak.                                                30
NURSE
　Jesu, what haste! Can you not stay awhile?
　Do you not see that I am out of breath?
JULIET
　How art thou out of breath, when thou hast breath
　To say to me that thou art out of breath?
　The excuse that thou dost make in this delay          35

38. **stay the circumstance:** wait for the details
40. **simple:** foolish
44. **talked on: talked** about
45. **flower:** best example
47. **What:** an interjection here introducing a question
53. **o' t' other:** on the **other**
54. **Beshrew:** curse (here, a mild imprecation); **about:** hither and thither
59. **honest:** honorable
66. **God's lady:** the Virgin Mary
67. **hot:** impatient; **Marry, come up, I trow:** an expression of irritation

Helen of Troy. (2.4.44)
From [Guillaume Rouillé,] . . . *Promptuarii iconum* . . . (1553).

Is longer than the tale thou dost excuse.
Is thy news good or bad? Answer to that.
Say either, and I'll stay the circumstance.
Let me be satisfied; is 't good or bad?

NURSE   Well, you have made a simple choice. You know     40
  not how to choose a man. Romeo? No, not he.
  Though his face be better than any man's, yet his leg
  excels all men's, and for a hand and a foot and a
  body, though they be not to be talked on, yet they
  are past compare. He is not the flower of courtesy,     45
  but I'll warrant him as gentle as a lamb. Go thy
  ways, wench. Serve God. What, have you dined at
  home?

JULIET
No, no. But all this did I know before.
What says he of our marriage? What of that?     50

NURSE
Lord, how my head aches! What a head have I!
It beats as it would fall in twenty pieces.
My back o' t' other side! Ah, my back, my back!
Beshrew your heart for sending me about
To catch my death with jaunting up and down.     55

JULIET
I' faith, I am sorry that thou art not well.
Sweet, sweet, sweet nurse, tell me, what says my
  love?

NURSE   Your love says, like an honest gentleman, and a
  courteous, and a kind, and a handsome, and, I     60
  warrant, a virtuous—Where is your mother?

JULIET
Where is my mother? Why, she is within.
Where should she be? How oddly thou repliest:
"Your love says, like an honest gentleman,
Where is your mother?"     65

NURSE                           O God's lady dear,
Are you so hot? Marry, come up, I trow.

70. **coil:** fuss

73. **hie you:** hurry

75. **wanton:** uncontrollable, rebellious

76. **They'll ... straight:** i.e., they turn red immediately

79. **climb a bird's nest:** i.e., **climb** up to your bedroom

81. **bear the burden:** (1) do your own work; (2) bear the weight of your lover; **soon at night:** i.e., tonight

**2.6** Juliet meets Romeo at Friar Lawrence's cell. After expressing their mutual love, they exit with the Friar to be married.

———————————

3. **But ... can:** i.e., no matter **what sorrow** comes

4. **countervail:** i.e., outweigh

6. **Do thou but close:** if you will only join

Is this the poultice for my aching bones?
Henceforward do your messages yourself.

JULIET
Here's such a coil. Come, what says Romeo?     70

NURSE
Have you got leave to go to shrift today?

JULIET   I have.

NURSE
Then hie you hence to Friar Lawrence' cell.
There stays a husband to make you a wife.
Now comes the wanton blood up in your cheeks;     75
They'll be in scarlet straight at any news.
Hie you to church. I must another way,
To fetch a ladder by the which your love
Must climb a bird's nest soon when it is dark.
I am the drudge and toil in your delight,     80
But you shall bear the burden soon at night.
Go. I'll to dinner. Hie you to the cell.

JULIET
Hie to high fortune! Honest nurse, farewell.

*They exit.*

Not going to turn out so well.

⌈Scene 6⌉

*Enter Friar ⌈Lawrence⌉ and Romeo.*

FRIAR LAWRENCE
So smile the heavens upon this holy act
That after-hours with sorrow chide us not.

ROMEO
Amen, amen. But come what sorrow can,
It cannot countervail the exchange of joy
That one short minute gives me in her sight.     5
Do thou but close our hands with holy words,
Then love-devouring death do what he dare,
It is enough I may but call her mine.

FRIAR LAWRENCE
These violent delights have violent ends

10. **powder:** gunpowder

12. **in his own:** in its **own**

13. **confounds:** destroys

15. **Too swift:** i.e., that which goes too fast (Proverbial: "The more haste, the worse speed [i.e., success].")

18. **gossamers:** cobwebs

19. **idles:** move idly; **wanton:** playful

20. **light:** insubstantial; **vanity:** transitory human experience

21. **confessor:** accented on the first and third syllables

24. **measure:** quantity

25. **that:** i.e., if; **more:** greater

26. **blazon:** describe; proclaim

28. **Unfold:** reveal

29. **in either:** in each other; **by:** by means of

30. **Conceit:** understanding

31. **Brags of his:** boasts of its

32. **but:** only; **count:** enumerate

34. **sum up sum:** calculate the total

36. **by your leaves:** i.e., begging **your** pardons

37. **Till . . . one:** i.e., until I, on behalf of the **Church,** make you a married couple

And in their triumph die, like fire and powder, 10
Which, as they kiss, consume. The sweetest honey
Is loathsome in his own deliciousness
And in the taste confounds the appetite.
Therefore love moderately. Long love doth so.
Too swift arrives as tardy as too slow. 15

fire
shed

*Enter Juliet.*

Here comes the lady. O, so light a foot
Will ne'er wear out the everlasting flint.
A lover may bestride the gossamers
That idles in the wanton summer air,
And yet not fall, so light is vanity. 20

JULIET
Good even to my ghostly confessor.

FRIAR LAWRENCE
Romeo shall thank thee, daughter, for us both.

JULIET
As much to him, else is his thanks too much.

ROMEO
Ah, Juliet, if the measure of thy joy
Be heaped like mine, and that thy skill be more 25
To blazon it, then sweeten with thy breath
This neighbor air, and let rich ⌜music's⌝ tongue
Unfold the imagined happiness that both
Receive in either by this dear encounter.

JULIET
Conceit, more rich in matter than in words, 30
Brags of his substance, not of ornament.
They are but beggars that can count their worth,
But my true love is grown to such excess
I cannot sum up sum of half my wealth.

FRIAR LAWRENCE
Come, come with me, and we will make short work, 35
For, by your leaves, you shall not stay alone
Till Holy Church incorporate two in one.
⌜*They exit.*⌝

*The Tragedy of*

# ROMEO

## AND

# JULIET

ACT 3

**3.1** Mercutio and Benvolio encounter Tybalt on the street. As soon as Romeo arrives, Tybalt tries to provoke him to fight. When Romeo refuses, Mercutio answers Tybalt's challenge. They duel and Mercutio is fatally wounded. Romeo then avenges Mercutio's death by killing Tybalt in a duel. Benvolio tries to persuade the Prince to excuse Romeo's slaying of Tybalt; however, the Capulets demand that Romeo pay with his life; the Prince instead banishes Romeo from Verona.

––––––––––

2. **Capels:** Capulets

6. **claps me:** i.e., **claps** (just as **draws him** [line 9] is Mercutio's way of saying "**draws** his **sword**")

8–9. **by . . . cup:** i.e., **by the** time his **second** drink has had an effect on him

9. **drawer:** waiter

13–14. **as soon moved . . . moved:** i.e., **as soon** provoked **to be** angry **and as** irritable

16. **an:** if; **two:** Mercutio deliberately misconstrues Benvolio's "**to**" as "**two.**"

21. **nuts:** hazelnuts

# ⌈ACT 3⌉

## ⌈Scene 1⌉

*Enter Mercutio, Benvolio, and ⌈their⌉ men.*

BENVOLIO
I pray thee, good Mercutio, let's retire.
The day is hot, the Capels ⌈are⌉ abroad,
And if we meet we shall not 'scape a brawl,
For now, these hot days, is the mad blood stirring.

MERCUTIO  Thou art like one of these fellows that, when    5
he enters the confines of a tavern, claps me his
sword upon the table and says "God send me no
need of thee" and, by the operation of the second
cup, draws him on the drawer when indeed there is
no need.    10

BENVOLIO  Am I like such a fellow?

MERCUTIO  Come, come, thou art as hot a jack in thy
mood as any in Italy, and as soon moved to be
moody, and as soon moody to be moved.

BENVOLIO  And what to?    15

MERCUTIO  Nay, an there were two such, we should
have none shortly, for one would kill the other.
Thou—why, thou wilt quarrel with a man that
hath a hair more or a hair less in his beard than
thou hast. Thou wilt quarrel with a man for crack-    20
ing nuts, having no other reason but because thou
hast hazel eyes. What eye but such an eye would spy
out such a quarrel? Thy head is as full of quarrels as

115

24. **meat:** food

24–25. **hath ... quarreling:** has **been beaten** into the state of a rotten **egg** (i.e., has been made addleheaded) as a consequence of your **quarreling**

29. **doublet:** close-fitting jacket (See picture, below.)

31. **tutor me from:** teach me to avoid

33. **fee simple:** title to full ownership

35. **simple:** foolish

46. **thou consortest:** you associate

47. **Consort:** play music with (A **consort** is a company of musicians. Mercutio links musicians to **minstrels,** who were classed with vagabonds.)

49. **fiddlestick:** probably his rapier

50. **Zounds:** i.e., by Christ's wounds, a strong oath

51. **haunt:** meeting place

Elizabethan Englishmen in doublet and hose. (3.1.29)
From Robert Greene, *A quip for an vpstart courtier* . . . (1620).

an egg is full of meat, and yet thy head hath been
beaten as addle as an egg for quarreling. Thou hast      25
quarreled with a man for coughing in the street
because he hath wakened thy dog that hath lain
asleep in the sun. Didst thou not fall out with a tailor
for wearing his new doublet before Easter? With
another, for tying his new shoes with old ribbon?        30
And yet thou wilt tutor me from quarreling?

BENVOLIO  An I were so apt to quarrel as thou art, any
man should buy the fee simple of my life for an
hour and a quarter.

MERCUTIO  The fee simple? O simple!                      35

*Enter Tybalt, Petruchio, and others.*

BENVOLIO  By my head, here comes the Capulets.

MERCUTIO  By my heel, I care not.

TYBALT, ⌜*to his companions*⌝
Follow me close, for I will speak to them.—
Gentlemen, good e'en. A word with one of you.

MERCUTIO  And but one word with one of us? Couple it     40
with something. Make it a word and a blow.

TYBALT  You shall find me apt enough to that, sir, an
you will give me occasion.

MERCUTIO  Could you not take some occasion without
giving?                                                  45

TYBALT  Mercutio, thou consortest with Romeo.

MERCUTIO  Consort? What, dost thou make us minstrels? An thou make minstrels of us, look to hear
nothing but discords. Here's my fiddlestick; here's
that shall make you dance. Zounds, consort!              50

BENVOLIO
We talk here in the public haunt of men.
Either withdraw unto some private place,
Or reason coldly of your grievances,
Or else depart. Here all eyes gaze on us.

57. **my man:** i.e., the one I wish to fight (Mercutio plays on the word's meaning of servant, attendant.)

58. **your livery:** the uniform of your servants

59. **field:** i.e., place for a duel

64–65. **appertaining rage / To: rage** appropriate in response **to**

70. **devise:** think out, imagine

71. **of:** i.e., for

72. **tender:** regard

75. **Alla stoccato:** literally, "at the thrust," presumably Mercutio's derisive nickname for Tybalt, the fencing expert; **carries it away:** i.e., wins (because Romeo refuses to fight)

76. **ratcatcher:** "prince of cats" (See note to 2.4.20, above.)

79. **withal:** with

80. **use:** treat; **dry-beat:** thrash

MERCUTIO
Men's eyes were made to look, and let them gaze.    55
I will not budge for no man's pleasure, I.

*Enter Romeo.*

TYBALT
Well, peace be with you, sir. Here comes my man.
MERCUTIO
But I'll be hanged, sir, if he wear your livery.
Marry, go before to field, he'll be your follower.
Your Worship in that sense may call him "man."    60
TYBALT
Romeo, the love I bear thee can afford
No better term than this: thou art a villain.
ROMEO
Tybalt, the reason that I have to love thee
Doth much excuse the appertaining rage
To such a greeting. Villain am I none.    65
Therefore farewell. I see thou knowest me not.
TYBALT
Boy, this shall not excuse the injuries
That thou hast done me. Therefore turn and draw.
ROMEO
I do protest I never injured thee
But love thee better than thou canst devise    70
Till thou shalt know the reason of my love.
And so, good Capulet, which name I tender
As dearly as mine own, be satisfied.
MERCUTIO
O calm, dishonorable, vile submission!
*Alla stoccato* carries it away.         ⌜*He draws.*⌝    75
Tybalt, you ratcatcher, will you walk?
TYBALT   What wouldst thou have with me?
MERCUTIO   Good king of cats, nothing but one of your
    nine lives, that I mean to make bold withal, and, as
    you shall use me hereafter, dry-beat the rest of the    80

81. **pilcher:** A "pilch" is, literally, a leather garment; here, a scabbard.

86. **passado:** a fencing step forward with a thrust

90. **bandying:** fighting

94. **sped:** done for, destroyed

95. **hath nothing:** i.e., has suffered no wound

98. **villain:** i.e., villein, servant

103. **peppered:** finished off, destroyed

106. **book of arithmetic:** i.e., the fencing manual (See picture, page 124.)

A street fight. (3.1.86 SD)
From Andreas Friedrich, *Emblemes noueeaux . . .* (1617).

eight. Will you pluck your sword out of his pilcher
by the ears? Make haste, lest mine be about your
ears ere it be out.

TYBALT   I am for you.                    ⌜*He draws.*⌝

ROMEO
Gentle Mercutio, put thy rapier up.                        85

MERCUTIO   Come, sir, your *passado*.        ⌜*They fight.*⌝

ROMEO
Draw, Benvolio, beat down their weapons.
                                   ⌜*Romeo draws.*⌝
Gentlemen, for shame forbear this outrage!
Tybalt! Mercutio! The Prince expressly hath
Forbid this bandying in Verona streets.                     90
Hold, Tybalt! Good Mercutio!
           ⌜*Romeo attempts to beat down their rapiers.*
                        *Tybalt stabs Mercutio.*⌝
⌜PETRUCHIO⌝   Away, Tybalt!
           ⌜*Tybalt, Petruchio, and their followers exit.*⌝

MERCUTIO   I am hurt.
A plague o' both houses! I am sped.
Is he gone and hath nothing?                               95

BENVOLIO                              What, art thou hurt?

MERCUTIO
Ay, ay, a scratch, a scratch. Marry, 'tis enough.
Where is my page?—Go, villain, fetch a surgeon.
                                   ⌜*Page exits.*⌝

ROMEO
Courage, man, the hurt cannot be much.

MERCUTIO   No, 'tis not so deep as a well, nor so wide as    100
a church door, but 'tis enough. 'Twill serve. Ask for
me tomorrow, and you shall find me a grave man. I
am peppered, I warrant, for this world. A plague o'
both your houses! Zounds, a dog, a rat, a mouse, a
cat, to scratch a man to death! A braggart, a rogue, a   105
villain that fights by the book of arithmetic! Why the
devil came you between us? I was hurt under your
arm.

112. **worms' meat:** food for worms
114. **near ally:** close relative
115. **very:** true, sincere
118. **cousin:** i.e., kinsman by marriage
120. **in my temper softened valor's steel:** i.e., has made my disposition soft **temper:** temperament (with a glancing reference to the hardening or tempering of **steel**)
121. **brave:** splendid
122. **aspired:** risen up to
123. **Which:** i.e., Mercutio's **spirit; untimely:** prematurely
124. **on more . . . depend:** waits in suspense on the future
125. **others:** future days
128. **respective lenity:** considerate mercifulness
129. **conduct:** guide
131. **late:** recently

ROMEO  I thought all for the best.

MERCUTIO
  Help me into some house, Benvolio,
  Or I shall faint. A plague o' both your houses!    110
  They have made worms' meat of me.
  I have it, and soundly, too. Your houses!
                ⌜*All but Romeo*⌝ *exit.*

ROMEO
  This gentleman, the Prince's near ally,
  My very friend, hath got this mortal hurt    115
  In my behalf. My reputation stained
  With Tybalt's slander—Tybalt, that an hour
  Hath been my cousin! O sweet Juliet,
  Thy beauty hath made me effeminate
  And in my temper softened valor's steel.    120

            *Enter Benvolio.*

BENVOLIO
  O Romeo, Romeo, brave Mercutio is dead.
  That gallant spirit hath aspired the clouds,
  Which too untimely here did scorn the earth.

ROMEO
  This day's black fate on more days doth depend.
  This but begins the woe others must end.    125

          ⌜*Enter Tybalt.*⌝

BENVOLIO
  Here comes the furious Tybalt back again.

ROMEO
  ⌜Alive⌝ in triumph, and Mercutio slain!
  Away to heaven, respective lenity,
  And ⌜fire-eyed⌝ fury be my conduct now.—
  Now, Tybalt, take the "villain" back again    130
  That late thou gavest me, for Mercutio's soul
  Is but a little way above our heads,
  Staying for thine to keep him company.
  Either thou or I, or both, must go with him.

139. **up:** i.e., **up** in arms
140. **amazed:** astounded; **doom thee death:** condemn you to **death**
142. **Fortune's:** the goddess Fortuna's; **fool:** plaything (See note to 3.5.60.)
150. **discover:** reveal
151. **manage:** course

# VINCENTIO
## SAVIOLO
his Practiſe.

*In two Bookes.*

*The firſt intreating of the vſe of the Rapier and Dagger.*

*The ſecond, of Honor and honorable Quarrels.*

LONDON
Printed by IOHN WOLFE.
1 5 9 5.

A fencing manual. (3.1.106)
From Vincentio Saviolo, . . . *His practiſe . . . of the use of the rapier and dagger . . . of honor and honorable quarrels* . . . (1595).

TYBALT
  Thou wretched boy that didst consort him here          135
  Shalt with him hence.
ROMEO                    This shall determine that.
                          *They fight. Tybalt falls.*

BENVOLIO
  Romeo, away, begone!
  The citizens are up, and Tybalt slain.    Theus 1/6
  Stand not amazed. The Prince will doom thee death    140
  If thou art taken. Hence, be gone, away.
ROMEO
  O, I am Fortune's fool!
BENVOLIO                    Why dost thou stay?
                          *Romeo exits.*

              *Enter Citizens.*

CITIZEN
  Which way ran he that killed Mercutio?
  Tybalt, that murderer, which way ran he?            145
BENVOLIO
  There lies that Tybalt.
CITIZEN, ⌐*to Tybalt*⌐      Up, sir, go with me.
  I charge thee in the Prince's name, obey.

*Enter Prince, old Montague, Capulet, their Wives and all.*

PRINCE
  Where are the vile beginners of this fray?
BENVOLIO
  O noble prince, I can discover all                  150
  The unlucky manage of this fatal brawl.
  There lies the man, slain by young Romeo,
  That slew thy kinsman, brave Mercutio.
LADY CAPULET
  Tybalt, my cousin, O my brother's child!
  O prince! O cousin! Husband! O, the blood is spilled  155
  Of my dear kinsman! Prince, as thou art true,

161. **fair:** politely; **bethink:** reflect upon
162. **nice:** trivial, trifling; **withal:** in addition
165. **take truce with:** placate; **spleen:** i.e., anger
166. **tilts:** strikes
172. **Retorts it:** sends it back again
177. **envious:** malicious
178. **stout:** valiant
180. **entertained:** contemplated
186. **Affection:** i.e., inclination toward them

For blood of ours, shed blood of Montague.
O cousin, cousin!

PRINCE
Benvolio, who began this bloody fray?

BENVOLIO
Tybalt, here slain, whom Romeo's hand did slay— 160
Romeo, that spoke him fair, bid him bethink
How nice the quarrel was, and urged withal
Your high displeasure. All this utterèd
With gentle breath, calm look, knees humbly bowed
Could not take truce with the unruly spleen 165
Of Tybalt, deaf to peace, but that he tilts
With piercing steel at bold Mercutio's breast,
Who, all as hot, turns deadly point to point
And, with a martial scorn, with one hand beats
Cold death aside and with the other sends 170
It back to Tybalt, whose dexterity
Retorts it. Romeo he cries aloud
"Hold, friends! Friends, part!" and swifter than his
   tongue
His ⌐agile⌐ arm beats down their fatal points, 175
And 'twixt them rushes; underneath whose arm
An envious thrust from Tybalt hit the life
Of stout Mercutio, and then Tybalt fled.
But by and by comes back to Romeo,
Who had but newly entertained revenge, 180
And to 't they go like lightning, for ere I
Could draw to part them was stout Tybalt slain,
And, as he fell, did Romeo turn and fly.
This is the truth, or let Benvolio die.

LADY CAPULET
He is a kinsman to the Montague. 185
Affection makes him false; he speaks not true.
Some twenty of them fought in this black strife,
And all those twenty could but kill one life.
I beg for justice, which thou, prince, must give.
Romeo slew Tybalt; Romeo must not live. 190

192. **his dear blood:** i.e., Mercutio's **blood**

194. **concludes but:** only **concludes; should end: should** have ended

198. **I:** The Prince switches from the royal "we" of line 197 to express a personal, rather than merely official, interest in the feud.

199. **My blood:** i.e., my kinsman (Mercutio)

200. **amerce:** punish

203. **Nor tears:** i.e., neither **tears; purchase out:** i.e., buy impunity for

206. **attend:** pay attention to, heed

**3.2** Juliet longs for Romeo to come to her. The Nurse arrives with the news that Romeo has killed Tybalt and has been banished. Juliet at first feels grief for the loss of her cousin Tybalt and verbally attacks Romeo, but then renounces these feelings and devotes herself to grief for Romeo's banishment. The Nurse promises to bring Romeo to Juliet that night.

---

1–2. **Gallop . . . lodging:** addressed to the horses of Phoebus, the sun god, urging speed (See picture, page 86.)

2. **wagoner:** charioteer

3. **Phaëton:** the son of Phoebus, allowed to drive the chariot of the sun but unable to control the horses (See picture, page 136.)

5. **close curtain:** i.e., **curtain** of secrecy

6. **runaways':** perhaps, vagabonds'; **wink:** i.e., shut, close

9. **By:** i.e., by the light of

PRINCE
  Romeo slew him; he slew Mercutio.
  Who now the price of his dear blood doth owe?
⌜MONTAGUE⌝
  Not Romeo, Prince; he was Mercutio's friend.
  His fault concludes but what the law should end,
  The life of Tybalt.                                          195
PRINCE               And for that offense
  Immediately we do exile him hence.
  I have an interest in your hearts' proceeding:
  My blood for your rude brawls doth lie a-bleeding.
  But I'll amerce you with so strong a fine          200
  That you shall all repent the loss of mine.
  ⌜I⌝ will be deaf to pleading and excuses.
  Nor tears nor prayers shall purchase out abuses.
  Therefore use none. Let Romeo hence in haste,
  Else, when he is found, that hour is his last.          205
  Bear hence this body and attend our will.
  Mercy but murders, pardoning those that kill.
                ⌜*They*⌝ *exit,* ⌜*the Capulet men*
                   *bearing off Tybalt's body.*⌝


⌜Scene 2⌝

*Enter Juliet alone.*

JULIET
  Gallop apace, you fiery-footed steeds,
  Towards Phoebus' lodging. Such a wagoner
  As Phaëton would whip you to the west
  And bring in cloudy night immediately.
  Spread thy close curtain, love-performing night,          5
  That runaways' eyes may wink, and Romeo
  Leap to these arms, untalked of and unseen.
  Lovers can see to do their amorous rites
  By their own beauties, or, if love be blind,

10. **civil:** i.e., soberly dressed

12. **learn:** teach

14–15. **Hood . . . mantle:** i.e., cover my blushes with your dark cloak (The language is from falconry. An untamed [**unmanned**] falcon beat its wings [**bating**] unless its head was covered with a hood.) See picture, below.

15. **strange:** unfamiliar

16. **Think:** i.e., and **think**

23. **I:** often changed by editors to "he" (See longer note, page 247.)

28. **mansion:** dwelling place

33 SD. **cords:** i.e., the rope ladder

A hooded falcon. (3.2.14)
From Antonio Francesco Doni, *L'academia Peregrina* . . . (1552).

It best agrees with night. Come, civil night,        10
Thou sober-suited matron all in black,
And learn me how to lose a winning match
Played for a pair of stainless maidenhoods.
Hood my unmanned blood, bating in my cheeks,
With thy black mantle till strange love grow bold,        15
Think true love acted simple modesty.
Come, night. Come, Romeo. Come, thou day in
    night,
For thou wilt lie upon the wings of night
Whiter than new snow upon a raven's back.        20
Come, gentle night; come, loving black-browed
    night,
Give me my Romeo, and when I shall die,        *face*
Take him and cut him out in little stars,        *shadow*
And he will make the face of heaven so fine        25
That all the world will be in love with night
And pay no worship to the garish sun.
O, I have bought the mansion of a love
But not possessed it, and, though I am sold,
Not yet enjoyed. So tedious is this day        30
As is the night before some festival
To an impatient child that hath new robes
And may not wear them.

                *Enter Nurse with cords.*

                        O, here comes my nurse,
And she brings news, and every tongue that speaks        35
But Romeo's name speaks heavenly eloquence.—
Now, nurse, what news? What hast thou there? The
    cords
That Romeo bid thee fetch?
NURSE                        Ay, ay, the cords.        40
            ⌜*Dropping the rope ladder.*⌝
JULIET
Ay me, what news? Why dost thou wring thy hands?

42. **weraday:** welladay, an expression of sorrow

45. **envious:** malicious

52. **"I":** pronounced the same as **ay**, which means "yes"

53. **cockatrice:** a mythical serpent (with the head, wings, and feet of a cock) whose look could kill (See picture, below.)

55. **those eyes:** i.e., Romeo's **eyes**

57. **weal:** well-being, happiness

59. **God save the mark:** a superstitious expression

60. **corse:** i.e., corpse

62. **gore:** clotted

63. **bankrout:** i.e., bankrupt

65. **Vile . . . resign:** i.e., let my body (itself, according to the Bible, originally made from dust or **vile earth**) be committed **to** the **earth**

66. **press . . . bier:** i.e., weigh down a single **bier**

A cockatrice. (3.2.53)
From Joachim Camerarius,
. . . *Symbolorum et emblematum* . . . (1605).

NURSE
Ah weraday, he's dead, he's dead, he's dead!
We are undone, lady, we are undone.
Alack the day, he's gone, he's killed, he's dead.

JULIET
Can heaven be so envious?                                    45

NURSE                          Romeo can,
Though heaven cannot. O Romeo, Romeo,
Whoever would have thought it? Romeo!

JULIET
What devil art thou that dost torment me thus?
This torture should be roared in dismal hell.                50
Hath Romeo slain himself? Say thou but "Ay,"
And that bare vowel "I" shall poison more
Than the death-darting eye of cockatrice.
I am not I if there be such an "I,"
Or those eyes ⌜shut⌝ that makes thee answer "Ay."          55
If he be slain, say "Ay," or if not, "No."
Brief sounds determine my weal or woe.

NURSE
I saw the wound. I saw it with mine eyes
(God save the mark!) here on his manly breast—
A piteous corse, a bloody piteous corse,                     60
Pale, pale as ashes, all bedaubed in blood,
All in gore blood. I swoonèd at the sight.

JULIET
O break, my heart, poor bankrout, break at once!
To prison, eyes; ne'er look on liberty.
Vile earth to earth resign; end motion here,                 65
And thou and Romeo press one heavy bier.

NURSE
O Tybalt, Tybalt, the best friend I had!
O courteous Tybalt, honest gentleman,
That ever I should live to see thee dead!

JULIET
What storm is this that blows so contrary?                   70

73. **dreadful . . . doom:** i.e., let the **trumpet** be blown to announce the Last Judgment, or Doomsday (See picture, page 142.)

79. **hid with:** hidden by

80. **dragon:** See picture, below. **keep:** dwell in; **fair:** beautiful

82. **wolvish-ravening:** i.e., wolfishly devouring

83. **show:** appearance

84. **Just:** exact; **justly:** truly

87. **bower:** i.e., give a dwelling to

89–90. **book . . . bound:** See picture, page 38.

94. **naught:** evil; **dissemblers:** deceivers

95. **aqua vitae:** strong drink, usually brandy

Dragon. (3.2.80)
From Ulisse Aldrovandi,
*. . . Serpentum, et draconum historiae libri duo . . .* [1639].

Is Romeo slaughtered and is Tybalt dead?
My dearest cousin, and my dearer lord?
Then, dreadful trumpet, sound the general doom,
For who is living if those two are gone?

NURSE
Tybalt is gone and Romeo banishèd.                    75
Romeo that killed him—he is banishèd. *banished*

JULIET
O God, did Romeo's hand shed Tybalt's blood?

⌜NURSE⌝
It did, it did, alas the day, it did.

⌜JULIET⌝
O serpent heart hid with a flow'ring face!
Did ever dragon keep so fair a cave?                  80
Beautiful tyrant, fiend angelical!
Dove-feathered raven, wolvish-ravening lamb!
Despisèd substance of divinest show!
Just opposite to what thou justly seem'st,
A ⌜damnèd⌝ saint, an honorable villain.               85
O nature, what hadst thou to do in hell
When thou didst bower the spirit of a fiend
In mortal paradise of such sweet flesh?
Was ever book containing such vile matter
So fairly bound? O, that deceit should dwell          90
In such a gorgeous palace!

NURSE                          There's no trust,
No faith, no honesty in men. All perjured,
All forsworn, all naught, all dissemblers.
Ah, where's my man? Give me some aqua vitae.          95
These griefs, these woes, these sorrows make me
     old.
Shame come to Romeo!

JULIET                          Blistered be thy tongue
For such a wish! He was not born to shame.            100
Upon his brow shame is ashamed to sit,
For 'tis a throne where honor may be crowned

107. **poor my lord:** i.e., **my poor lord**

110. **wherefore:** why

113. **Your . . . woe:** i.e., **tears** (line 112) are properly the tribute (i.e., tax) paid to sorrow

120. **fain:** gladly

128. **needly:** necessarily; **ranked:** classified (but with a sense of "drawn up in ranks," a military usage picked up in line 132 below.)

131. **Which . . . moved:** i.e., **which might have** provoked ordinary mourning **modern:** everyday

132. **a rearward:** the rearguard of a marching army. (In the first rank or vanguard is the statement **"Tybalt's dead"**; behind it, in the rear, is **"Romeo is banishèd."**)

136. **bound:** boundary

Phaëton. (3.2.3)
From Ovid, . . . *Metamorphoseos* . . . (1527).

Sole monarch of the universal Earth.
O, what a beast was I to chide at him!

NURSE
Will you speak well of him that killed your cousin?        105

JULIET
Shall I speak ill of him that is my husband?
Ah, poor my lord, what tongue shall smooth thy
    name
When I, thy three-hours wife, have mangled it?
But wherefore, villain, didst thou kill my cousin?        110
That villain cousin would have killed my husband.
Back, foolish tears, back to your native spring;
Your tributary drops belong to woe,
Which you, mistaking, offer up to joy.
My husband lives, that Tybalt would have slain,        115
And Tybalt's dead, that would have slain my
    husband.
All this is comfort. Wherefore weep I then?
Some word there was, worser than Tybalt's death,
That murdered me. I would forget it fain,        120
But, O, it presses to my memory
Like damnèd guilty deeds to sinners' minds:
"Tybalt is dead and Romeo banishèd."
That "banishèd," that one word "banishèd,"
Hath slain ten thousand Tybalts. Tybalt's death        125
Was woe enough if it had ended there;
Or, if sour woe delights in fellowship
And needly will be ranked with other griefs,
Why followed not, when she said "Tybalt's dead,"
"Thy father" or "thy mother," nay, or both,        130
Which modern lamentation might have moved?
But with a rearward following Tybalt's death,
"Romeo is banishèd." To speak that word
Is father, mother, Tybalt, Romeo, Juliet,
All slain, all dead. "Romeo is banishèd."        135
There is no end, no limit, measure, bound,

137. **that word's death:** i.e., the **death** expressed by the **word banishèd; sound:** (1) express; (2) measure (i.e., by taking soundings to determine its depth)

145. **you are beguiled:** your hopes are cheated

151. **Hie:** hurry

152. **wot:** know

**3.3** Friar Lawrence tells Romeo that his punishment for killing Tybalt is banishment, not death. Romeo responds that death is preferable to banishment from Juliet. When the Nurse enters and tells Romeo that Juliet is grief-stricken, Romeo attempts suicide. Friar Lawrence then says that Romeo may spend the night with Juliet and leave for exile in Mantua next morning. The Friar promises that Balthasar will bring Romeo news of Verona and suggests that Romeo can expect in time that the Prince may relent and allow him to return to Verona.

———————

2. **Affliction . . . parts:** i.e., it is as if disaster were in love with your attractive qualities

In that word's death. No words can that woe sound.
Where is my father and my mother, nurse?

NURSE
Weeping and wailing over Tybalt's corse.
Will you go to them? I will bring you thither.          140

JULIET
Wash they his wounds with tears? Mine shall be
    spent,
When theirs are dry, for Romeo's banishment.—
Take up those cords.
                ⌜*The Nurse picks up the rope ladder.*⌝
                        Poor ropes, you are beguiled,          145
Both you and I, for Romeo is exiled.
He made you for a highway to my bed,
But I, a maid, die maiden-widowèd.
Come, cords—come, nurse. I'll to my wedding bed,
And death, not Romeo, take my maidenhead!          150

NURSE
Hie to your chamber. I'll find Romeo
To comfort you. I wot well where he is.
Hark you, your Romeo will be here at night.
I'll to him. He is hid at Lawrence' cell.

JULIET
O, find him!          ⌜*Giving the Nurse a ring.*⌝          155
        Give this ring to my true knight
And bid him come to take his last farewell.
                                ⌜*They*⌝ *exit.*


                        ⌜Scene 3⌝

                *Enter Friar* ⌜*Lawrence.*⌝

FRIAR LAWRENCE
Romeo, come forth; come forth, thou fearful man.
Affliction is enamored of thy parts,
And thou art wedded to calamity.

4. **doom:** sentence, judgment

5. **craves acquaintance at my hand:** is anxious to meet me (literally, to shake hands with me)

11. **vanished:** disappeared (a reference to words as mere breath that vanish as soon as spoken)

14. **his:** its

17. **patient:** calm

18. **without:** outside

21. **world's exile: exile from the world**

22. **mistermed:** misnamed

26. **Thy fault . . . death:** i.e., your crime is punishable by **death** under **our law**

27. **part:** side; **rushed aside:** shoved **aside**

Verona.
From Pietro Bertelli, *Theatrum vrbium Italicarum* . . . (1599).

⌈*Enter Romeo.*⌉

ROMEO
Father, what news? What is the Prince's doom?
What sorrow craves acquaintance at my hand          5
That I yet know not?

FRIAR LAWRENCE          Too familiar
Is my dear son with such sour company.
I bring thee tidings of the Prince's doom.

ROMEO
What less than doomsday is the Prince's doom?          10

FRIAR LAWRENCE
A gentler judgment vanished from his lips:
Not body's death, but body's banishment.

ROMEO
Ha, banishment? Be merciful, say "death,"
For exile hath more terror in his look,
Much more than death. Do not say "banishment."          15

FRIAR LAWRENCE
Here from Verona art thou banishèd.
Be patient, for the world is broad and wide.

ROMEO
There is no world without Verona walls
But purgatory, torture, hell itself.
Hence "banishèd" is "banished from the world,"          20
And world's exile is death. Then "banishèd"
Is death mistermed. Calling death "banishèd,"
Thou cutt'st my head off with a golden ax
And smilest upon the stroke that murders me.

FRIAR LAWRENCE
O deadly sin, O rude unthankfulness!          25
Thy fault our law calls death, but the kind prince,
Taking thy part, hath rushed aside the law
And turned that black word "death" to
    "banishment."
This is dear mercy, and thou seest it not.          30

36. **courtship:** status as a courtier
40. **vestal:** i.e., virginal
41. **Still:** always; **their own kisses:** i.e., the **kisses** each lip gives the other
48. **mean:** means; **mean:** sordid
51. **attends:** accompanies
53. **professed:** self-proclaimed
55. **fond:** foolish
60. **Yet:** still

Doomsday. (3.2.73)
From Thomas Fisher, the etching of the wall painting of Doomsday in the Guild Chapel at Stratford-upon-Avon (1807).

ROMEO
   'Tis torture and not mercy. Heaven is here
   Where Juliet lives, and every cat and dog
   And little mouse, every unworthy thing,
   Live here in heaven and may look on her,
   But Romeo may not. More validity,             35
   More honorable state, more courtship lives
   In carrion flies than Romeo. They may seize
   On the white wonder of dear Juliet's hand
   And steal immortal blessing from her lips,
   Who even in pure and vestal modesty        40
   Still blush, as thinking their own kisses sin;
   But Romeo may not; he is banishèd.
   Flies may do this, but I from this must fly.
   They are free men, but I am banishèd.
   And sayest thou yet that exile is not death?    45
   Hadst thou no poison mixed, no sharp-ground
      knife,
   No sudden mean of death, though ne'er so mean,
   But "banishèd" to kill me? "Banishèd"?
   O friar, the damnèd use that word in hell.     50
   Howling attends it. How hast thou the heart,
   Being a divine, a ghostly confessor,
   A sin absolver, and my friend professed,
   To mangle me with that word "banishèd"?

FRIAR LAWRENCE
   ⌜Thou⌝ fond mad man, hear me a little speak.   55

ROMEO
   O, thou wilt speak again of banishment.

FRIAR LAWRENCE
   I'll give thee armor to keep off that word,
   Adversity's sweet milk, philosophy,
   To comfort thee, though thou art banishèd.

ROMEO
   Yet "banishèd"? Hang up philosophy.        60
   Unless philosophy can make a Juliet,

62. **Displant:** uproot
65. **when that:** when
66. **dispute:** reason; **of:** about; **estate:** condition
70. **Doting:** in love
81. **By and by:** soon (addressed to the person knocking)
82. **simpleness:** foolishness

Displant a town, reverse a prince's doom,
It helps not, it prevails not. Talk no more.

FRIAR LAWRENCE
O, then I see that ⌈madmen⌉ have no ears.

ROMEO
How should they when that wise men have no eyes? 65

FRIAR LAWRENCE
Let me dispute with thee of thy estate.

ROMEO
Thou canst not speak of that thou dost not feel.
Wert thou as young as I, Juliet thy love,
An hour but married, Tybalt murderèd,
Doting like me, and like me banishèd, 70
Then mightst thou speak, then mightst thou tear thy
    hair
And fall upon the ground as I do now,
                    ⌈*Romeo throws himself down.*⌉
Taking the measure of an unmade grave.
                    *Knock* ⌈*within.*⌉

FRIAR LAWRENCE
Arise. One knocks. Good Romeo, hide thyself. 75

ROMEO
Not I, unless the breath of heartsick groans,
Mistlike, enfold me from the search of eyes.
                                        *Knock.*

FRIAR LAWRENCE
Hark, how they knock!—Who's there?—Romeo,
    arise.
Thou wilt be taken.—Stay awhile.—Stand up. 80
                                        *Knock.*
Run to my study.—By and by.—God's will,
What simpleness is this?—I come, I come.
                                        *Knock.*
Who knocks so hard? Whence come you? What's
    your will?

92. **even:** exactly; **case:** plight

93. **woeful sympathy:** i.e., harmony (between Romeo and Juliet) in their grief

106. **My concealed lady:** i.e., she who is secretly my wife (**concealed** accented on the first syllable); **canceled:** annulled (because of his banishment)

109. **on Romeo:** i.e., on the name "Romeo"

NURSE, ⌜*within*⌝
    Let me come in, and you shall know my errand.          85
    I come from Lady Juliet.
FRIAR LAWRENCE, ⌜*admitting the Nurse*⌝
                              Welcome, then.

                    ⌜*Enter Nurse.*⌝

NURSE
    O holy friar, O, tell me, holy friar,
    Where's my lady's lord? Where's Romeo?
FRIAR LAWRENCE
    There on the ground, with his own tears made          90
      drunk.
NURSE
    O, he is even in my mistress' case,
    Just in her case. O woeful sympathy!
    Piteous predicament! Even so lies she,
    Blubb'ring and weeping, weeping and blubb'ring.—          95
    Stand up, stand up. Stand an you be a man.
    For Juliet's sake, for her sake, rise and stand.
    Why should you fall into so deep an O?
ROMEO   Nurse.
NURSE
    Ah sir, ah sir, death's the end of all.          100
ROMEO, ⌜*rising up*⌝
    Spakest thou of Juliet? How is it with her?
    Doth not she think me an old murderer,
    Now I have stained the childhood of our joy
    With blood removed but little from her own?
    Where is she? And how doth she? And what says          105
    My concealed lady to our canceled love?
NURSE
    O, she says nothing, sir, but weeps and weeps,
    And now falls on her bed, and then starts up,
    And "Tybalt" calls, and then on Romeo cries,
    And then down falls again.          110

112. **level:** aim

116. **sack:** destroy by plundering and pillaging

122. **Unseemly:** improper (even for a **woman**); **seeming:** apparent

123. **ill-beseeming . . . both:** i.e., unnatural animal in appearing to be **both** a **woman** and **a man**

125. **tempered:** adjusted

129. **railest thou on:** do you heap scorn upon, revile

132–35. **thou shamest . . . wit:** In these lines the Friar shows, in turn, how Romeo is shaming his form as a man, his love for Juliet, and his intelligence (**wit**). Like a **usurer** (one who, contrary to the morality of the time, lent money to get interest), Romeo has an abundance of wealth (his **shape, love,** and **wit**) but does not use any of it properly. The idea is elaborated in lines 136–44. **Which, like:** who, **like**

136. **but . . . wax:** no better than a wax figure

137. **Digressing from:** if it swerves away from

138. **dear love sworn: love** you have **sworn** is **dear**

139. **Killing:** if it kills

141. **conduct:** management

142. **powder:** gunpowder; **flask:** powder **flask**

144. **thou dismembered . . . defense:** i.e., you are blown to pieces by your own weapons

146. **thou . . . dead:** i.e., you were just now willing to die

ROMEO                          As if that name,
  Shot from the deadly level of a gun,
  Did murder her, as that name's cursèd hand
  Murdered her kinsman.—O, tell me, friar, tell me,
  In what vile part of this anatomy                    115
  Doth my name lodge? Tell me, that I may sack
  The hateful mansion.          ⌜*He draws his dagger.*⌝
FRIAR LAWRENCE          Hold thy desperate hand!
  Art thou a man? Thy form cries out thou art.
  Thy tears are womanish; thy wild acts ⌜denote⌝      120
  The unreasonable fury of a beast.
  Unseemly woman in a seeming man,
  And ill-beseeming beast in seeming both!
  Thou hast amazed me. By my holy order,
  I thought thy disposition better tempered.           125
  Hast thou slain Tybalt? Wilt thou slay thyself,
  And slay thy lady that in thy life ⌜lives,⌝
  By doing damnèd hate upon thyself?
  Why railest thou on thy birth, the heaven, and earth,
  Since birth and heaven and earth all three do meet   130
  In thee at once, which thou at once wouldst lose?
  Fie, fie, thou shamest thy shape, thy love, thy wit,
  Which, like a usurer, abound'st in all
  And usest none in that true use indeed
  Which should bedeck thy shape, thy love, thy wit.     135
  Thy noble shape is but a form of wax,
  Digressing from the valor of a man;
  Thy dear love sworn but hollow perjury,
  Killing that love which thou hast vowed to cherish;
  Thy wit, that ornament to shape and love,            140
  Misshapen in the conduct of them both,
  Like powder in a skilless soldier's flask,
  Is set afire by thine own ignorance,
  And thou dismembered with thine own defense.
  What, rouse thee, man! Thy Juliet is alive,          145
  For whose dear sake thou wast but lately dead:

147. **happy:** fortunate; **would:** wanted to

150. **exile:** accent on the second syllable

154. **fortune:** i.e., good **fortune**

155. **such:** i.e., **such** ungrateful persons

156. **decreed:** decided

158. **look:** i.e., be sure that; **watch:** guards stationed at the city gates

159. **pass to:** i.e., leave Verona for

161. **blaze:** make public; **friends:** relatives (the warring Capulets and Montagues)

165. **Commend me:** i.e., offer my respects

167. **apt unto:** inclined to do

Mantua.
From Pietro Bertelli, *Theatrum vrbium Italicarum* . . . (1599).

There art thou happy. Tybalt would kill thee,
But thou slewest Tybalt: there art thou happy.
The law that threatened death becomes thy friend
And turns it to exile: there art thou happy. 150
A pack of blessings light upon thy back;
Happiness courts thee in her best array;
But, like a ⌜misbehaved⌝ and sullen wench,
Thou ⌜pouts upon⌝ thy fortune and thy love.
Take heed, take heed, for such die miserable. 155
Go, get thee to thy love, as was decreed.
Ascend her chamber. Hence and comfort her.
But look thou stay not till the watch be set,
For then thou canst not pass to Mantua,
Where thou shalt live till we can find a time 160
To blaze your marriage, reconcile your friends,
Beg pardon of the Prince, and call thee back
With twenty hundred thousand times more joy
Than thou went'st forth in lamentation.—
Go before, nurse. Commend me to thy lady, 165
And bid her hasten all the house to bed,
Which heavy sorrow makes them apt unto.
Romeo is coming.

NURSE
O Lord, I could have stayed here all the night
To hear good counsel. O, what learning is!— 170
My lord, I'll tell my lady you will come.

ROMEO
Do so, and bid my sweet prepare to chide.

NURSE
Here, sir, a ring she bid me give you, sir.
⌜*Nurse gives Romeo a ring.*⌝
Hie you, make haste, for it grows very late.
⌜*She exits.*⌝

ROMEO
How well my comfort is revived by this! 175

176–77. **here stands all your state:** your condition depends on the following

180. **find out your man:** search **out your** servant

181–82. **signify . . . to you:** i.e., let **you** know **every** piece of **good** fortune

185. **brief:** quickly

**3.4** Paris again approaches Capulet about marrying Juliet. Capulet, saying that Juliet will do as she is told, promises Paris that she will marry him in three days.

———

1. **fallen out:** happened

2. **move our daughter:** i.e., persuade Juliet

6. **but:** except

12. **mewed up to:** shut up with (The term **mewed up** is from falconry and means "caged.") **heaviness:** grief

13. **desperate tender:** bold (or risky) offer

FRIAR LAWRENCE
  Go hence, good night—and here stands all your
    state:
  Either be gone before the watch be set
  Or by the break of day ⌜disguised⌝ from hence.
  Sojourn in Mantua. I'll find out your man,                    180
  And he shall signify from time to time
  Every good hap to you that chances here.
  Give me thy hand. 'Tis late. Farewell. Good night.

ROMEO
  But that a joy past joy calls out on me,
  It were a grief so brief to part with thee.                    185
  Farewell.

                               *They exit.*


⌜Scene 4⌝

*Enter old Capulet, his Wife, and Paris.*

CAPULET
  Things have fallen out, sir, so unluckily
  That we have had no time to move our daughter.
  Look you, she loved her kinsman Tybalt dearly,
  And so did I. Well, we were born to die.
  'Tis very late. She'll not come down tonight.                   5
  I promise you, but for your company,
  I would have been abed an hour ago.

PARIS
  These times of woe afford no times to woo.—
  Madam, good night. Commend me to your
    daughter.                                                  10

LADY CAPULET
  I will, and know her mind early tomorrow.
  Tonight she's mewed up to her heaviness.

CAPULET
  Sir Paris, I will make a desperate tender
  Of my child's love. I think she will ⌜be⌝ ruled

17. **son:** future son-in-law
18. **mark you me?:** i.e., do you hear?
26. **We'll . . . ado:** i.e., we won't make a fuss
27. **late:** recently
28. **held him carelessly:** i.e., esteemed him little
35. **against:** in anticipation of
37. **Afore me:** a mild oath

**3.5** Romeo and Juliet separate at the first light of day. Almost immediately her mother comes to announce that Juliet must marry Paris. When Juliet refuses, her father becomes enraged and vows to put her out on the streets. The Nurse recommends that Juliet forget the banished Romeo and regard Paris as a more desirable husband. Juliet is secretly outraged at the Nurse's advice and decides to seek Friar Lawrence's help.

———————

0 SD. **aloft:** i.e., in the gallery above the stage, as at a window
3. **fearful:** anxious

A nightingale. (3.5.2)
From Konrad Gesner, . . . *Historiae animalium* . . . (1585–1604).

In all respects by me. Nay, more, I doubt it not.—          15
Wife, go you to her ere you go to bed.
Acquaint her here of my son Paris' love,
And bid her—mark you me?—on Wednesday
    next—
But soft, what day is this?

PARIS                              Monday, my lord.

CAPULET
Monday, ha ha! Well, Wednesday is too soon.
O' Thursday let it be.—O' Thursday, tell her,
She shall be married to this noble earl.—
Will you be ready? Do you like this haste?          25
⌐We'll¬ keep no great ado: a friend or two.
For hark you, Tybalt being slain so late,
It may be thought we held him carelessly,
Being our kinsman, if we revel much.
Therefore we'll have some half a dozen friends,          30
And there an end. But what say you to Thursday?

PARIS
My lord, I would that Thursday were tomorrow.

CAPULET
Well, get you gone. O' Thursday be it, then.
⌐*To Lady Capulet.*¬ Go you to Juliet ere you go to bed.
Prepare her, wife, against this wedding day.—          35
Farewell, my lord.—Light to my chamber, ho!
Afore me, it is so very late that we
May call it early by and by.—Good night.

                                        *They exit.*


⌐Scene 5¬

*Enter Romeo and Juliet aloft.*


JULIET
Wilt thou be gone? It is not yet near day.
It was the nightingale, and not the lark,
That pierced the fearful hollow of thine ear.

7. **envious:** malicious

9. **Night's candles:** i.e., the stars

13. **exhaled:** drew up as a gas (**A meteor** was thought to be a fiery gas drawn up by **the sun.**)

18. **so thou:** i.e., if thou

19. **the morning's eye:** See 2.3.1, where the morn is "gray-eyed."

20. **reflex . . . brow:** reflection of the moon (Cynthia is goddess of the moon. See picture, below.)

23. **care, will:** desire

28. **sharps:** discordant notes (above the true pitch)

29. **division:** a rapid, melodious passage of music

33. **affray:** frighten

34. **hunt's-up:** i.e., an early morning song

Cynthia. (3.5.20)
From Robert Whitcombe, *Janua divorum . . .* (1678).

Nightly she sings on yond pomegranate tree.
Believe me, love, it was the nightingale. 5

ROMEO
It was the lark, the herald of the morn,
No nightingale. Look, love, what envious streaks
Do lace the severing clouds in yonder east.
Night's candles are burnt out, and jocund day
Stands tiptoe on the misty mountain-tops. 10
I must be gone and live, or stay and die.

JULIET
Yond light is not daylight, I know it, I.
It is some meteor that the sun ⌐exhaled⌐
To be to thee this night a torchbearer
And light thee on thy way to Mantua. 15
Therefore stay yet. Thou need'st not to be gone.

ROMEO
Let me be ta'en; let me be put to death.
I am content, so thou wilt have it so.
I'll say yon gray is not the morning's eye;
'Tis but the pale reflex of Cynthia's brow. 20
Nor that is not the lark whose notes do beat
The vaulty heaven so high above our heads.
I have more care to stay than will to go.
Come death and welcome. Juliet wills it so.
How is 't, my soul? Let's talk. It is not day. 25

JULIET
It is, it is. Hie hence, begone, away!
It is the lark that sings so out of tune,
Straining harsh discords and unpleasing sharps.
Some say the lark makes sweet division.
This doth not so, for she divideth us. 30
Some say the lark and loathèd toad ⌐changed⌐ eyes.
O, now I would they had changed voices too,
Since arm from arm that voice doth us affray,
Hunting thee hence with hunt's-up to the day.
O, now begone. More light and light it grows. 35

46. **by this count:** according to this calculation; **much in years:** i.e., very old

54. **ill-divining:** prophetic of evil

55. **Methinks:** I think

59. **Dry . . . blood:** i.e., we are pale with grief (**Sorrow** is represented as thirsty [**dry**] because it was believed that each sorrowful sigh consumed a drop of **blood** from the heart.)

Larks. (3.5.6)
From Konrad Gesner, . . . *Historiae animalium* . . . (1585–1604).

ROMEO
　　More light and light, more dark and dark our woes.

*Enter Nurse.*

NURSE  Madam.
JULIET  Nurse?
NURSE
　　Your lady mother is coming to your chamber.
　　The day is broke; be wary; look about.    ⌜*She exits.*⌝    40
JULIET
　　Then, window, let day in, and let life out

ROMEO
　　Farewell, farewell. One kiss and I'll descend.
⌜*They kiss, and Romeo descends.*⌝

JULIET
　　Art thou gone so? Love, lord, ay husband, friend!
　　I must hear from thee every day in the hour,
　　For in a minute there are many days.
　　O, by this count I shall be much in years    45
　　Ere I again behold my Romeo.
ROMEO  Farewell.
　　I will omit no opportunity
　　That may convey my greetings, love, to thee.    50
JULIET
　　O, think'st thou we shall ever meet again?
ROMEO
　　I doubt it not; and all these woes shall serve
　　For sweet discourses in our times to come.
⌜JULIET⌝
　　O God, I have an ill-divining soul!
　　Methinks I see thee, now thou art so low,    55
　　As one dead in the bottom of a tomb.
　　Either my eyesight fails or thou lookest pale.
ROMEO
　　And trust me, love, in my eye so do you.
　　Dry sorrow drinks our blood. Adieu, adieu.  *He exits.*

**60. Fortune:** The goddess Fortuna was thought to control the fate of humans, but in a whimsical, unpredictable way. (See picture, below.) **fickle:** inconstant, changeable

**62. faith:** constancy

**67. not down: not** yet in bed

**68. procures:** i.e., brings

**68 SD. descends:** While Romeo, at 42 SD, presumably uses the rope ladder of 3.2, Juliet would descend to the main stage behind the scenes, and reenter there.

**76. shows . . . wit:** always manifests a lack of intelligence

**77. feeling:** strongly felt

Fortune spinning her wheel. (3.1.142; 3.5.60)
From Guido delle Colonne, *The hystorye, sege and dystruccyon of Troye,* trans. John Lydgate (1513).

JULIET
  O Fortune, Fortune, all men call thee fickle.                    60
  If thou art fickle, what dost thou with him
  That is renowned for faith? Be fickle, Fortune,
  For then I hope thou wilt not keep him long,
  But send him back.

              *Enter ⌜Lady Capulet.⌝*

LADY CAPULET          Ho, daughter, are you up?                    65
JULIET
  Who is 't that calls? It is my lady mother.
  Is she not down so late or up so early?
  What unaccustomed cause procures her hither?
                              ⌜*Juliet descends.*⌝

LADY CAPULET
  Why, how now, Juliet?
JULIET                  Madam, I am not well.                      70
LADY CAPULET
  Evermore weeping for your cousin's death?
  What, wilt thou wash him from his grave with tears?
  An if thou couldst, thou couldst not make him live.
  Therefore have done. Some grief shows much of
      love,                                                        75
  But much of grief shows still some want of wit.
JULIET
  Yet let me weep for such a feeling loss.
LADY CAPULET
  So shall you feel the loss, but not the friend
  Which you weep for.
JULIET                  Feeling so the loss,                       80
  I cannot choose but ever weep the friend.
LADY CAPULET
  Well, girl, thou weep'st not so much for his death
  As that the villain lives which slaughtered him.
JULIET
  What villain, madam?

88. **grieve:** (1) incense with anger; (2) afflict with longing (From here to line 107, Juliet's words say what her mother expects her to say of a hated Montague but, through wordplay, also say what Juliet truly feels about Romeo.)

90. **reach:** (1) grasp; (2) touch

91. **Would:** I wish that

94. **runagate:** runaway, fugitive

95. **dram:** a small draught (here, of poison)

99. **—dead—:** By suspending this word between dashes, editions since Alexander Pope's (1725) have been able to show Juliet's double meaning. She may be read to say "till I behold him dead," or to say "dead is my poor heart."

100. **kinsman:** (1) Tybalt; (2) Romeo

101. **find out but:** only **find out**

102. **temper:** (1) mix; (2) dilute and thereby turn it from poison into a sleeping potion

106. **wreak:** (1) avenge; (2) bestow

107. **his body that:** the **body** of the man who

112. **careful:** full of care (for you)

LADY CAPULET                    That same villain, Romeo.                    85
JULIET, ⌜*aside*⌝
  Villain and he be many miles asunder.—
  God pardon ⌜him.⌝ I do with all my heart,
  And yet no man like he doth grieve my heart.
LADY CAPULET
  That is because the traitor murderer lives.
JULIET
  Ay, madam, from the reach of these my hands.                    90
  Would none but I might venge my cousin's death!
LADY CAPULET
  We will have vengeance for it, fear thou not.
  Then weep no more. I'll send to one in Mantua,
  Where that same banished runagate doth live,
  Shall give him such an unaccustomed dram                    95
  That he shall soon keep Tybalt company.
  And then, I hope, thou wilt be satisfied.
JULIET
  Indeed, I never shall be satisfied
  With Romeo till I behold him—dead—
  Is my poor heart, so for a kinsman vexed.                    100
  Madam, if you could find out but a man
  To bear a poison, I would temper it,
  That Romeo should, upon receipt thereof,
  Soon sleep in quiet. O, how my heart abhors
  To hear him named and cannot come to him                    105
  To wreak the love I bore my cousin
  Upon his body that hath slaughtered him.
LADY CAPULET
  Find thou the means, and I'll find such a man.
  But now I'll tell thee joyful tidings, girl.
JULIET
  And joy comes well in such a needy time.                    110
  What are they, beseech your ladyship?
LADY CAPULET
  Well, well, thou hast a careful father, child,

113. **heaviness:** i.e., grief

114. **sorted out:** selected; **sudden day:** i.e., **a day** that is about to come soon

116. **in happy time:** i.e., how opportune

134. **conduit:** fountain

136. **counterfeits:** imitates; **bark:** small sailboat

141. **Without a sudden calm:** i.e., unless suddenly there's **a calm; overset:** capsize

A criminal drawn on a hurdle to execution. (3.5.160)
From *The life and death of Mr. Edmund Geninges priest . . .* (1614).

One who, to put thee from thy heaviness,
Hath sorted out a sudden day of joy
That thou expects not, nor I looked not for.            115

JULIET
Madam, in happy time! What day is that?

LADY CAPULET
Marry, my child, early next Thursday morn
The gallant, young, and noble gentleman,
The County Paris, at Saint Peter's Church
Shall happily make thee there a joyful bride.            120

JULIET
Now, by Saint Peter's Church, and Peter too,
He shall not make me there a joyful bride!
I wonder at this haste, that I must wed
Ere he that should be husband comes to woo.
I pray you, tell my lord and father, madam,            125
I will not marry yet, and when I do I swear
It shall be Romeo, whom you know I hate,
Rather than Paris. These are news indeed!

LADY CAPULET
Here comes your father. Tell him so yourself,
And see how he will take it at your hands.            130

*Enter Capulet and Nurse.*

CAPULET
When the sun sets, the earth doth drizzle dew,
But for the sunset of my brother's son
It rains downright.
How now, a conduit, girl? What, still in tears?
Evermore show'ring? In one little body            135
Thou counterfeits a bark, a sea, a wind.
For still thy eyes, which I may call the sea,
Do ebb and flow with tears; the bark thy body is,
Sailing in this salt flood; the winds thy sighs,
Who, raging with thy tears and they with them,            140
Without a sudden calm, will overset

144. **she will ... thanks:** i.e., she refuses any part in it, saying "No, thank you"

146. **Soft:** i.e., wait a moment; **take me with you:** i.e., let me understand you

148. **count her:** regard herself as

149. **wrought:** produced

150. **bride:** i.e., bridegroom

151. **proud you:** i.e., **proud** that **you**

153. **for hate ... love:** i.e., **for** what I hate when it is intended as **love**

154. **Chopped logic:** quibbling

156. **minion:** darling (here, a contemptuous term)

158. **fettle:** prepare; **'gainst:** in anticipation of

160. **hurdle:** a wooden frame on which criminals were drawn through the streets to execution (See picture, page 164.)

161. **green-sickness:** a form of anemia thought to affect girls in puberty, making them pale; **carrion:** a term of contempt (literally, dead flesh); **baggage:** good-for-nothing woman

162. **tallow:** animal fat used in candles (another reference to Juliet's paleness)

Thy tempest-tossèd body.—How now, wife?
Have you delivered to her our decree?

LADY CAPULET
Ay, sir, but she will none, she ⌜gives⌝ you thanks.
I would the fool were married to her grave.                    145

CAPULET
Soft, take me with you, take me with you, wife.
How, will she none? Doth she not give us thanks?
Is she not proud? Doth she not count her blessed,
Unworthy as she is, that we have wrought
So worthy a gentleman to be her bride?                         150

JULIET
Not proud you have, but thankful that you have.
Proud can I never be of what I hate,
But thankful even for hate that is meant love.

CAPULET
How, how, how, how? Chopped logic? What is this?
"Proud," and "I thank you," and "I thank you not,"            155
And yet "not proud"? Mistress minion you,
Thank me no thankings, nor proud me no prouds,
But fettle your fine joints 'gainst Thursday next
To go with Paris to Saint Peter's Church,
Or I will drag thee on a hurdle thither.                       160
Out, you green-sickness carrion! Out, you baggage!
You tallow face!

LADY CAPULET     Fie, fie, what, are you mad?

JULIET, ⌜*kneeling*⌝
Good father, I beseech you on my knees,
Hear me with patience but to speak a word.                     165

CAPULET
Hang thee, young baggage, disobedient wretch!
I tell thee what: get thee to church o' Thursday,
Or never after look me in the face.
Speak not; reply not; do not answer me.
My fingers itch.—Wife, we scarce thought us                   170
   blessed

175. **hilding:** good-for-nothing

177. **to blame:** blameworthy, deserving rebuke; **rate:** berate, scold

179. **smatter:** chatter; **gossips:** women friends

181. **God 'i' g' eden:** exclamation of annoyance (literally, God give you good evening)

184. **gravity:** serious remarks (said contemptuously); **bowl:** drinking vessel

187. **God's bread:** an oath on the sacrament of communion (a strong oath)

188. **tide:** season

189. **still:** always, constantly

192. **demesnes:** property; **nobly ligned:** i.e., noble by lineal descent, by birth

193. **parts:** qualities

195. **puling:** feebly wailing

196. **mammet:** doll; **in her fortune's tender:** i.e., when she is offered (tendered) good fortune

198. **pardon me:** excuse me from marrying

199. **pardon you:** give you permission to leave

201. **do not use:** am not accustomed

202. **advise:** ponder, consider

That God had lent us but this only child,
But now I see this one is one too much,
And that we have a curse in having her.
Out on her, hilding.                                              175
NURSE                    God in heaven bless her!
  You are to blame, my lord, to rate her so.
CAPULET
  And why, my Lady Wisdom? Hold your tongue.
  Good Prudence, smatter with your gossips, go.
NURSE
  I speak no treason.                                              180
⌜CAPULET⌝          O, God 'i' g' eden!
⌜NURSE⌝
  May not one speak?
CAPULET                    Peace, you mumbling fool!
  Utter your gravity o'er a gossip's bowl,
  For here we need it not.                                         185
LADY CAPULET   You are too hot.
CAPULET   God's bread, it makes me mad.
  Day, night, hour, tide, time, work, play,
  Alone, in company, still my care hath been
  To have her matched. And having now provided       190
  A gentleman of noble parentage,
  Of fair demesnes, youthful, and nobly ⌜ligned,⌝
  Stuffed, as they say, with honorable parts,
  Proportioned as one's thought would wish a man—
  And then to have a wretched puling fool,                        195
  A whining mammet, in her fortune's tender,
  To answer "I'll not wed. I cannot love.
  I am too young. I pray you, pardon me."
  But, an you will not wed, I'll pardon you!
  Graze where you will, you shall not house with me.  200
  Look to 't; think on 't. I do not use to jest.
  Thursday is near. Lay hand on heart; advise.
  An you be mine, I'll give you to my friend.

207. **bethink you:** reflect seriously; **I'll not be forsworn:** i.e., **I'll not** take back my words

217. **on Earth:** i.e., alive

220. **By leaving Earth:** by dying (She has vowed to be his wife until death parts them.)

221–22. **practice stratagems/Upon:** set traps for

226. **all the world to nothing:** i.e., I would bet **all** against **nothing**

227. **challenge:** claim

232. **dishclout:** dishrag

233. **quick:** lively

234. **Beshrew:** i.e., the devil take (a mild oath)

An you be not, hang, beg, starve, die in the streets,
For, by my soul, I'll ne'er acknowledge thee,                    205
Nor what is mine shall never do thee good.
Trust to 't; bethink you. I'll not be forsworn.

                                                *He exits.*

JULIET
Is there no pity sitting in the clouds
That sees into the bottom of my grief?—
O sweet my mother, cast me not away.                             210
Delay this marriage for a month, a week,
Or, if you do not, make the bridal bed
In that dim monument where Tybalt lies.

LADY CAPULET
Talk not to me, for I'll not speak a word.
Do as thou wilt, for I have done with thee.                      215

                                                *She exits.*

JULIET, ⌜*rising*⌝
O God! O nurse, how shall this be prevented?
My husband is on Earth, my faith in heaven.
How shall that faith return again to Earth
Unless that husband send it me from heaven
By leaving Earth? Comfort me; counsel me.—                       220
Alack, alack, that heaven should practice stratagems
Upon so soft a subject as myself.—
What sayst thou? Hast thou not a word of joy?
Some comfort, nurse.

NURSE                              Faith, here it is.              225
Romeo is banished, and all the world to nothing
That he dares ne'er come back to challenge you,
Or, if he do, it needs must be by stealth.
Then, since the case so stands as now it doth,
I think it best you married with the County.                     230
O, he's a lovely gentleman!
Romeo's a dishclout to him. An eagle, madam,
Hath not so green, so quick, so fair an eye
As Paris hath. Beshrew my very heart,

How she changes moods just like

237–38. **'twere . . . him:** i.e., he is **as good** as **dead** since you live **here** (rather than with him) and have **no use of him**

240. **both:** i.e., heart and soul

241. **Amen:** Juliet's "**Amen**" transforms the Nurse's **beshrew them both** into a solemn curse. (See note to line 234, above.)

246. **absolved:** forgiven (given absolution)

248. **Ancient damnation:** old damned one

249. **thus forsworn:** i.e., to break my marriage vows to Romeo

251. **above compare:** beyond comparison

253. **bosom:** i.e., secrets; **twain:** separate

255. **myself:** I

I think you are happy in this second match,                    235
For it excels your first, or, if it did not,
Your first is dead, or 'twere as good he were
As living here and you no use of him.

JULIET
Speak'st thou from thy heart?

NURSE
And from my soul too, else beshrew them both.              240

JULIET  Amen.

NURSE  What?

JULIET
Well, thou hast comforted me marvelous much.
Go in and tell my lady I am gone,
Having displeased my father, to Lawrence' cell              245
To make confession and to be absolved.

NURSE
Marry, I will; and this is wisely done.        ⌜*She exits.*⌝

JULIET
Ancient damnation, O most wicked fiend!
Is it more sin to wish me thus forsworn
Or to dispraise my lord with that same tongue               250
Which she hath praised him with above compare
So many thousand times? Go, counselor.
Thou and my bosom henceforth shall be twain.
I'll to the Friar to know his remedy.
If all else fail, myself have power to die.                    255
                                        *She exits.*

*I wonder how many times [BJ] wanted to die in this book*

*The Tragedy of*

# ROMEO

## AND

# JULIET

---

ACT 4

**4.1**  Paris is talking with Friar Lawrence about the coming wedding when Juliet arrives. After Paris leaves, she threatens suicide if Friar Lawrence cannot save her from marrying Paris. Friar Lawrence gives her a potion that will make her appear as if dead the morning of the wedding. He assures her that when she awakes in the vault, Romeo will be there to take her away.

---

2. **father:** i.e., prospective father-in-law

3. **I am . . . haste:** "**His haste** shall not be abated by my slowness," (Samuel Johnson)

7. **talk of:** conversation about

8. **Venus:** goddess of love (See picture, page 178.)

10. **That . . . sway:** i.e., **that she** lets **her sorrow** master her

11. **marriage:** pronounced as a three-syllable word

13–14. **Which . . . society:** i.e., **her tears,** to **which** she is **too much** disposed (**minded**) when she is **alone, may be** driven away **by** company (**society**)

# ⌜ACT 4⌝

## ⌜Scene 1⌝

*Enter Friar ⌜Lawrence⌝ and County Paris.*

FRIAR LAWRENCE
　On Thursday, sir? The time is very short.
PARIS
　My father Capulet will have it so,
　And I am nothing slow to slack his haste.
FRIAR LAWRENCE
　You say you do not know the lady's mind?
　Uneven is the course. I like it not.　　　　　　　　　5
PARIS
　Immoderately she weeps for Tybalt's death,
　And therefore have I little talk of love,
　For Venus smiles not in a house of tears.
　Now, sir, her father counts it dangerous
　That she do give her sorrow so much sway,　　　　　10
　And in his wisdom hastes our marriage
　To stop the inundation of her tears,
　Which, too much minded by herself alone,
　May be put from her by society.
　Now do you know the reason of this haste.　　　　　15
FRIAR LAWRENCE, ⌜*aside*⌝
　I would I knew not why it should be slowed.—
　Look, sir, here comes the lady toward my cell.

*Enter Juliet.*

177

18. **Happily:** fortunately
24. **I should confess:** i.e., I would be confessing
28. **price:** value
33. **report:** statement

Venus. (4.1.8)
From Vincenzo Cartari, *Le vere e noue imagini* . . . (1615).

**PARIS**
Happily met, my lady and my wife.

**JULIET**
That may be, sir, when I may be a wife.

**PARIS**
That "may be" must be, love, on Thursday next.                    20

**JULIET**
What must be shall be.

**FRIAR LAWRENCE**                    That's a certain text.

**PARIS**
Come you to make confession to this father?

**JULIET**
To answer that, I should confess to you.

**PARIS**
Do not deny to him that you love me.                    25

**JULIET**
I will confess to you that I love him.

**PARIS**
So will you, I am sure, that you love me.

**JULIET**
If I do so, it will be of more price
Being spoke behind your back than to your face.

**PARIS**
Poor soul, thy face is much abused with tears.                    30

**JULIET**
The tears have got small victory by that,
For it was bad enough before their spite.

**PARIS**
Thou wrong'st it more than tears with that report.

**JULIET**
That is no slander, sir, which is a truth,
And what I spake, I spake it to my face.                    35

**PARIS**
Thy face is mine, and thou hast slandered it.

**JULIET**
It may be so, for it is not mine own.—

40. **pensive:** sorrowful, sad

41. **entreat:** ask for

42. **shield:** prevent that

43. **rouse you:** awaken you (with music, as was customary on the wedding day)

46. **past care: past** being taken **care** of; **past** any concern for taking **care** of myself (Many texts follow the First Quarto and print "past cure.")

48. **strains . . . wits:** forces me beyond the limits of my ingenuity

49. **prorogue:** postpone

54. **Do thou but call:** only **call**

57–58. **sealed . . . label . . . deed:** A **label** was a strip of parchment that attached a seal to a **deed. deed:** a legal document or contract

60. **this:** i.e., the knife; **both: hand** (line 57) and **heart** (line 59)

62. **present counsel:** immediate advice

63. **extremes:** extreme difficulties

65. **commission:** authority; **art:** learning

66. **issue . . . honor:** i.e., honorable conclusion

Are you at leisure, holy father, now,
Or shall I come to you at evening Mass?

FRIAR LAWRENCE
My leisure serves me, pensive daughter, now.— 40
My lord, we must entreat the time alone.

PARIS
God shield I should disturb devotion!—
Juliet, on Thursday early will I rouse you.
Till then, adieu, and keep this holy kiss. *He exits.*

JULIET
O, shut the door, and when thou hast done so, 45
Come weep with me, past hope, past care, past help.

FRIAR LAWRENCE
O Juliet, I already know thy grief.
It strains me past the compass of my wits.
I hear thou must, and nothing may prorogue it,
On Thursday next be married to this County. 50

JULIET
Tell me not, friar, that thou hearest of this,
Unless thou tell me how I may prevent it.
If in thy wisdom thou canst give no help,
Do thou but call my resolution wise,
And with this knife I'll help it presently. 55
⌜*She shows him her knife.*⌝
God joined my heart and Romeo's, thou our hands;
And ere this hand, by thee to Romeo's sealed,
Shall be the label to another deed,
Or my true heart with treacherous revolt
Turn to another, this shall slay them both. 60
Therefore out of thy long-experienced time
Give me some present counsel, or, behold,
'Twixt my extremes and me this bloody knife
Shall play the umpire, arbitrating that
Which the commission of thy years and art 65
Could to no issue of true honor bring.
Be not so long to speak. I long to die
If what thou speak'st speak not of remedy.

69. **Hold:** stop, wait

70. **craves . . . execution:** demands as reckless action

71. **As . . . desperate: as that** action **is** unbearable

74. **is it:** i.e., **it is**

76. **That . . . it:** i.e., you who would meet **death** itself in order to escape **this shame**

80. **thievish ways:** roads infested with thieves

82. **charnel house:** house for storing the bones of the dead (See picture, below.)

83. **O'ercovered quite:** entirely covered up

84. **reeky:** reeking; **chapless:** jawless

86. **hide me:** i.e., **hide; shroud:** See picture, page 184.

95. **being then:** once you are

96. **distilling:** (1) distilled; (2) infusing (the body); **liquor:** liquid

99. **his native:** its natural; **surcease:** cease

A charnel house. (4.1.82)
From Richard Day, *A booke of Christian prayers . . .* (1590).

FRIAR LAWRENCE
    Hold, daughter, I do spy a kind of hope,
    Which craves as desperate an execution     70
    As that is desperate which we would prevent.
    If, rather than to marry County Paris,
    Thou hast the strength of will to ⌜slay⌝ thyself,
    Then is it likely thou wilt undertake
    A thing like death to chide away this shame,     75
    That cop'st with death himself to 'scape from it;
    And if thou darest, I'll give thee remedy.

JULIET
    O, bid me leap, rather than marry Paris,
    From off the battlements of any tower,
    Or walk in thievish ways, or bid me lurk     80
    Where serpents are. Chain me with roaring bears,
    Or hide me nightly in a charnel house,
    O'ercovered quite with dead men's rattling bones,
    With reeky shanks and yellow ⌜chapless⌝ skulls.
    Or bid me go into a new-made grave     85
    And hide me with a dead man in his ⌜shroud⌝
    (Things that to hear them told have made me
        tremble),
    And I will do it without fear or doubt,
    To live an unstained wife to my sweet love.     90

FRIAR LAWRENCE
    Hold, then. Go home; be merry; give consent
    To marry Paris. Wednesday is tomorrow.
    Tomorrow night look that thou lie alone;
    Let not the Nurse lie with thee in thy chamber.
                           ⌜*Holding out a vial.*⌝
    Take thou this vial, being then in bed,     95
    And this distilling liquor drink thou off;
    When presently through all thy veins shall run
    A cold and drowsy humor; for no pulse
    Shall keep his native progress, but surcease.
    No warmth, no ⌜breath⌝ shall testify thou livest.     100

102. **paly:** pale
104. **supple government:** flexibility
105. **stark:** rigid
112. **uncovered:** bare-faced
115. **against:** in preparation for the time at which
116. **drift:** purpose
118. **watch:** keep watch over
121. **inconstant toy:** whim that interferes with your firmness of purpose
122. **Abate:** lessen
124. **prosperous:** successful
127–28. **help afford:** provide **help**

A corpse in a shroud. (4.1.86)
From Richard Day, *A booke of Christian prayers* . . . (1590).

The roses in thy lips and cheeks shall fade
To ⌜paly⌝ ashes, thy eyes' windows fall
Like death when he shuts up the day of life.
Each part, deprived of supple government,
Shall, stiff and stark and cold, appear like death,          105
And in this borrowed likeness of shrunk death
Thou shalt continue two and forty hours
And then awake as from a pleasant sleep.
Now, when the bridegroom in the morning comes
To rouse thee from thy bed, there art thou dead.            110
Then, as the manner of our country is,
⌜In⌝ thy best robes uncovered on the bier
Thou ⌜shalt⌝ be borne to that same ancient vault
Where all the kindred of the Capulets lie.
In the meantime, against thou shalt awake,                  115
Shall Romeo by my letters know our drift,
And hither shall he come, and he and I
Will watch thy ⌜waking,⌝ and that very night
Shall Romeo bear thee hence to Mantua.
And this shall free thee from this present shame,           120
If no inconstant toy nor womanish fear
Abate thy valor in the acting it.

JULIET
Give me, give me! O, tell not me of fear!

FRIAR LAWRENCE, ⌜*giving Juliet the vial*⌝
Hold, get you gone. Be strong and prosperous
In this resolve. I'll send a friar with speed               125
To Mantua with my letters to thy lord.

JULIET
Love give me strength, and strength shall help
     afford.
Farewell, dear father.
                    ⌜*They*⌝ *exit* ⌜*in different directions.*⌝

**4.2**   Capulet energetically directs preparations for the wedding. When Juliet returns from Friar Lawrence and pretends to have learned obedience, Capulet is so delighted that he moves the wedding up to the next day and goes off to tell Paris the new date.

---

   0 SD. **Servingmen, two or three:** i.e., **two or three servingmen**
   2. **cunning:** skilled
   3. **none ill:** no incompetent ones; **try:** test (to see)
   6–7. **'tis . . . fingers:** proverbial
   10. **unfurnished:** unprovided
   14. **peevish:** obstinate; **harlotry:** good-for-nothing (often—but probably not here—with reference to a harlot, or whore); **it:** i.e., she
   18. **learned me:** i.e., **learned**

⌜Scene 2⌝

*Enter Father Capulet, Mother, Nurse, and Servingmen,*
*two or three.*

CAPULET
  So many guests invite as here are writ.
                    ⌜*One or two of the Servingmen exit*
                              *with Capulet's list.*⌝
  Sirrah, go hire me twenty cunning cooks.
SERVINGMAN  You shall have none ill, sir, for I'll try if
  they can lick their fingers.
CAPULET  How canst thou try them so?                    5
SERVINGMAN  Marry, sir, 'tis an ill cook that cannot lick
  his own fingers. Therefore he that cannot lick his
  fingers goes not with me.
CAPULET  Go, begone.          ⌜*Servingman exits.*⌝
  We shall be much unfurnished for this time.—      10
  What, is my daughter gone to Friar Lawrence?
NURSE  Ay, forsooth.
CAPULET
  Well, he may chance to do some good on her.
  A peevish ⌜self-willed⌝ harlotry it is.

*Enter Juliet.*

NURSE
  See where she comes from shrift with merry look.     15
CAPULET
  How now, my headstrong, where have you been
     gadding?
JULIET
  Where I have learned me to repent the sin
  Of disobedient opposition
  To you and your behests, and am enjoined           20
  By holy Lawrence to fall prostrate here     ⌜*Kneeling.*⌝
  To beg your pardon. Pardon, I beseech you.
  Henceforward I am ever ruled by you.

25. **this knot:** the marriage of Juliet and Paris
27. **becomèd:** fitting, becoming
29. **on 't:** of it
33. **bound:** obliged
34. **closet:** private room
35–36. **sort . . . furnish me:** select **such** clothes as you think suitable for me to wear
43. **deck up her:** array or adorn **her**
47. **prepare up him: prepare him**
48. **Against:** in anticipation of

**CAPULET**
Send for the County. Go tell him of this.
I'll have this knot knit up tomorrow morning.          25

**JULIET**
I met the youthful lord at Lawrence' cell
And gave him what becomèd love I might,
Not stepping o'er the bounds of modesty.

**CAPULET**
Why, I am glad on 't. This is well. Stand up.
                         ⌜*Juliet rises.*⌝
This is as 't should be.—Let me see the County.          30
Ay, marry, go, I say, and fetch him hither.—
Now, afore God, this reverend holy friar,
All our whole city is much bound to him.

**JULIET**
Nurse, will you go with me into my closet
To help me sort such needful ornaments                    35
As you think fit to furnish me tomorrow?

**LADY CAPULET**
No, not till Thursday. There is time enough.

**CAPULET**
Go, nurse. Go with her. We'll to church tomorrow.
                   ⌜*Juliet and the Nurse*⌝ *exit.*

**LADY CAPULET**
We shall be short in our provision.
'Tis now near night.                                      40

**CAPULET**                    Tush, I will stir about,
And all things shall be well, I warrant thee, wife.
Go thou to Juliet. Help to deck up her.
I'll not to bed tonight. Let me alone.
I'll play the housewife for this once.—What ho!—          45
They are all forth. Well, I will walk myself
To County Paris, to prepare up him
Against tomorrow. My heart is wondrous light
Since this same wayward girl is so reclaimed.
                                    ⌜*They*⌝ *exit.*

**4.3** Juliet sends the Nurse away for the night. After facing her terror at the prospect of awaking in her family's burial vault, Juliet drinks the potion that Friar Lawrence has given her.

---

1. **those attires are:** this apparel is; **gentle:** a complimentary epithet
4. **state:** condition
5. **cross:** full of contradictions
7. **culled:** chosen
7–8. **necessaries . . . behooveful:** i.e., necessary and useful things
8. **state:** display

⌜Scene 3⌝

*Enter Juliet and Nurse.*

JULIET
  Ay, those attires are best. But, gentle nurse,
  I pray thee leave me to myself tonight,
  For I have need of many orisons
  To move the heavens to smile upon my state,
  Which, well thou knowest, is cross and full of sin.    5

*Enter ⌜Lady Capulet.⌝*

LADY CAPULET
  What, are you busy, ho? Need you my help?
JULIET
  No, madam, we have culled such necessaries
  As are behooveful for our state tomorrow.
  So please you, let me now be left alone,
  And let the Nurse this night sit up with you,    10
  For I am sure you have your hands full all
  In this so sudden business.
LADY CAPULET                Good night.
  Get thee to bed and rest, for thou hast need.
             ⌜*Lady Capulet and the Nurse*⌝ *exit.*

JULIET
  Farewell.—God knows when we shall meet again.    15
  I have a faint cold fear thrills through my veins
  That almost freezes up the heat of life.
  I'll call them back again to comfort me.—
  Nurse!—What should she do here?
  My dismal scene I needs must act alone.    20
  Come, vial.           ⌜*She takes out the vial.*⌝
  What if this mixture do not work at all?
  Shall I be married then tomorrow morning?
             ⌜*She takes out her knife*
            *and puts it down beside her.*⌝
  No, no, this shall forbid it. Lie thou there.
  What if it be a poison which the Friar    25

26. **Subtly:** craftily; **ministered:** provided
29. **should not:** i.e., **should not** be
30. **still been tried:** always been proven
36. **strangled:** suffocated
37. **like:** i.e., likely that
38. **conceit of:** thoughts (or images) of
40. **As:** i.e., **as** being
43. **green in earth:** freshly interred in the vault
48. **mandrakes:** plants whose forked roots make them resemble the human body, and which were thought to shriek when **torn out of the** ground (See picture, below.)
49. **That:** i.e., so **that**
54. **rage:** madness; **great kinsman's:** e.g., great-grandfather's or great-uncle's
57. **spit:** impale
58. **Stay:** wait

A mandrake. (4.3.48)
From Rembert Dodoens, *Purgantium . . . herbarum historiae . . .* (1574).

Subtly hath ministered to have me dead,
Lest in this marriage he should be dishonored
Because he married me before to Romeo?
I fear it is. And yet methinks it should not,
For he hath still been tried a holy man.                          30
How if, when I am laid into the tomb,
I wake before the time that Romeo
Come to redeem me? There's a fearful point.
Shall I not then be stifled in the vault,
To whose foul mouth no healthsome air breathes in,    35
And there die strangled ere my Romeo comes?
Or, if I live, is it not very like
The horrible conceit of death and night,
Together with the terror of the place—
As in a vault, an ancient receptacle                             40
Where for this many hundred years the bones
Of all my buried ancestors are packed;
Where bloody Tybalt, yet but green in earth,
Lies fest'ring in his shroud; where, as they say,
At some hours in the night spirits resort—            45
Alack, alack, is it not like that I,
So early waking, what with loathsome smells,
And shrieks like mandrakes torn out of the earth,
That living mortals, hearing them, run mad—
O, if I ⌈wake,⌉ shall I not be distraught,                       50
Environèd with all these hideous fears,
And madly play with my forefathers' joints,
And pluck the mangled Tybalt from his shroud,
And, in this rage, with some great kinsman's bone,
As with a club, dash out my desp'rate brains?           55
O look, methinks I see my cousin's ghost
Seeking out Romeo that did spit his body
Upon a rapier's point! Stay, Tybalt, stay!
Romeo, Romeo, Romeo! Here's drink. I drink to
   thee.          ⌈*She drinks and falls upon her bed*          60
               *within the curtains.*⌉

**4.4**   The Capulets and the Nurse stay up all night to get ready for the wedding. Capulet, hearing Paris approach with musicians, orders the Nurse to wake Juliet.

---

2.  **pastry:** room where **pastry** is made
3.  **second cock hath crowed:** i.e., it is after 3 A.M. (Conventionally, the cock crowed first at midnight, then at 3 A.M., and then one hour before daybreak.)
5.  **baked meats:** meat pies
7.  **cot-quean:** i.e., a man who meddles in women's kitchen tasks (Some editors assign this speech to Lady Capulet on the grounds that the Nurse would not be free to speak to Capulet in this way.)
9.  **For:** because of; **watching:** staying awake
12. **mouse-hunt:** i.e., chaser of women (literally, a mouse hunter like a cat or weasel)
13. **watch . . . watching:** keep you in sight in order to prevent you from "mouse hunting"
14. **A jealous hood:** i.e., one who wears jealousy like a cap

⌈Scene 4⌉

*Enter ⌈Lady Capulet⌉ and Nurse.*

LADY CAPULET
  Hold, take these keys, and fetch more spices, nurse.
NURSE
  They call for dates and quinces in the pastry.

*Enter old Capulet.*

CAPULET
  Come, stir, stir, stir! The second cock hath crowed.
  The curfew bell hath rung. 'Tis three o'clock.—
  Look to the baked meats, good Angelica.          5
  Spare not for cost.
NURSE                     Go, you cot-quean, go,
  Get you to bed. Faith, you'll be sick tomorrow
  For this night's watching.
CAPULET
  No, not a whit. What, I have watched ere now      10
  All night for lesser cause, and ne'er been sick.
LADY CAPULET
  Ay, you have been a mouse-hunt in your time,
  But I will watch you from such watching now.
                    *Lady ⌈Capulet⌉ and Nurse exit.*
CAPULET
  A jealous hood, a jealous hood!

*Enter three or four ⌈Servingmen⌉ with spits and logs
            and baskets.*

                          Now fellow,          15
    What is there?
⌈FIRST SERVINGMAN⌉
  Things for the cook, sir, but I know not what.
CAPULET
  Make haste, make haste.      ⌈*First Servingman exits.*⌉
                    Sirrah, fetch drier logs.
  Call Peter. He will show thee where they are.      20

23. **Mass:** i.e., by the **Mass; whoreson:** literally, whore's son, but here only a kind of familiar address
24. **loggerhead:** blockhead
26. **straight:** straightaway, immediately
29. **trim:** dress

**4.5** The Nurse finds Juliet in the deathlike trance caused by the Friar's potion and announces Juliet's death. Juliet's parents and Paris join the Nurse in lamentation. Friar Lawrence interrupts them and begins to arrange Juliet's funeral. The scene closes with an exchange of wordplay between Capulet's servant Peter and Paris's musicians.

———————

1. **Fast:** i.e., **fast** asleep
5. **pennyworths:** little bits (of sleep)
8. **set up his rest:** firmly decided (with a sexual implication for which the Nurse then asks forgiveness, only to introduce further sexual implications with **take** [line 12] and **fright you up** [line 13])
10. **Marry:** a mild interjection (originally an oath on the Virgin Mary)

⌜SECOND SERVINGMAN⌝
    I have a head, sir, that will find out logs
    And never trouble Peter for the matter.

CAPULET
    Mass, and well said. A merry whoreson, ha!
    Thou shalt be loggerhead.
                    ⌜*Second Servingman exits.*⌝
                    Good ⌜faith,⌝ 'tis day.    25
    The County will be here with music straight,
                            *Play music.*
    For so he said he would. I hear him near.—
    Nurse!—Wife! What ho!—What, nurse, I say!

                  *Enter Nurse.*

    Go waken Juliet. Go and trim her up.
    I'll go and chat with Paris. Hie, make haste,    30
    Make haste. The bridegroom he is come already.
    Make haste, I say.
                          ⌜*He exits.*⌝


               ⌜Scene 5⌝

NURSE, ⌜*approaching the bed*⌝
    Mistress! What, mistress! Juliet!—Fast, I warrant
      her, she—
    Why, lamb, why, lady! Fie, you slugabed!
    Why, love, I say! Madam! Sweetheart! Why, bride!—
    What, not a word?—You take your pennyworths    5
      now.
    Sleep for a week, for the next night, I warrant,
    The County Paris hath set up his rest
    That you shall rest but little.—God forgive me,
    Marry, and amen! How sound is she asleep!    10
    I needs must wake her.—Madam, madam, madam!
    Ay, let the County take you in your bed,

13. **Will . . . be?:** i.e., won't you wake up
18. **weraday:** exclamation of sorrow
19. **aqua vitae:** strong drink, usually brandy
23. **heavy:** sorrowful
30. **Out, alas:** expressions of sorrow

Mourners with corpse on bier. (4.5)
From Tommaso Porcacchi, *Funerali antichi . . .* (1591).

He'll fright you up, i' faith.—Will it not be?
⌜*She opens the bed's curtains.*⌝
What, dressed, and in your clothes, and down
　again?　　　　　　　　　　　　　　　　　　　15
I must needs wake you. Lady, lady, lady!—
Alas, alas! Help, help! My lady's dead.—
O, weraday, that ever I was born!—
Some aqua vitae, ho!—My lord! My lady!

⌜*Enter Lady Capulet.*⌝

LADY CAPULET
　What noise is here?　　　　　　　　　　　　　20
NURSE　　　　　　　　O lamentable day!
LADY CAPULET
　What is the matter?
NURSE　　　　　　　　Look, look!—O heavy day!
LADY CAPULET
　O me! O me! My child, my only life,
　Revive, look up, or I will die with thee.　　　25
　Help, help! Call help.

Enter ⌜*Capulet.*⌝

CAPULET
　For shame, bring Juliet forth. Her lord is come.
NURSE
　She's dead, deceased. She's dead, alack the day!
LADY CAPULET
　Alack the day, she's dead, she's dead, she's dead.
CAPULET
　Ha, let me see her! Out, alas, she's cold.　　30
　Her blood is settled, and her joints are stiff.
　Life and these lips have long been separated.
　Death lies on her like an untimely frost
　Upon the sweetest flower of all the field.
NURSE
　O lamentable day!　　　　　　　　　　　　35

43. **deflowerèd by him:** i.e., sexually visited by **Death**

46. **living:** livelihood

47. **thought long to see:** i.e., **long** looked forward to seeing

49. **unhappy:** disastrous (From this line to the Friar's interruption at line 71, four characters each have a speech lamenting Juliet's "death." It has been suggested that the four ought to deliver their lines simultaneously, as may just possibly be indicated by this stage direction in the First Quarto: "All at once cry out and wring their hands.")

51. **lasting:** everlasting

54. **catched:** snatched

61. **Beguiled:** disappointed, cheated

Death as a bridegroom. (3.2.150; 4.5.44–45)
From *Todten-Tantz . . .* (1696).

LADY CAPULET         O woeful time!

CAPULET
  Death, that hath ta'en her hence to make me wail,
  Ties up my tongue and will not let me speak.

*Enter Friar ⌈Lawrence⌉ and the County ⌈Paris, with*
*Musicians.⌉*

FRIAR LAWRENCE
  Come, is the bride ready to go to church?

CAPULET
  Ready to go, but never to return.—                    40
  O son, the night before thy wedding day
  Hath Death lain with thy wife. There she lies,
  Flower as she was, deflowerèd by him.
  Death is my son-in-law; Death is my heir.
  My daughter he hath wedded. I will die              45
  And leave him all. Life, living, all is Death's.

PARIS
  Have I thought ⌈long⌉ to see this morning's face,
  And doth it give me such a sight as this?

LADY CAPULET
  Accursed, unhappy, wretched, hateful day!
  Most miserable hour that e'er time saw                50
  In lasting labor of his pilgrimage!
  But one, poor one, one poor and loving child,
  But one thing to rejoice and solace in,
  And cruel death hath catched it from my sight!

NURSE
  O woe, O woeful, woeful, woeful day!                  55
  Most lamentable day, most woeful day
  That ever, ever I did yet behold!
  O day, O day, O day, O hateful day!
  Never was seen so black a day as this!
  O woeful day, O woeful day!                           60

PARIS
  Beguiled, divorcèd, wrongèd, spited, slain!

66. **Uncomfortable:** distressing

67. **solemnity:** festival (Juliet's wedding)

71. **Confusion's:** ruin's

72. **confusions:** outbursts, commotions

73. **Had part:** i.e., each **had** a share; **maid:** maiden

77. **her promotion:** her material advancement

78. **heaven:** supreme happiness; **advanced:** raised in rank or station

79. **advanced:** lifted up

81. **ill:** badly

82. **she is well:** i.e., **she is** happy in heaven (**"She is well"** was a phrase indicating that someone had died.)

85. **rosemary:** an aromatic plant, symbol of remembrance (associated with both funerals and weddings) See picture, page 204.

88. **fond:** foolish

89. **reason's merriment:** i.e., cause for reason's rejoicing

90. **ordainèd festival:** planned to be festive

91. **office:** function

93. **cheer:** food and drink

94. **sullen dirges:** mournful funeral songs

Most detestable death, by thee beguiled,
By cruel, cruel thee quite overthrown!
O love! O life! Not life, but love in death!

CAPULET
Despised, distressèd, hated, martyred, killed!          65
Uncomfortable time, why cam'st thou now
To murder, murder our solemnity?
O child! O child! My soul and not my child!
Dead art thou! Alack, my child is dead,
And with my child my joys are burièd.          70

FRIAR LAWRENCE
Peace, ho, for shame! Confusion's ⌜cure⌝ lives not
In these confusions. Heaven and yourself
Had part in this fair maid. Now heaven hath all,
And all the better is it for the maid.
Your part in her you could not keep from death,          75
But heaven keeps his part in eternal life.
The most you sought was her promotion,
For 'twas your heaven she should be advanced;
And weep you now, seeing she is advanced
Above the clouds, as high as heaven itself?          80
O, in this love you love your child so ill
That you run mad, seeing that she is well.
She's not well married that lives married long,
But she's best married that dies married young.
Dry up your tears, and stick your rosemary          85
On this fair corse, and, as the custom is,
And in her best array, bear her to church,
For though ⌜fond⌝ nature bids us all lament,
Yet nature's tears are reason's merriment.

CAPULET
All things that we ordainèd festival          90
Turn from their office to black funeral:
Our instruments to melancholy bells,
Our wedding cheer to a sad burial feast,
Our solemn hymns to sullen dirges change,

100. **lour:** frown

101. **Move:** provoke

102. **put up:** i.e., **put** away

104. **case:** event

105. **the case may be amended:** (1) the situation might be improved; (2) **the case** in which I keep my instrument might be mended

106. **"Heart's ease":** the name of a popular song

110–11. **"My heart is full":** part of a line from a popular song

111. **merry dump:** a contradiction in terms, since a **dump** is a sad song

117. **give it you:** i.e., beat you

119. **gleek:** jest, jeer

119–20. **give you the minstrel:** call you a **minstrel**

Rosemary. (4.5.85)
From *The grete herball* . . . (1529).

Our bridal flowers serve for a buried corse,                    95
And all things change them to the contrary.

FRIAR LAWRENCE
Sir, go you in, and, madam, go with him,
And go, Sir Paris. Everyone prepare
To follow this fair corse unto her grave.
The heavens do lour upon you for some ill.                      100
Move them no more by crossing their high will.
        ⌜*All but the Nurse and the Musicians*⌝ *exit.*

⌜FIRST MUSICIAN⌝
Faith, we may put up our pipes and be gone.

NURSE
Honest good fellows, ah, put up, put up,
For, well you know, this is a pitiful case.

⌜FIRST MUSICIAN⌝
Ay, ⌜by⌝ my troth, the case may be amended.                    105
                                    ⌜*Nurse* ⌝ *exits.*

*Enter* ⌜*Peter.* ⌝

PETER  Musicians, O musicians, "Heart's ease,"
   "Heart's ease." O, an you will have me live, play
   "Heart's ease."

⌜FIRST MUSICIAN⌝  Why "Heart's ease?"

PETER  O musicians, because my heart itself plays "My  110
   heart is full." O, play me some merry dump to
   comfort me.

⌜FIRST MUSICIAN⌝  Not a dump, we. 'Tis no time to play
   now.

PETER  You will not then?                                      115

⌜FIRST MUSICIAN⌝  No.

PETER  I will then give it you soundly.

⌜FIRST MUSICIAN⌝  What will you give us?

PETER  No money, on my faith, but the gleek. I will give
   you the minstrel.                                           120

⌜FIRST MUSICIAN⌝  Then will I give you the serving-
   creature.

124. **carry no crochets:** i.e., tolerate none of your whims (**Crochets** also meant quarter notes.) **re, fa:** names of musical notes

125. **note:** pay attention to

128. **put out:** display

129. **have at you:** i.e., I'll attack you

132–34. **When griping . . . sound:** from a song by Richard Edwardes published in 1576 **griping:** distressing **dumps:** low spirits

136. **Catling:** a small catgut string for a fiddle

139. **Prates:** i.e., he just chatters; **Rebeck:** a fiddle

141. **sound:** play

142. **Soundpost:** a peg of wood fixed underneath the bridge of a violin or fiddle

144. **cry you mercy:** i.e., beg your pardon; **say:** i.e., speak, because you can only sing

146. **sounding:** playing

148. **lend redress:** make amends

149. **this same:** i.e., **this** man (Peter)

151. **tarry:** wait; **stay:** i.e., **stay** for

PETER  Then will I lay the serving-creature's dagger on
your pate. I will carry no crochets. I'll *re* you, I'll *fa*
you. Do you note me?                                      125
⌜FIRST MUSICIAN⌝  An you *re* us and *fa* us, you note us.
SECOND ⌜MUSICIAN⌝  Pray you, put up your dagger and
put out your wit.
⌜PETER⌝  Then have at you with my wit. I will dry-beat
you with an iron wit, and put up my iron dagger.        130
Answer me like men.
    ⌜*Sings.*⌝ *When griping griefs the heart doth wound*
          ⌜*And doleful dumps the mind oppress,*⌝
          *Then music with her silver sound—*
Why "silver sound"? Why "music with her silver          135
sound"? What say you, Simon Catling?
⌜FIRST MUSICIAN⌝  Marry, sir, because silver hath a
sweet sound.
PETER  Prates.—What say you, Hugh Rebeck?
SECOND ⌜MUSICIAN⌝  I say "silver sound" because musi-   140
cians sound for silver.
PETER  Prates too.—What say you, James Soundpost?
THIRD ⌜MUSICIAN⌝  Faith, I know not what to say.
PETER  O, I cry you mercy. You are the singer. I will say
for you. It is "music with her silver sound" because      145
musicians have no gold for sounding:
    ⌜*Sings.*⌝     *Then music with her silver sound*
              *With speedy help doth lend redress.*
                                              *He exits.*
⌜FIRST MUSICIAN⌝  What a pestilent knave is this same!
SECOND ⌜MUSICIAN⌝  Hang him, Jack. Come, we'll in     150
here, tarry for the mourners, and stay dinner.
                                          ⌜*They*⌝ *exit.*

*The Tragedy of*

# ROMEO

## AND

# JULIET

ACT 5

**5.1**  Romeo's man, Balthasar, arrives in Mantua with news of Juliet's death. Romeo sends him to hire horses for their immediate return to Verona. Romeo then buys poison so that he can join Juliet in death in the Capulets' burial vault.

————

1. **trust . . . sleep:** depend on the illusory hopes provided by dreams, as if they were true

2. **at hand:** soon

3. **bosom's . . . throne:** i.e., perhaps, my heart **sits lightly in** my breast

7. **gives . . . leave:** permits **a dead man**

12. **shadows:** i.e., images, dreams

## ⌈ACT 5⌉

⌈Scene 1⌉

*Enter Romeo.*

ROMEO
If I may trust the flattering truth of sleep,
My dreams presage some joyful news at hand.
My bosom's ⌈lord⌉ sits lightly in his throne,
And all this day an unaccustomed spirit
Lifts me above the ground with cheerful thoughts.   5
I dreamt my lady came and found me dead
(Strange dream that gives a dead man leave to
    think!)
And breathed such life with kisses in my lips
That I revived and was an emperor.   10
Ah me, how sweet is love itself possessed
When but love's shadows are so rich in joy!

*Enter Romeo's man ⌈Balthasar, in riding boots.⌉*

News from Verona!—How now, Balthasar?
Dost thou not bring me letters from the Friar?
How doth my lady? Is my father well?   15
How doth my Juliet? That I ask again,
For nothing can be ill if she be well.
BALTHASAR
Then she is well and nothing can be ill.
Her body sleeps in Capels' monument,
And her immortal part with angels lives.   20

211

22. **presently took post:** immediately departed on a post-horse (See note to line 27, below.)

24. **office:** duty

25. **deny:** repudiate; **stars:** fate, destiny; the influence of **stars** and planets on human affairs (See Prologue, line 6, page 7.)

27. **post-horses:** horses kept at inns for the use of travelers

28. **patience:** self-control

29. **import:** portend, forebode

31. **deceived:** mistaken

38. **for means:** by what **means**; **mischief:** evildoing, wickedness

40. **apothecary:** druggist (See picture, page 214.)

41. **late:** recently

42. **weeds:** clothes: **overwhelming:** overhanging

43. **Culling of simples:** selecting medicinal herbs; **Meager were his looks:** he looked emaciated

45. **needy:** poverty-stricken

45–47. **tortoise ... fishes:** Other writings of the period suggest that apothecaries decorated their shops with the remains of alligators and other such curiosities.

50. **of roses:** made of compressed rose petals

I saw her laid low in her kindred's vault
And presently took post to tell it you.
O, pardon me for bringing these ill news,
Since you did leave it for my office, sir.

ROMEO
Is it e'en so?—Then I deny you, stars!— 25
Thou knowest my lodging. Get me ink and paper,
And hire post-horses. I will hence tonight.

BALTHASAR
I do beseech you, sir, have patience.
Your looks are pale and wild and do import
Some misadventure. 30

ROMEO                  Tush, thou art deceived.
Leave me, and do the thing I bid thee do.
Hast thou no letters to me from the Friar?

BALTHASAR
No, my good lord.

ROMEO                  No matter. Get thee gone, 35
And hire those horses. I'll be with thee straight.
                              ⌜*Balthasar*⌝ *exits.*

Well, Juliet, I will lie with thee tonight.
Let's see for means. O mischief, thou art swift
To enter in the thoughts of desperate men.
I do remember an apothecary 40
(And hereabouts he dwells) which late I noted
In tattered weeds, with overwhelming brows,
Culling of simples. Meager were his looks.
Sharp misery had worn him to the bones.
And in his needy shop a tortoise hung, 45
An alligator stuffed, and other skins
Of ill-shaped fishes; and about his shelves,
A beggarly account of empty boxes,
Green earthen pots, bladders, and musty seeds,
Remnants of packthread, and old cakes of roses 50
Were thinly scattered to make up a show.
Noting this penury, to myself I said

54. **Whose . . . Mantua:** i.e., the **sale** of which **in Mantua** is penalized by immediate execution

55. **caitiff:** miserable

63. **ducats:** valuable gold coins

64. **dram:** a small draught; **soon-speeding gear:** quick-working stuff

66. **That:** i.e., so **that**

67. **trunk:** body

70. **mortal:** deadly

71. **any he:** i.e., anyone; **utters:** sells

74. **Need and oppression:** i.e., oppressive **need**

75. **Contempt and beggary:** i.e., contemptible **beggary**

77. **affords:** provides

An apothecary. (5.1.40)
From Ambroise Paré, *The workes of . . .* (1634).

"An if a man did need a poison now,
Whose sale is present death in Mantua,
Here lives a caitiff wretch would sell it him." 55
O, this same thought did but forerun my need,
And this same needy man must sell it me.
As I remember, this should be the house.
Being holiday, the beggar's shop is shut.—
What ho, Apothecary! 60

⌐*Enter Apothecary.*⌐

APOTHECARY　　　　　Who calls so loud?

ROMEO
Come hither, man. I see that thou art poor.
　　　　　　　　　　⌐*He offers money.*⌐
Hold, there is forty ducats. Let me have
A dram of poison, such soon-speeding gear
As will disperse itself through all the veins, 65
That the life-weary taker may fall dead,
And that the trunk may be discharged of breath
As violently as hasty powder fired
Doth hurry from the fatal cannon's womb.

APOTHECARY
Such mortal drugs I have, but Mantua's law 70
Is death to any he that utters them.

ROMEO
Art thou so bare and full of wretchedness,
And fearest to die? Famine is in thy cheeks,
Need and oppression starveth in thy eyes,
Contempt and beggary hangs upon thy back. 75
The world is not thy friend, nor the world's law.
The world affords no law to make thee rich.
Then be not poor, but break it, and take this.

APOTHECARY
My poverty, but not my will, consents.

ROMEO
I ⌐pay⌐ thy poverty and not thy will. 80

90. **cordial:** invigorating drink

**5.2**   Friar John enters, bringing with him the letter that he was to have delivered to Romeo. He tells why he was unable to deliver the letter. Friar Lawrence anxiously goes to the tomb to be there when Juliet comes out of her trance.

---

2. **This same:** i.e., **this**
5. **Going:** i.e., as I was **going; a barefoot brother:** i.e., another Franciscan friar (See picture, below.)
6. **associate:** accompany
7. **Here:** i.e., who was **here**
8. **finding:** i.e., I **finding; searchers:** i.e., officials
10. **pestilence:** plague
12. **speed:** i.e., journey

A barefoot brother. (5.2.5)
From Niccolo Catalano, *Fiume del terrestre paradiso* . . . (1652).

APOTHECARY, ⌜*giving him the poison*⌝
  Put this in any liquid thing you will
  And drink it off, and if you had the strength
  Of twenty men, it would dispatch you straight.
ROMEO, ⌜*handing him the money*⌝
  There is thy gold, worse poison to men's souls,
  Doing more murder in this loathsome world          85
  Than these poor compounds that thou mayst not
    sell.
  I sell thee poison; thou hast sold me none.
  Farewell, buy food, and get thyself in flesh.
                       ⌜*Apothecary exits.*⌝
  Come, cordial and not poison, go with me          90
  To Juliet's grave, for there must I use thee.
                           ⌜*He exits.*⌝


⌜*Scene 2*⌝

*Enter Friar John.*

FRIAR JOHN
  Holy Franciscan friar, brother, ho!

*Enter* ⌜*Friar*⌝ *Lawrence.*

FRIAR LAWRENCE
  This same should be the voice of Friar John. —
  Welcome from Mantua. What says Romeo?
  Or, if his mind be writ, give me his letter.
FRIAR JOHN
  Going to find a barefoot brother out,          5
  One of our order, to associate me,
  Here in this city visiting the sick,
  And finding him, the searchers of the town,
  Suspecting that we both were in a house
  Where the infectious pestilence did reign,          10
  Sealed up the doors and would not let us forth,
  So that my speed to Mantua there was stayed.

13. **bare:** i.e., bore, carried
17. **my brotherhood:** my vocation as friar
18. **nice:** trivial; **charge:** importance
19. **dear:** precious; dire, costly
21. **crow:** crowbar
26. **beshrew:** i.e., reprove (literally, curse)
27. **accidents:** events, happenings

**5.3** Paris visits Juliet's tomb and, when Romeo arrives, challenges him. Romeo and Paris fight and Paris is killed. Romeo, in the tomb, takes poison, dying as he kisses Juliet. As Friar Lawrence enters the tomb, Juliet awakes to find Romeo lying dead. Frightened by a noise, the Friar flees the tomb. Juliet kills herself with Romeo's dagger. Alerted by Paris's page, the watch arrives and finds the bodies. When the Prince, the Capulets, and Montague arrive, Friar Lawrence gives an account of the marriage of Romeo and Juliet. Their deaths lead Montague and Capulet to declare that the families' hostility is at an end.

1. **aloof:** at a distance
2. **it:** i.e., the **torch**
3. **lay thee all along:** i.e., stretch out

FRIAR LAWRENCE
　Who bare my letter, then, to Romeo?
FRIAR JOHN
　I could not send it—here it is again—
　　　　　　　　　　　⌐*Returning the letter.*⌐
　Nor get a messenger to bring it thee,　　　　　　15
　So fearful were they of infection.
FRIAR LAWRENCE
　Unhappy fortune! By my brotherhood,
　The letter was not nice but full of charge,
　Of dear import, and the neglecting it
　May do much danger. Friar John, go hence.　　20
　Get me an iron crow and bring it straight
　Unto my cell.
FRIAR JOHN
　Brother, I'll go and bring it thee.　　　*He exits.*
FRIAR LAWRENCE
　Now must I to the monument alone.
　Within this three hours will fair Juliet wake.　25
　She will beshrew me much that Romeo
　Hath had no notice of these accidents.
　But I will write again to Mantua,
　And keep her at my cell till Romeo come.
　Poor living corse, closed in a dead man's tomb!　30
　　　　　　　　　　　　　　　　*He exits.*


⌐Scene 3⌐

*Enter Paris and his Page.*

PARIS
　Give me thy torch, boy. Hence and stand aloof.
　Yet put it out, for I would not be seen.
　Under yond ⌐yew⌐ trees lay thee all along,
　Holding thy ear close to the hollow ground.
　So shall no foot upon the churchyard tread　　5
　(Being loose, unfirm, with digging up of graves)

11. **adventure:** venture, take the risk
14. **sweet water:** scented **water; dew:** dampen
15. **wanting:** lacking
20. **cross:** impede, thwart
21. **Muffle:** wrap up and thereby hide
22. **wrenching iron:** i.e., crowbar
25. **charge:** command
27. **course:** proceedings
32. **dear:** important
33. **jealous:** suspicious

But thou shalt hear it. Whistle then to me
As signal that thou hearest something approach.
Give me those flowers. Do as I bid thee. Go.

PAGE, ⌜*aside*⌝
I am almost afraid to stand alone                               10
Here in the churchyard. Yet I will adventure.
                              ⌜*He moves away from Paris.*⌝

PARIS, ⌜*scattering flowers*⌝
Sweet flower, with flowers thy bridal bed I strew
(O woe, thy canopy is dust and stones!)
Which with sweet water nightly I will dew,
Or, wanting that, with tears distilled by moans.        15
The obsequies that I for thee will keep
Nightly shall be to strew thy grave and weep.
                              ⌜*Page*⌝ *whistles.*
The boy gives warning something doth approach.
What cursèd foot wanders this way tonight,
To cross my obsequies and true love's rite?             20
What, with a torch? Muffle me, night, awhile.
                              ⌜*He steps aside.*⌝

        *Enter Romeo and* ⌜*Balthasar.*⌝

ROMEO
Give me that mattock and the wrenching iron.
Hold, take this letter. Early in the morning
See thou deliver it to my lord and father.
Give me the light. Upon thy life I charge thee,         25
Whate'er thou hearest or seest, stand all aloof
And do not interrupt me in my course.
Why I descend into this bed of death
Is partly to behold my lady's face,
But chiefly to take thence from her dead finger        30
A precious ring, a ring that I must use
In dear employment. Therefore hence, begone.
But, if thou, jealous, dost return to pry
In what I farther shall intend to do,

39. **empty:** hungry

43. **For all this same:** i.e., **all** the **same**

44. **fear:** distrust; **doubt:** suspect

45. **detestable:** accented on the first and third syllables; **maw, womb:** stomach

48. **in despite:** maliciously (because the stomach-tomb is already **gorged** [line 46])

52. **villainous shame:** i.e., shameful villainy

By heaven, I will tear thee joint by joint 35
And strew this hungry churchyard with thy limbs.
The time and my intents are savage-wild,
More fierce and more inexorable far
Than empty tigers or the roaring sea.

⌜BALTHASAR⌝
I will be gone, sir, and not trouble you. 40

ROMEO
So shalt thou show me friendship. Take thou that.
⌜*Giving money.*⌝
Live and be prosperous, and farewell, good fellow.

⌜BALTHASAR, *aside*⌝
For all this same, I'll hide me hereabout.
His looks I fear, and his intents I doubt.
⌜*He steps aside.*⌝

ROMEO, ⌜*beginning to force open the tomb*⌝
Thou detestable maw, thou womb of death, 45
Gorged with the dearest morsel of the earth,
Thus I enforce thy rotten jaws to open,
And in despite I'll cram thee with more food.

PARIS
This is that banished haughty Montague
That murdered my love's cousin, with which grief 50
It is supposèd the fair creature died,
And here is come to do some villainous shame
To the dead bodies. I will apprehend him.
⌜*Stepping forward.*⌝
Stop thy unhallowed toil, vile Montague.
Can vengeance be pursued further than death? 55
Condemnèd villain, I do apprehend thee.
Obey and go with me, for thou must die.

ROMEO
I must indeed, and therefore came I hither.
Good gentle youth, tempt not a desp'rate man.
Fly hence and leave me. Think upon these gone. 60
Let them affright thee. I beseech thee, youth,

68. **commination:** threat (This word, first adopted into an edition of *Romeo and Juliet* by G. W. Williams, is in the Church of England's Book of Common Prayer in "A Commination Against Sinners." Q2 has "commiration," Q1 has "coniurations," and Q3, Q4, and F1 have "commisseration." Most editions follow Capell's "conjuration," which is based on Q1.)

71. **watch:** watchmen, guards

78. **should have:** was to **have**

83. **triumphant:** glorious

84. **lantern:** a turret with many windows (See picture, below.)

86. **feasting presence:** chamber where a monarch would entertain

A lantern. (5.3.84)
From Sebastiano Serlio, *Tutte l'opere d'architettura . . .* (1584).

Put not another sin upon my head
By urging me to fury. O, begone!
By heaven, I love thee better than myself,
For I come hither armed against myself.                    65
Stay not, begone, live, and hereafter say
A madman's mercy bid thee run away.

PARIS
I do defy thy ⌜commination⌝
And apprehend thee for a felon here.

ROMEO
Wilt thou provoke me? Then have at thee, boy!            70
                        ⌜*They draw and fight.*⌝

⌜PAGE⌝
O Lord, they fight! I will go call the watch.
                                ⌜*He exits.*⌝

PARIS
O, I am slain! If thou be merciful,
Open the tomb; lay me with Juliet.        ⌜*He dies.*⌝

ROMEO
In faith, I will.—Let me peruse this face.
Mercutio's kinsman, noble County Paris!                   75
What said my man when my betossèd soul
Did not attend him as we rode? I think
He told me Paris should have married Juliet.
Said he not so? Or did I dream it so?
Or am I mad, hearing him talk of Juliet,                  80
To think it was so?—O, give me thy hand,
One writ with me in sour misfortune's book!
I'll bury thee in a triumphant grave.—
                        ⌜*He opens the tomb.*⌝
A grave? O, no. A lantern, slaughtered youth,
For here lies Juliet, and her beauty makes               85
This vault a feasting presence full of light.—
Death, lie thou there, by a dead man interred.
                        ⌜*Laying Paris in the tomb.*⌝
How oft when men are at the point of death

90. **light'ning:** sudden lifting of the spirits

94. **ensign:** military flag or banner

97. **sheet:** shroud

98. **more:** greater

100. **his:** i.e., Romeo's

106. **still:** always

110. **set . . . rest:** venture everything (from the card game primero); also, rest here forever

114–15. **seal . . . death:** The legal language that begins with **seal** is carried through in **bargain** (contract) and **engrossing** (monopolizing, buying up in quantity).

116. **conduct:** guide

117. **pilot:** i.e., **pilot** of a sailing vessel (**bark**) (Romeo here addresses himself.)

119. **true**: truthful, honest

Have they been merry, which their keepers call
A light'ning before death! O, how may I                    90
Call this a light'ning?—O my love, my wife,
Death, that hath sucked the honey of thy breath,
Hath had no power yet upon thy beauty.
Thou art not conquered. Beauty's ensign yet
Is crimson in thy lips and in thy cheeks,                   95
And death's pale flag is not advancèd there.—
Tybalt, liest thou there in thy bloody sheet?
O, what more favor can I do to thee
Than with that hand that cut thy youth in twain
To sunder his that was thine enemy?                        100
Forgive me, cousin.—Ah, dear Juliet,
Why art thou yet so fair? Shall I believe
That unsubstantial death is amorous,
And that the lean abhorrèd monster keeps
Thee here in dark to be his paramour?                      105
For fear of that I still will stay with thee
And never from this ⌜palace⌝ of dim night
Depart again. Here, here will I remain
With worms that are thy chambermaids. O, here
Will I set up my everlasting rest                          110
And shake the yoke of inauspicious stars
From this world-wearied flesh! Eyes, look your last.
Arms, take your last embrace. And, lips, O, you
The doors of breath, seal with a righteous kiss
A dateless bargain to engrossing death.                    115
                              ⌜*Kissing Juliet.*⌝
Come, bitter conduct, come, unsavory guide!
Thou desperate pilot, now at once run on
The dashing rocks thy seasick weary bark!
Here's to my love. ⌜*Drinking.*⌝ O true apothecary,
Thy drugs are quick. Thus with a kiss I die.              120
                              ⌜*He dies.*⌝

*Enter Friar* ⌜*Lawrence*⌝ *with lantern, crow, and spade.*

121. **be my speed:** i.e., help me
137. **fearfully:** in a way that caused fear
140. **ill unthrifty:** evil and unlucky

A yew tree. (5.3.3, 141)
From John Gerard, *The herball* . . . (1597).

FRIAR LAWRENCE
  Saint Francis be my speed! How oft tonight
  Have my old feet stumbled at graves!—Who's there?
⌜BALTHASAR⌝
  Here's one, a friend, and one that knows you well.
FRIAR LAWRENCE
  Bliss be upon you. Tell me, good my friend,
  What torch is yond that vainly lends his light          125
  To grubs and eyeless skulls? As I discern,
  It burneth in the Capels' monument.
⌜BALTHASAR⌝
  It doth so, holy sir, and there's my master,
  One that you love.
FRIAR LAWRENCE          Who is it?          130
⌜BALTHASAR⌝                    Romeo.
FRIAR LAWRENCE
  How long hath he been there?
⌜BALTHASAR⌝                    Full half an hour.
FRIAR LAWRENCE
  Go with me to the vault.
⌜BALTHASAR⌝                I dare not, sir.          135
  My master knows not but I am gone hence,
  And fearfully did menace me with death
  If I did stay to look on his intents.
FRIAR LAWRENCE
  Stay, then. I'll go alone. Fear comes upon me.
  O, much I fear some ill unthrifty thing.          140
⌜BALTHASAR⌝
  As I did sleep under this ⌜yew⌝ tree here,
  I dreamt my master and another fought,
  And that my master slew him.
FRIAR LAWRENCE, ⌜*moving toward the tomb*⌝
                    Romeo!—
  Alack, alack, what blood is this which stains          145
  The stony entrance of this sepulcher?
  What mean these masterless and gory swords

150. **unkind:** (1) unnatural; (2) cruel

151. **lamentable:** accented on the first and third syllables

153. **comfortable:** comfort-bringing

167. **timeless:** (1) untimely, premature; (2) eternal

168. **churl:** selfish one, miser

171. **with a restorative:** i.e., with Romeo's kiss, which should be for her like a restorative medicine

174. **happy dagger:** i.e., **dagger** I am fortunate to find

To lie discolored by this place of peace?
Romeo! O, pale! Who else? What, Paris too?
And steeped in blood? Ah, what an unkind hour          150
Is guilty of this lamentable chance!
The lady stirs.

JULIET
O comfortable friar, where is my lord?
I do remember well where I should be,
And there I am. Where is my Romeo?                     155

FRIAR LAWRENCE
I hear some noise.—Lady, come from that nest
Of death, contagion, and unnatural sleep.
A greater power than we can contradict
Hath thwarted our intents. Come, come away.
Thy husband in thy bosom there lies dead,              160
And Paris, too. Come, I'll dispose of thee
Among a sisterhood of holy nuns.
Stay not to question, for the watch is coming.
Come, go, good Juliet. I dare no longer stay.

JULIET
Go, get thee hence, for I will not away.               165
                                        *He exits.*
What's here? A cup closed in my true love's hand?
Poison, I see, hath been his timeless end.—
O churl, drunk all, and left no friendly drop
To help me after! I will kiss thy lips.
Haply some poison yet doth hang on them,               170
To make me die with a restorative. ⌜*She kisses him.*⌝
Thy lips are warm!

            *Enter* ⌜*Paris's Page*⌝ *and Watch.*

⌜FIRST⌝ WATCH   Lead, boy. Which way?

JULIET
Yea, noise? Then I'll be brief. O, happy dagger,
This is thy sheath. There rust, and let me die.        175
      ⌜*She takes Romeo's dagger, stabs herself, and dies.*⌝

179. **attach:** arrest
185. **ground:** earth; **woes:** i.e., the corpses
186. **ground:** cause; **woes:** sorrows
187. **circumstance:** details; **descry:** discover
190. **in safety:** i.e., securely
194. **great:** i.e., cause for **great**
196. **our person:** The Prince uses the royal "we."

⌜PAGE⌝
  This is the place, there where the torch doth burn.

⌜FIRST⌝ WATCH
  The ground is bloody.—Search about the
    churchyard.
  Go, some of you; whoe'er you find, attach.
                       ⌜*Some watchmen exit.*⌝
  Pitiful sight! Here lies the County slain,          180
  And Juliet bleeding, warm, and newly dead,
  Who here hath lain this two days burièd.—
  Go, tell the Prince. Run to the Capulets.
  Raise up the Montagues. Some others search.
                         ⌜*Others exit.*⌝
  We see the ground whereon these woes do lie,    185
  But the true ground of all these piteous woes
  We cannot without circumstance descry.

   *Enter* ⌜*Watchmen with*⌝ *Romeo's man* ⌜*Balthasar.*⌝

⌜SECOND⌝ WATCH
  Here's Romeo's man. We found him in the
    churchyard.

⌜FIRST⌝ WATCH
  Hold him in safety till the Prince come hither.    190

   *Enter Friar* ⌜*Lawrence*⌝ *and another Watchman.*

THIRD WATCH
  Here is a friar that trembles, sighs, and weeps.
  We took this mattock and this spade from him
  As he was coming from this churchyard's side.

⌜FIRST⌝ WATCH
  A great suspicion. Stay the Friar too.

   *Enter the Prince* ⌜*with Attendants.*⌝

PRINCE
  What misadventure is so early up          195
  That calls our person from our morning rest?

201. **startles:** i.e., sounds startlingly
205. **know:** learn
211. **mista'en:** mistaken (its proper place); **his house:** its sheath
215. **warns:** summons

*Enter ⌜Capulet and Lady Capulet.⌝*

CAPULET
  What should it be that is so ⌜shrieked⌝ abroad?
LADY CAPULET
  O, the people in the street cry "Romeo,"
  Some "Juliet," and some "Paris," and all run
  With open outcry toward our monument.                    200
PRINCE
  What fear is this which startles in ⌜our⌝ ears?
⌜FIRST⌝ WATCH
  Sovereign, here lies the County Paris slain,
  And Romeo dead, and Juliet, dead before,
  Warm and new killed.
PRINCE
  Search, seek, and know how this foul murder           205
    comes.
⌜FIRST⌝ WATCH
  Here is a friar, and ⌜slaughtered⌝ Romeo's man,
  With instruments upon them fit to open
  These dead men's tombs.
CAPULET
  O heavens! O wife, look how our daughter bleeds!   210
  This dagger hath mista'en, for, lo, his house
  Is empty on the back of Montague,
  And it mis-sheathèd in my daughter's bosom.
LADY CAPULET
  O me, this sight of death is as a bell
  That warns my old age to a sepulcher.                    215

*Enter Montague.*

PRINCE
  Come, Montague, for thou art early up
  To see thy son and heir now ⌜early⌝ down.
MONTAGUE
  Alas, my liege, my wife is dead tonight.

223. **press:** hurry, thrust yourself forward

224. **outrage:** outcry

226. **spring:** source; **head:** fountainhead, source

230. **let . . . patience:** i.e., **let** calmness master your misfortunes

231. **parties of suspicion:** i.e., suspicious **parties**

232. **greatest:** i.e., most suspicious

234. **make:** i.e., provide evidence

235–36. **impeach . . . excused:** i.e., accuse **myself** of that for which I should be condemned and clear **myself** of that of which I should be found innocent

238. **date of breath:** lifetime

242. **stol'n:** secret

247. **perforce:** under compulsion

249. **mean:** means

Grief of my son's exile hath stopped her breath.
What further woe conspires against mine age?     220
PRINCE  Look, and thou shalt see.
MONTAGUE, ⌜*seeing Romeo dead*⌝
O thou untaught! What manners is in this,
To press before thy father to a grave?
PRINCE
Seal up the mouth of outrage for awhile,
Till we can clear these ambiguities     225
And know their spring, their head, their true
   descent,
And then will I be general of your woes
And lead you even to death. Meantime forbear,
And let mischance be slave to patience.—     230
Bring forth the parties of suspicion.
FRIAR LAWRENCE
I am the greatest, able to do least,
Yet most suspected, as the time and place
Doth make against me, of this direful murder.
And here I stand, both to impeach and purge     235
Myself condemnèd and myself excused.
PRINCE
Then say at once what thou dost know in this.
FRIAR LAWRENCE
I will be brief, for my short date of breath
Is not so long as is a tedious tale.
Romeo, there dead, was husband to that Juliet,     240
And she, there dead, ⌜that⌝ Romeo's faithful wife.
I married them, and their stol'n marriage day
Was Tybalt's doomsday, whose untimely death
Banished the new-made bridegroom from this city,
For whom, and not for Tybalt, Juliet pined.     245
You, to remove that siege of grief from her,
Betrothed and would have married her perforce
To County Paris. Then comes she to me,
And with wild looks bid me devise some mean

252. **art:** i.e., skill in medicine
256. **as this:** i.e., **this**
262. **prefixèd:** predetermined
264. **closely:** secretly
272. **desperate:** in despair
275. **is privy:** knows the secret
277. **some . . . time:** i.e., an **hour** or so **before** its **time** (to end)
279. **still:** always
282. **in post:** in haste

To rid her from this second marriage,                                   250
Or in my cell there would she kill herself.
Then gave I her (so tutored by my art)
A sleeping potion, which so took effect
As I intended, for it wrought on her
The form of death. Meantime I writ to Romeo          255
That he should hither come as this dire night
To help to take her from her borrowed grave,
Being the time the potion's force should cease.
But he which bore my letter, Friar John,
Was stayed by accident, and yesternight                     260
Returned my letter back. Then all alone
At the prefixèd hour of her waking
Came I to take her from her kindred's vault,
Meaning to keep her closely at my cell
Till I conveniently could send to Romeo.                      265
But when I came, some minute ere the time
Of her awakening, here untimely lay
The noble Paris and true Romeo dead.
She wakes, and I entreated her come forth
And bear this work of heaven with patience.              270
But then a noise did scare me from the tomb,
And she, too desperate, would not go with me
But, as it seems, did violence on herself.
All this I know, and to the marriage
Her nurse is privy. And if aught in this                          275
Miscarried by my fault, let my old life
Be sacrificed some hour before his time
Unto the rigor of severest law.

PRINCE
We still have known thee for a holy man.—
Where's Romeo's man? What can he say to this?        280

BALTHASAR
I brought my master news of Juliet's death,
And then in post he came from Mantua
To this same place, to this same monument.

284. **he . . . father:** i.e., **he** instructed **me** to **give his father early** this morning

285. **going:** i.e., as he was **going**

288. **that raised:** i.e., who alerted

290. **what made your master:** i.e., **what** was **your master** doing

299. **therewithal:** i.e., with the poison

303. **your joys:** i.e., your children

304. **winking at:** closing my eyes to

307. **jointure:** the present given the bride by the groom's family

310. **ray:** i.e., array, dress (**Ray** is the reading of the Second Quarto; the alternative and more familiar reading, "raise," is found in the Fourth Quarto and the Folio. But Montague is evidently promising to gold-plate the figure of Juliet that would customarily lie on top of her tomb or sarcophagus. Compare the "gilded monuments" of Shakespeare's Sonnet 55.)

311. **whiles:** as long as

312. **figure:** statue; **at . . . set:** be valued as greatly

Handshake of reconciliation. (5.3.306)
From John Bulwer, *Chirologia . . .* (1644).

This letter he early bid me give his father
And threatened me with death, going in the vault,　285
If I departed not and left him there.

PRINCE
Give me the letter. I will look on it.—
⌈*He takes Romeo's letter.*⌉
Where is the County's page, that raised the
watch?—
Sirrah, what made your master in this place?　290

PAGE
He came with flowers to strew his lady's grave
And bid me stand aloof, and so I did.
Anon comes one with light to ope the tomb,
And by and by my master drew on him,
And then I ran away to call the watch.　295

PRINCE
This letter doth make good the Friar's words,
Their course of love, the tidings of her death;
And here he writes that he did buy a poison
Of a poor 'pothecary, and therewithal
Came to this vault to die and lie with Juliet.　300
Where be these enemies?—Capulet, Montague,
Sec what a scourge is laid upon your hate,
That heaven finds means to kill your joys with love,
And I, for winking at your discords too,
Have lost a brace of kinsmen. All are punished.　305

CAPULET
O brother Montague, give me thy hand.
This is my daughter's jointure, for no more
Can I demand.

MONTAGUE　　　But I can give thee more,
For I will ray her statue in pure gold,　310
That whiles Verona by that name is known,
There shall no figure at such rate be set
As that of true and faithful Juliet.

314. **Romeo's:** i.e., **Romeo's** statue

CAPULET
  As rich shall Romeo's by his lady's lie,
  Poor sacrifices of our enmity.                   315
PRINCE
  A glooming peace this morning with it brings.
  The sun for sorrow will not show his head.
  Go hence to have more talk of these sad things.
  Some shall be pardoned, and some punishèd.
  For never was a story of more woe           320
  Than this of Juliet and her Romeo.

                        ⌈*All exit.*⌉

# Longer Notes

2.2.44–45. **O . . . man:** Here our edition departs from long-standing editorial tradition in following the Second Quarto, as is our practice whenever possible throughout this edition. The Second Quarto version of these lines contains the metrically defective line "Belonging to a man," which has only three metrical feet (x / | x x | x /), rather than the five usually found in Shakespeare's blank verse. The editorial tradition since Edmond Malone in 1790 has regarded such a metrically defective line as unacceptable and has followed him in resorting to the First Quarto in order to fill out the line. At this point the First Quarto reads

> Whats *Mountague*? It is nor hand nor foote,
> Nor arme, nor face, nor any other part.
> Whats in a name? That which we call a Rose,
> By any other name would smell as sweet:

Malone picked up the words "nor any other part" from the First Quarto, reversed the phrases "belonging to a man" and "O, be some other name," and inserted the First Quarto phrase after "Nor arm nor face." He thus created a passage that made sense and that contained no metrically defective line. Since Malone, editors have generally printed in their editions a combination of the First Quarto and the Second:

> What's Montague? It is nor hand nor foot,
> Nor arm nor face, nor any other part
> Belonging to a man. O, be some other name!
> What's in a name? That which we call a rose
> By any other word would smell as sweet.

Because this editorial reconstruction of the text seems excessively intrusive, because the Second Quarto seems to make good sense as it stands, and because the present scene is not without metrically defective lines in the middle of speeches (e.g., 2.2.11), we have followed the Second Quarto reading of the lines. (See page lix.)

**2.2.179. My dear:** Here the Second Quarto has Romeo call Juliet "My Neece," words that are unintelligible in this context and that editors must emend. No one has found an alternative that has been widely persuasive among editors. In printing "My dear," we follow the Fourth Quarto of 1623. Among other proposed readings are "Madame" from the First Quarto, "My sweete" from the Second Folio of 1632, "My novice," "My—," (followed by the interpolation of a speech prefix for the Nurse, who is then made to deliver from "within" or offstage the line "Madam"), and "My niesse" (an obsolete form of the word *nyas*, which means "young hawk." Editors who follow this emendation note that Juliet has called Romeo a **tassel-gentle** or male falcon at line 170.)

**2.3.1–4. The gray-eyed . . . wheels:** As recorded in the Textual Notes, in the Second Quarto these same four lines (with slight variations) are also given to Romeo just after 2.2.203. The Second Quarto also prints duplicate versions of parts of speeches elsewhere. (See 3.3.41–46 and 5.3.102 and 108 in the Textual Notes.) Under the influence of the belief that many plays, including *Romeo and Juliet* as it appears in the Second Quarto, were printed directly from Shakespeare's own working papers (usually termed "foul papers"; see "The Publication of Shakespeare's Plays," pages xlix–lii), many modern editors have assumed that these duplications were created by Shakespeare himself during his composition of the play and inadvertently left standing by him. However, more recent research has called attention to the presence of duplicate versions of speeches in playhouse manuscripts, with the duplications written in other hands than those of dramatists, and sometimes with the duplications left standing without any marks of deletion. Thus, as editors, we are now aware that such duplications may arise in various ways.

3.2.23. **when I shall die:** Many earlier editors adopted the Fourth Quarto's reading "hee" for the Second Quarto's **I** that is printed in this edition. However, recent editors and critics have shown that the Second Quarto's reading is altogether possible by interpreting the passage and its place in the play in terms of that reading. They interpret the passage both as Juliet's fantasy of sharing sexual climax with Romeo (according to the early modern use of **die** to refer to achievement of such climax) and as Juliet's premonition of their shared death. Such editors and critics have also understood Juliet's extravagant characterization of the living Romeo's starlike beauty in this passage to be parallel to his representation of her beauty in analogous terms at 2.2.15–23, where he speaks of the living Juliet's eyes in the heavens as stars.

# Textual Notes

The reading of the present text appears to the left of the square bracket. The earliest sources of readings not in **Q2,** the quarto of 1599 (upon which this edition is based, except for 1.2.55–1.3.37, which are based on the 1597 quarto), are indicated as follows: **Q1** is the quarto of 1597; **Q3** is that of 1609; **Q4** is that of 1623; and **F** is the Shakespeare First Folio of 1623, in which *Romeo and Juliet* is a slightly edited reprint of Q3. **Ed.** is an earlier editor of Shakespeare, from the editor of the Second Folio of 1632 to the present. No sources are given for emendations of punctuation or for correction of obvious typographical errors, such as turned letters that produce no known word. **SD** means stage direction; **SP** means speech prefix; **uncorr.** means the uncorrected, or first state in Q2; **corr.** means the corrected, or second state in Q2; ~ refers to a word already quoted; ∧ indicates the omission of a punctuation mark.

**1.1.** 28. in] Q1; *omit* Q2 33. SD *Enter . . . Servingman.*] this ed.; *Enter two other seruing men.* Q2 74. SP CITIZENS] Ed.; *Offi.* Q2 77. SP LADY CAPULET] Ed.; *Wife.* Q2 78. SD *2 lines later in* Q2 82. SP LADY MONTAGUE] Ed.; M. *Wife.* 2. Q2 94. Verona's] *Neronas* Q2 118. SP LADY MONTAGUE] Ed.; *Wife* Q2 122. drove] Q3 (draue); driue Q2 123. sycamore] Syramour Q2 150. his] Q3; is Q2 182. create] Q1; created Q2 184. wellseeming] Q4; welseeing Q2 223. rich in beauty] ~, ~~ Q2 226. makes] Q4; make Q2

**1.2.** 0. SD *a Servingman*] Ed.; *the Clowne* Q2 21. guest ∧] ~: Q2 23. welcome,] ~ ∧ Q2 32. on] Q2 (one) 38. SD *Capulet . . . exit.*] Ed.; *Exit.* Q2 39–40.

written here] ~.~ Q2   48. One] Q2 (On)   71. *Vitruvio*]
Ed.; Vtruuio Q1, Q2   75. *and*] Q1; *omit* Q2   84. thee]
Q1; you Q2

**1.3.**   0. SD *Lady Capulet*] Ed.; *Capulets wife* Q1, Q2
1, 8, 13, 17. SP LADY CAPULET] Ed.; *Wife.* Q1, Q2   1.
daughter?] ~ʌ Q1   12. an] Q2; a Q1   19. shall] Q1; stal
Q2   34. the] Q2; *omit* Q1   54, 68, 75, 83, 85, 102. SP
LADY CAPULET] Ed.; *Old La.* Q2   70 disposition] Ed.; dis-
positions Q2   71, 72. honor] Q1; houre Q2   77. mothers. . . . count ʌ] ~ ʌ . . . ~. Q2   101. bigger.] ~ ʌ Q2
105. it] Q1; *omit* Q2   105. SD *Servingman*] F; *Seruing.*
Q2   111. SP LADY CAPULET] Ed.; *Mo.* Q2

**1.4.**   7–8. Q1; *omit* Q2   23. SP MERCUTIO] Q4; *Hora-
tio* Q2   39. done] Q1; dum Q2   42. your] F; you Q2
47. lights; . . . light] Ed.; ~ ʌ . . . lights Q2   48. judg-
ment] indgement Q2   49. five 2] Ed.; fine Q2   62.
atomi] Q1; ottamie Q2   71. maid] Q1; man Q2   76.
love;] ~. Q2   79. on] Q2 (one)   81. breaths] Q1
(breathes); breath Q2   86. he dreams] *stet* Q2   95. elf-
locks] Q1; Elklocks Q2   118. forfeit] fofreit Q2   120.
sail] Q1; sute Q2

**1.5.**   0. SD *napkins*] F; *Napkins.* | *Enter* Romeo. Q2
1, 7, 13. SP FIRST SERVINGMAN] Ed.; *Ser.* Q2   4. SP SEC-
OND SERVINGMAN] Ed.; 1. Q2   12. SP THIRD SERVINGMAN]
Ed.; 2. Q2   15. SP THIRD SERVINGMAN] Ed.; 3. Q2   17.
SD *They . . . aside.*] this ed.; *Exeunt.* Q2   18, 40, 46.
SP CAPULET] Q1; 1. *Capu.* Q2   19. a bout] Ed.; about
Q2   21. mistresses] mistesses Q2   29. gentlemen.] ~ ʌ
Q2   39, 44. SP CAPULET'S COUSIN] Ed.; 2. *Capu.* Q2   41.
Lucentio] Q1; *Lucientio* Q2   95. you.] ~ ʌ Q2   106. pil-
grims, ready] Q1; Pylgrims did readie Q2   156. this?]
this. Q2 *uncorr.* (tis.); tis ʌ Q2 *corr.*

**2. Chor.**   4. matched] Q3; match Q2

**2.1.**   8. SP MERCUTIO] Q1; *omit* Q2   9. Romeo] Q1;
*Mer. Romeo* Q2   11. one] Q2 (on)   12. pronounce]
Q1; prouaunt Q2   13. "dove"] Q1; day Q2   15. heir]

Q1; her Q2    16. Abraham ∧ Cupid,] ~:~ ∧ Q2; trim] Q1;
true Q2    36. SP MERCUTIO] Q3; *Mar.* Q2    41. open-arse]
Ed.; open, or Q2    46. SD *They exit.*] Q4; *Exit.* Q2

**2.2.**    16. do] Q1; to Q2    46. name? That] ~ ∧ ~ Q2
48. were] Q3; wene Q2    70. kinsmen] kismen Q2    88.
washed] Q1; washeth Q2    97. false. . . . perjuries,]~
∧ . . . ~. Q2    104. havior] Q1; behauior Q2    106.
more] Q1; *omit* Q2    115. circled] Q1; circle Q2    155.
lord] Q1; L. Q2    159–60. Madam . . . come] Ed.; (by
and by I come) Madam. Q2    173. mine] Q1; *omit* Q2
179. dear] Q4; Neece Q2    202. SP ROMEO] Q1; *Iu.* Q2
203. Would] Q4; *Ro.* Would Q2    203. rest.] Q1; rest |
The grey eyde morne smiles on the frowning night, |
Checkring the Easterne Clouds with streaks of light, |
And darknesse fleckted like a drunkard reeles, | From
forth daies pathway, made by *Tytans* wheeles. Q2.

**2.3.**    1 *and throughout until* 5.2. SP FRIAR LAWRENCE]
Ed.; *Fri.* Q2    2. Check'ring] Q2 2.2.203 (above); Check-
ing Q2 2.3.2    4. fiery] Q1; burning Q2    13. many ∧ vir-
tues] ~, ~ Q2    55. wounded. Both ∧] ~ ∧ ~, Q2    71.
Young] yonng Q2    91. now ∧] ~. Q2

**2.4.**    0. SD *Enter*] *Bnter* Q2    7. kinsman] kisman Q2
19. SP BENVOLIO] Q1; *Ro.* Q2    30. phantasimes] Ed.;
phantacies Q2    34–35. "pardon-me"'s] Q1; pardons
mees Q2    41. Petrarch] Petrach Q2    103. SD *one-half
line later in* Q2    165. quivers.] ~, Q2    212. Ah,] A ∧ Q2
212. dog's name. *R*] Q3; dog, name *R.* Q2    213. the—
No] ~ ∧ ~ Q2    219. SD *They exit.*] Q1 *(Ex. omnes.);*
*Exit.* Q2

**2.5.**    7. Love] F; loue Q2    11. three] Q3; there Q2    15.
And] Q4; *M.* And Q2    41. he.]~ ∧ Q2    59. and] Q2 (An)

**2.6.**    27. music's] Q4; musicke Q2

**3.1.**    2. are] Q1; *omit* Q2    70. thou] thon Q2    91.
SD *Romeo . . . Mercutio.*] this ed.; *omit* Q2; *Tibalt vnder
Romeos arme thrusts Mercutio, in and flyes.* Q1    92.
SP PETRUCHIO] Ed.; *omit* Q2, *which sets this speech as*

*a* SD   113. soundly, too. Your] Ed.; soundly ∧ to ∧
your Q2   113. SD *All . . . exit.*] Ed.; *Exit.* Q2   122. gal-
lant] gallanr Q2   127. Alive] Q1; He gan Q2   129: fire-
eyed] Q1; fier end Q2   144, 147. SP CITIZEN] Ed.; *Citti.*
*(Citi.* 147) Q2   145. murderer] mutherer Q2   153,
156. kinsman] kisman Q2   154, 185. SP LADY CAPULET]
Ed.; *Capu. Wi. (Ca. Wi.* 185) Q2   163. displeasure.] ~
∧ Q2   175. agile] Q1; aged Q2   185. kinsman] kisman
Q2   193. SP MONTAGUE] Q4; *Capu.* Q2   202. I] Q1; It
Q2   207. SD *They . . . body.*] this ed.; *Exit.* Q2

**3.2.**   1. SP JULIET] Q1; *omit* Q2   9. By] Q4; And by
Q2   33. SD *one-half line later in* Q2   48. it?] ~ ∧ Q2
53. death-darting] death arting Q2   55. shut] Ed.; shot
Q2   57. Brief ∧ sounds ∧] ~, ~, Q2   57. determine my]
Q2 *stet;* determine of my F   66. one] Q2 (on)   78. SP
NURSE] Q1; *omit* Q2   79. SP JULIET] Q1; *Nur.* Q2   80.
Did] Ed.; *Iu.* Did Q2   82. Dove-feathered] Ed.; Raue-
nous douefeatherd Q2   85. damnèd] Q4; dimme Q2
157. SD *They exit.*] Q1; *Exit.* Q2

**3.3.**   0. SD *Enter . . . Lawrence.*] Ed.; *Enter Frier
and* Romeo. Q2   20. is banished] Q3; is blanisht Q2
41–46. sin . . . Hadst] Ed.; sin. | This may flyes do, when
I from this must flie, | And sayest thou yet, that exile
is not death? | But *Romeo* may not, he is banished. |
Flies may do this, but I from this must flie: | They are
freemen, but I am banished. | Hadst Q2   53. absolver]
Q2 (obsoluer)   55. Thou] Q1; Then Q2   64. madmen]
Q1; mad man Q2   71. Then mightst] Q1; then might-
est Q2   74. SD *Knock within.*] Ed.; *Enter Nurse, and
knocke.* Q2   77. SD *Knock.*] Q4; *They knocke.* Q2   80.
SD *Knock.*] F; *Slud knock.* Q2   85. SP NURSE, *within*]
Ed.; *Enter Nurse. | Nur.* Q2   120. denote] Q1; deuote
Q2   127. lives] Ed.; lies Q2   146–47. dead: . . . happy.]
~ . . . . ~, Q2   153. misbehaved] Q1; mishaued Q2   154.
pouts upon] Q4; puts vp Q2   175. comfort] eomfort Q2
179. disguised] Q3; disguise Q2

**3.4.** 11. SP LADY CAPULET] Ed.; *La.* Q2    14. be] Q1;
me Q2    26. We'll∧] Q1; Well, Q2

**3.5.** 13. exhaled] Ed.; exhale Q2    19. the] the
the Q2    31. changed] Ed.; change Q2    36. SD *Enter
Nurse.*] Ed.; *Enter Madame and Nurse.* Q2    54. SP
JULIET] Q1; *Ro.* Q2    55. thee, now∧] ~∧~, Q2    64. SD
*Enter Lady Capulet.*] Ed.; *Enter Mother.* Q2    65, 69, 71,
78, 82, 85, 89, 92, 144, 163. SP LADY CAPULET] Ed.; *La.*
Q2    87. pardon] Q3; padon O2    87. him] Q4; *omit* Q2
99. him—dead—] ~. ~∧ Q2    108, 214. SP LADY CAPU-
LET] Ed.; *Mo.* Q2    112, 117, 129. SP LADY CAPULET] Ed.;
*M.* Q2    135. show'ring? . . . body∧] ~∧ . . . ~? Q2    136.
counterfeits∧] ~. Q2    144. gives] Q3; giue Q2    156.
proud? . . . you,] ~∧ . . . ~? Q2    166, 178, 183, 187. SP CAP-
ULET] Ed.; *Fa.* Q2    179. Prudence, smatter∧]~∧~, Q2
181. SP CAPULET O] Q1; Father, ô Q2    182. SP NURSE]
Q4; *omit* Q2    186. SP LADY CAPULET] Ed.; *Wi.* Q2    192.
ligned] Ed.; liand Q2    246. absolved] Q2 (obsolu'd)

**4.1.** 73. slay] Q1; stay Q2    79. off] Q2 (of)    84.
chapless] Q1; chapels Q2    86. shroud] Q4; *omit* Q2
100. breath] Q1; breast Q2    101. fade∧] ~: Q2    102.
paly] Q4; many Q2    102. fall ∧] ~: Q2    112. In] Q3; Is
Q2    112–13. bier | Thou] Ed.; Beere, | Be borne to buri-
all in thy kindreds graue: | Thou Q2    113. shalt] Q3;
shall O2    117. and] Q2 (an)    118. waking] Q3; walking Q2    123. fear] Q2 *uncorr.* (feare); fea re Q2 *corr.*
129. SD *They . . . directions.*] this ed.; *Exit.* Q2

**4.2.** 3, 6. SP SERVINGMAN] Ed.; *Ser.* Q2    14. self-
willed harlotry] Q3; selfewield harlottry Q2 *uncorr.;*
selfewieldhar lottry Q2 *corr.*    27. becomèd] Q4;
becomd Q2    37, 39. SP LADY CAPULET] Ed.; *Mo.* Q2    38,
41. SP CAPULET] Ed.; *Fa* Q2    38. SD *Juliet . . . exit.*] Q1;
*Exeunt.* Q2    49. SD *They exit.*] Q1; *Exit.* Q2

**4.3.** 5. SD *Lady Capulet*] Ed.; *Mother* Q2    6, 13.
SP LADY CAPULET] Ed.; *Mo.* Q2    14. SD *Lady . . . exit.*]
Ed.; *Exeunt.* Q2    50. wake] Q4; walke Q2    60. SD

*She . . . curtains.*] this ed.; *omit* Q2; *She fals vpon her bed within the Curtaines.* Q1

**4.4.** 0. SD *Lady Capulet*] Ed.; *Lady of the house* Q2 1, 12. SP LADY CAPULET] Ed.; *La.* Q2 13. SD *Lady Capulet*] Ed.; *Lady* Q2 14. SD *one-half line later in* Q2 17. SP FIRST SERVINGMAN] Ed.; *Fel.* Q2 18. haste.] ~ ∧ Q2 21. SP SECOND SERVINGMAN] Ed.; *Fel.* Q2 24. Thou] Q1; Twou Q2 25. faith] Q4; father Q2 26. SD *Play music.*] *1 line earlier in* Q2

**4.5.** 20, 22, 24, 29, 36, 49. SP LADY CAPULET] Ed.; *Mo.* (once *M.*) Q2 26. SD *Capulet*] Ed.; *Father* Q2 27, 30, 37, 40, 65, 90. SP CAPULET] Ed.; *Fa.* (once *Fat.*) Q2 43. deflowerèd] Ed.; deflowred Q2 46. all.] ~ ∧ Q2 47. long] Q1; loue Q2 57. behold] Q3; bedold Q2 71. cure] Ed.; care Q2 72. confusions.] ~ ∧ Q2 88. fond] Ed.; some Q2 101. SD *All . . . exit.*] Ed.; *Fxeunt manet.* Q2 102. SP FIRST MUSICIAN] Ed.; *Musi.* Q2 105. SP FIRST MUSICIAN] Ed.; *Fid.* Q2 105. by] Q1; my Q2 105. SD *Nurse exits.*] Q1 (*1 line earlier*); *Exit omnes.* Q2 105. SD *Peter*] Q4; *Will Kemp* Q2 109. SP FIRST MUSICIAN] Ed.; *Fidler.* Q2 113. SP FIRST MUSICIAN] Ed.; *Minstrels.* Q2 116, 118, 126, 137. SP FIRST MUSICIAN] Ed.; *Minst.* Q2 121. SP FIRST MUSICIAN] Ed.; *Minstrel.* Q2 127, 140. SP SECOND MUSICIAN] Ed.; *2. M.* Q2 129. SP PETER] Q4; *omit* Q2 129. wit. I] Q4; wit. | *Peter* I Q2 133. *And . . . oppress*] Q1; *omit* Q2 143. SP THIRD MUSICIAN] Ed.; *3. M.* Q2 149. SP FIRST MUSICIAN] Ed.; *Min.* Q2 150. SP SECOND MUSICIAN] Ed.; *M. 2.* Q2 151. SD *They exit.*] Q1; *Exit.* Q2

**5.1.** 3. lord] Q1; *L.* Q2 12. SD *Balthasar in riding boots*] this ed.; *Balthasar his man booted* Q1; *omit* Q2 16. Juliet] Q1; Lady *Iuliet* Q2 18, 28, 34. SP BALTHASAR] Q1; *Man.* Q2 25. e'en] Q2 (in) 36. SD *Exit., 2 lines earlier in* Q2 62. SP ROMEO] *Kom.* Q2 70, 79, 81. SP APOTHECARY] Q1; *Poti.* Q2 80. pay] Q1; pray Q2 91. SD *He exits.*] Ed.; *Exeunt.* Q2

**5.2.** 0. SD Q2 *adds "to Frier* Lawrence" 1, 5, 14, 23. SP FRIAR JOHN] Ed.; *Ioh.* (twice *Iohn.*) Q2 2, 13, 17, 24. SP FRIAR LAWRENCE] Ed.; *Law.* Q2

**5.3.** 3, 141. yew] Q1 (Ew, 3); young Q2 17. SD *Page whistles.*] Ed.; *Whistle Boy.* Q2 21. SD *Balthasar*] Q1; *Peter* Q2 25. light.] ~ ʌ Q2 40, 43. SP BALTHASAR] Q1 *(Balt.); Peter* Q2 41. friendship] Q3; friendshid Q2 45. SD *beginning to force open the tomb*] Ed.; *Romeo opens the tombe.* Q1; *omit* Q2 68. commination] Ed.; commiration Q2 70. SD *They draw and fight.*] *They fight.* Q1; *omit* Q2 71. SP PAGE] Ed.; *Boy* Q1; *omit* Q2, *which sets this speech as a stage direction* 102. Shall ] Ed.; I will beleeue | Shall Q2 107. palace] Q3; pallat Q2 107. night ʌ] ~. Q2 108. Depart again. Here] Q4; Depart againe, come lye thou in my arme, | Heer's to thy health, where ere thou tumblest in. | O true Appothecarie! | Thy drugs are quicke. Thus with a kisse I die. | Depart againe, here Q2 120. SD *Enter*] Q3; *Entrer* Q2 121 *and throughout* SP FRIAR LAWRENCE] Ed.; *Frier.* Q2 123, 128, 131, 133, 135, 141. SP BALTHASAR] Q4; *Man.* Q2 156. noise.] ~ ʌ Q2 165. SD *He exits.*] *1 line earlier in* Q2 172. SD *Paris' Page*] Ed.; *Boy* Q2 173, 177, 202, 207. SP FIRST WATCH] Ed.; *Watch* Q2 176. SP PAGE] Ed.; *Watch boy* Q2 188. SP SECOND] Ed.; *omit* Q2 190, 194. SP FIRST] Ed.; *Chief.* Q2 194. too] too too. Q2 196. SD *Capulet and Lady Capulet*] Ed.; *Capels* Q2 197. shrieked] Ed.; shrike Q2 198, 214. SP LADY CAPULET] Ed.; *Wife.* Q2 201. our] Ed.; your Q2 207. slaughtered] Q3; Slaughter Q2 209. tombs.] Tombes. *Enter Capulet and his wife.* Q2 213. mis-sheathèd] misssheathd Q2 217. early] Q1; earling Q2 235. impeach] Q2 *uncorr.;* i peach Q2 *corr.* 241. that] Q1; thats Q2 283. place, . . . monument.] ~. . . . ~ ʌ Q2 291. SP PAGE] F; *Boy* Q2 302. hate,]~? Q2

# *Romeo and Juliet:*
# A Modern Perspective

## Gail Kern Paster

Does *Romeo and Juliet* need an introduction? Of all Shakespeare's plays, it has been the most continuously popular since its first performance in the mid-1590s. It would seem, then, the most direct of Shakespeare's plays in its emotional impact. What could be easier to understand and what could be more moving than the story of two adolescents finding in their sudden love for each other a reason to defy their families' mutual hatred by marrying secretly? The tragic outcome of their blameless love (their "misadventured piteous overthrows") seems equally easy to understand: it results first from Tybalt's hotheaded refusal to obey the Prince's command and second from accidents of timing beyond any human ability to foresee or control. Simple in its story line, clear in its affirmation of the power of love over hate, *Romeo and Juliet* seems to provide both a timeless theme and universal appeal. Its immediacy stands in welcome contrast to the distance, even estrangement, evoked by other Shakespeare plays. No wonder it is often the first Shakespeare play taught in schools—on the grounds of its obvious relevance to the emotional and social concerns of young people.

Recent work by social historians on the history of private life in western European culture, however, offers a complicating perspective on the timelessness of *Romeo and Juliet.* At the core of the play's evident accessibility is the importance and privilege modern Western culture grants to desire, regarding it as

257

deeply expressive of individual identity and central to the personal fulfillment of women no less than men. But, as these historians have argued, such conceptions of desire reflect cultural changes in human consciousness—in ways of imagining and articulating the nature of desire.[1] In England until the late sixteenth century, individual identity had been imagined not so much as the result of autonomous, personal growth in consciousness but rather as a function of social station, an individual's place in a network of social and kinship structures. Furthermore, traditional culture distinguished sharply between the nature of identity for men and women. A woman's identity was conceived almost exclusively in relation to male authority and marital status. She was less an autonomous, desiring self than any male was; she was a daughter, wife, or widow expected to be chaste, silent, and, above all, obedient. It is a profound and necessary act of historical imagination, then, to recognize innovation in the moment when Juliet impatiently invokes the coming of night and the husband she has disobediently married: "Come, gentle night; come, loving black-browed night, / Give me my Romeo" (3.2.21–23).

Recognizing that the nature of desire and identity is subject to historical change and cultural innovation can provide the basis for rereading *Romeo and Juliet*. Instead of an uncomplicated, if lyrically beautiful, contest between young love and "ancient grudge," the play becomes a narrative that expresses an historical conflict between old forms of identity and new modes of desire, between authority and freedom, between parental will and romantic individualism. Furthermore, though the Chorus initially sets the lovers *as a pair* against the background of familial hatred, the reader attentive to social detail will be struck instead by Shakespeare's care in distinguishing between the circumstances of male and female lovers: "she as much in love, *her means much less* / To meet her new belovèd anywhere" (2. Chorus. 11–12, italics added). The story of "Juliet and her Romeo" may be a single narrative, but its clear internal division is drawn along the traditionally unequal lines of gender.

Because of such traditional notions of identity and gender, Elizabethan theatergoers might have recognized a paradox in the play's lyrical celebration of the beauty of awakened sexual desire in the adolescent boy and girl. By causing us to identify with Romeo and Juliet's desire for one another, the play affirms their love even while presenting it as a problem in social management. This is true not because Romeo and Juliet fall in love with forbidden or otherwise unavailable sexual partners; such is the usual state of affairs at the beginning of Shakespearean comedy, but those comedies end happily. Rather Romeo and Juliet's love is a social problem, unresolvable except by their deaths, because they dare to *marry* secretly in an age when legal, consummated marriage was irreversible. Secret marriage is the narrative device by which Shakespeare brings into conflict the new privilege claimed by individual desire and the traditional authority granted fathers to arrange their daughters' marriages. Secret marriage is the testing ground, in other words, of the new kind of importance being claimed by individual desire. Shakespeare's representation of the narrative outcome of this desire as tragic—here, as later in the secret marriage that opens *Othello*—may suggest something of Elizabethan society's anxiety about the social cost of romantic individualism.

The conflict between traditional authority and individual desire also provides the framework for Shakespeare's presentation of the Capulet-Montague feud. The feud, like the lovers' secret marriage, is another problem in social management, another form of socially problematic desire. We are never told what the families are fighting about or fighting for; in this sense the feud is both causeless and goal-less. The Chorus's first words insist not on the differences between the two families but on their similarity: they are two households "both alike in dignity." Later, after Prince Escalus has broken up the street brawl, they are "In penalty alike" (1.2.2). Ironically, then, they are not fighting over differences. Rather it is Shakespeare's careful insistence on the lack of difference between Montague and Capulet that provides a key to understanding the underlying social dynamic of the feud. Just as desire brings Romeo and Juliet together as lovers, desire in another form brings the Montague and Capulet males out on the street as fighters. The feud perpetuates a close bond of rivalry between these men that even the Prince's threat of punishment cannot sever: "Montague is *bound* as well as I," Capulet tells Paris (1.2.1). Indeed, the feud seems necessary to the structure of male-male relations in Verona. Feuding reinforces male identity—loyalty to one's male ancestors—at the same time that it clarifies the social structure: servants fight with servants, young noblemen with young noblemen, old men with old men.[2]

That the feud constitutes a relation of desire between Montague and Capulet is clear from the opening, when the servants Gregory and Sampson use bawdy innuendo to draw a causal link between their virility and their eagerness to fight Montagues: "A dog of that house shall move me to stand," i.e., to be sexually erect (1.1.12). The Montagues seem essential to Sampson's masculinity since, by besting Montague men, he can lay claim to Montague women as symbols of conquest. (This, of course, would be a reductive way of describing what Romeo does in secretly marrying a Capulet daughter.) The feud not only establishes a structure of relations between men based on competition and sexual aggression, but it seems to involve a particularly debased attitude toward women. No matter how comic the wordplay of the Capulet servants may be, we should not forget that the sexual triangle they imagine is based on fantasized rape: "I will push Montague's men from the wall and thrust his maids to the wall" (1.1.18–19). Gregory and Sampson are not interested in the "heads" of the Montague maidens, which might imply awareness of them as individuals. They are interested only in their "maidenheads." Their coarse view of woman as generic sexual object is reiterated in a wittier vein by Mercutio, who understands Romeo's experience of awakened desire only as a question of the sexual availability of his mistress: "O Romeo, that she were, O, that she were / An open-arse, thou a pop'rin pear" (2.1.40–41).

Feuding, then, is the form that male bonding takes in Verona, a bonding which seems linked to the derogation of woman. But Romeo, from the very opening of the play, is distanced both physically and emotionally from the feud, not appearing until the combatants and his parents are leaving the stage. His reaction to Benvolio's news of the fight seems to indicate that he is aware of the mechanisms of desire that are present in the feud: "Here's much to do with hate, but more with love" (1.1.180). But it also underscores his sense of alienation: "This love feel I, that feel no love in this" (187). He is alienated not only from the feud itself, one feels, but more importantly from the idea of sexuality that underlies it. Romeo subscribes to a different, indeed a competing view of woman—the idealizing view of the Petrarchan lover. In his melancholy, his desire for solitude, and his paradox-strewn language, Romeo identifies himself with the style of feeling and address that Renaissance culture named after the fourteenth-century Italian poet Francesco Petrarca or Petrarch, most famous for his sonnets to Laura. By identifying his beloved as perfect and perfectly chaste, the Petrarchan lover opposes the indiscriminate erotic appetite of a Gregory or Sampson. He uses the frustrating experience of intense, unfulfilled, and usually unrequited passion to refine his modes of feeling and to enlarge his experience of self.

It is not coincidental, then, that Shakespeare uses the language and self-involved behaviors of the Petrarchan lover to dramatize Romeo's experience of love. For Romeo as for Petrarch, love is the formation of an individualistic identity at odds with other kinds of identity: "I have lost myself. I am not here. / This is not Romeo. He's some other where" (1.1.205–6). Petrarchan desire for solitude explains Romeo's absence from the opening clash and his lack of interest in the activities of his gang of friends, whom he accompanies only reluctantly to the Capulet feast: "I'll be a candle holder and look on" (1.4.38). His physical isolation from his parents—with whom he exchanges no words in the course of the play—further suggests his shift from traditional, clan identity to the romantic individualism prefigured by Petrarch.

Shakespeare's comic irony is that such enlargement of self is itself a mark of conventionality, since Petrarchism in European literature was by the late sixteenth century very widespread. A more cutting irony is that the Petrarchan lover and his sensual opponent (Sampson or Gregory) have more in common than is first apparent. The Petrarchan lover, in emphasizing the often paralyzing intensity of his passion, is less interested in praising the remote mistress who inspires such devotion than he is in displaying his own poetic virtuosity and his capacity for self-denial. Such a love—like

Romeo's for Rosaline—is founded upon frustration and requires rejection. The lover is interested in affirming the uniqueness of his beloved only in theory. On closer look, she too becomes a generic object and he more interested in self-display. Thus the play's two languages of heterosexual desire—Petrarchan praise and anti-Petrarchan debasement—appear as opposite ends of a single continuum, as complementary discourses of woman, high and low. Even when Paris and old Capulet, discussing Juliet as prospective bride, vary the discourse to include a conception of woman as wife and mother, she remains an object of verbal and actual exchange.

In lyric poetry, the Petrarchan mistress remains a function of language alone, unheard, seen only as a collection of ideal parts, a center whose very absence promotes desire. Drama is a material medium, however. In drama, the Petrarchan mistress takes on embodiment and finds an answering voice, like Juliet's gently noting her sonneteer-pilgrim's conventionality: "You kiss by th' book" (1.5.122). In drama, the mistress may come surrounded by relatives and an inconveniently insistent social milieu. As was noted above, Shakespeare distinguishes sharply between the social circumstances of adolescent males and females. Thus one consequence of setting the play's domestic action solely within the Capulet household is to set Juliet, the "hopeful lady" of Capulet's "earth" (1.2.15), firmly into a familial context which, thanks to the Nurse's fondness for recollection and anecdote, is rich in domestic detail. Juliet's intense focus upon Romeo's surname—"What's Montague? . . . O, be some other name" (2.2.43, 44)—is a projection onto her lover of her own conflicted sense of tribal loyalty. Unlike Romeo, whose deepest emotional ties are to his gang of friends, and unlike the more mobile daughters of Shakespearean comedy who often come in pairs, Juliet lives isolated and confined, emotionally as well as physically, by her status as daughter. Her own passage into sexual maturity comes first by way of parental invitation to "think of marriage now" (1.3.75). Her father invites Paris, the man who wishes to marry Juliet, to attend a banquet and feast his eyes on female beauty: "Hear all, all see, / And like her most whose merit most shall be" (1.2.30–31). Juliet, in contrast, is invited to look only where her parents tell her:

I'll look to like, if looking liking move.
But no more deep will I endart mine eye
Than your consent gives strength to make it fly.
(1.3.103–5)

The logic of Juliet's almost instant disobedience in looking at, and liking, Romeo (rather than Paris) can be understood as the ironic fulfillment of the fears in traditional patriarchal culture about the uncontrollability of female desire, the alleged tendency of the female gaze to wander. Petrarchism managed the vexed question of female desire largely by wishing it out of existence, describing the mistress as one who, like the invisible Rosaline of this play, "will not stay the siege of loving terms, / Nor bide th' encounter of assailing eyes" (1.1.220–21). Once Romeo, in the Capulet garden, overhears Juliet's expression of desire, however, Juliet abandons the conventional denial of desire— "Fain would I dwell on form; fain, fain deny / What I have spoke. But farewell compliment" (2.2.93–94). She rejects the "strength" implied by parental sanction and the protection afforded by the Petrarchan celebration of chastity for a risk-taking experiment in desire that Shakespeare affirms by the beauty of the lovers' language in their four scenes together. Juliet herself asks Romeo the serious questions that Elizabethan society wanted only fathers to ask. She challenges social prescriptions, designed to contain erotic desire in marriage, by taking responsibility for her own marriage:

> If that thy bent of love be honorable,
> Thy purpose marriage, send me word tomorrow,
> By one that I'll procure to come to thee,
> Where and what time thou wilt perform the rite,
> And all my fortunes at thy foot I'll lay
> And follow thee my lord throughout the world.
>
> (2.2.150–55)

The irony in her pledge—an irony perhaps most obvious to a modern, sexually egalitarian audience—is that Romeo here is following Juliet on an uncharted narrative path to sexual fulfillment in unsanctioned marriage. Allowing her husband access to a bedchamber in her father's house, Juliet leads him into a sexual territory beyond the reach of dramatic representation. Breaking through the narrow oppositions of the play's two discourses of woman—as either anonymous sexual object (for Sampson and Gregory) or beloved woman exalted beyond knowing or possessing (for Petrarch)—she affirms her imaginative commitment to the cultural significance of desire as an individualizing force:

> Come, civil night,
> Thou sober-suited matron all in black,
> And learn me how to lose a winning match
> Played for a pair of stainless maidenhoods.
> Hood my unmanned blood, bating in my cheeks,
> With thy black mantle till strange love grow bold,
> Think true love acted simple modesty.
>
> (3.2.10–16)

Romeo, when he is not drawn by desire deeper and deeper into Capulet territory, wanders into the open square where the destinies of the play's other young men—and in part his own too—are enacted. Because the young man's deepest loyalty is to his friends, Romeo is not really asked to choose between Juliet and his family but between Juliet and Mercutio, who are opposed in the play's thematic structure. Thus one function of Mercutio's anti-Petrarchan skepticism about the idealization of woman is to offer resistance to the adult heterosexuality heralded by Romeo's union with Juliet, resistance on behalf of the regressive pull of adolescent male bonding—being "one of the guys." This distinction, as we have seen, is in part a question of speaking different discourses. Romeo easily picks up Mercutio's banter, even its sly innuendo against women. Mercutio himself regards Romeo's quickness at repartee as the hopeful sign of a return to a "normal" manly identity incompatible with his ridiculous role as lover:

Why, is not this better now than groaning for love? Now art thou sociable, now art thou Romeo, now art thou what thou art, by art as well as by nature. For this driveling love is like a great natural that runs lolling up and down to hide his bauble in a hole.

(2.4.90–95)

Implicit here is a central tenet of traditional misogyny that excessive desire for a woman is effeminizing. For Mercutio it is the effeminate lover in Romeo who refuses shamefully to answer Tybalt's challenge: "O calm, dishonorable, vile submission!" he exclaims furiously (3.1.74). Mercutio's death at Tybalt's hands causes Romeo temporarily to agree, obeying the regressive emotional pull of grief and guilt over his own part in Mercutio's defeat. "Why the devil came you between us?" Mercutio asks. "I was hurt under your arm" (3.1.106–8). Why, we might ask instead, should Mercutio have insisted on answering a challenge addressed only to Romeo? Romeo, however, displaces blame onto Juliet: "Thy beauty hath made me effeminate / And in my temper softened valor's steel" (3.1.119–20).

In terms of narrative structure, the death of Mercutio and Romeo's slaying of Tybalt interrupt the lovers' progress from secret marriage to its consummation, suggesting the incompatibility between romantic individualism and adolescent male bonding. The audience experiences this incompatibility as a sudden movement from comedy to tragedy. Suddenly Friar Lawrence must abandon hopes of using the love of Capulet and Montague as a force for social reintegration. Instead, he must desperately stave off Juliet's marriage to Paris, upon which her father insists, by making her counterfeit death and by subjecting her to entombment. The legal finality of consummated marriage—which was the basis for Friar Lawrence's hopes "to turn your households' rancor to pure love" (2.3.99)—becomes the instrument of tragic design. It is only the Nurse who would allow Juliet to accept Paris as husband; we are asked to judge such a prospect so unthinkable that we then agree imaginatively to Friar Lawrence's ghoulish device.

In terms of the play's symbolic vocabulary, Juliet's preparations to imitate death on the very bed where her sexual maturation from girl- to womanhood occurred confirms ironically her earlier premonition about Romeo: "If he be marrièd, / My grave is like to be my wedding bed" (1.5.148–49). Her brief journey contrasts sharply with those of Shakespeare's comic heroines who move out from the social confinement of daughterhood into a freer, less socially defined space (the woods outside Athens in *A Midsummer Night's Dream*, the Forest of Arden in *As You Like It*). There they can exercise a sanctioned, limited freedom in the romantic experimentation of courtship. Juliet is punished for such experimentation in part because hers is more radical; secret marriage symbolically is as irreversible as "real" death. Her journey thus becomes an internal journey in which her commitment to union with Romeo must face the imaginative challenge of complete, claustrophobic isolation and finally death in the Capulet tomb.

It is possible to see the lovers' story, as some critics have done, as Shakespeare's dramatic realization of the ruling metaphors of Petrarchan love poetry—particularly its fascination with "death-marked love" (Prologue. 9).[3] But, in pondering the implications of Shakespeare's moving his audience to identify with this narrative of initiative, desire, and power, we also do well to remember the psychosocial dynamics of drama. By heightening their powers of identification, drama gives the members of an audience an embodied image of the possible scope and form of their fears and desires. Here we have seen how tragic form operates to contain the complex play of desire/identification. The metaphors of Petrarchan idealization work as part of a complex, ambivalent discourse of woman whose ultimate social function is to encode the felt differences between men and women on which a dominant male power structure is based. Romeo and Juliet find a new discourse of romantic individualism in which Petrarchan idealization conjoins with the mutual avowal of sexual desire. But their union, as we have seen, imperils the traditional relations between males that is founded upon the exchange of women, whether the violent exchange Gregory and Sampson crudely imagine or the normative exchange planned by Capulet and Paris. Juliet, as the daughter whose erotic willfulness activates her father's transformation from concerned to tyrannical parent, is the greater rebel. Thus the secret marriage in which this new language of feeling is contained cannot here be granted the sanction of a comic outcome. When Romeo and Juliet reunite, it is only to see each other, dead, in the dim confines of the Capulet crypt. In this play the autonomy of romantic individualism remains "star-crossed."

1. The story of these massive shifts in European sensibility is told in a five-volume study titled *A History of Private Life*, gen. eds. Philippe Ariès and Georges Duby (Cambridge, Mass.: Harvard University Press, 1987–91). The study covers over three millennia in the history of western Europe. For the period most relevant to *Romeo and Juliet*, see vol. 3, *Passions of the Renaissance* (1989), ed. Roger Chartier, trans. Arthur Goldhammer, pp. 399–607.

2. The best extended discussion of the dynamic of the feud is Coppélia Kahn, *Man's Estate: Masculine Identity in Shakespeare* (Berkeley: University of California Press, 1981), pp. 83ff.

3. Nicholas Brooke, *Shakespeare's Early Tragedies* (London: Methuen, 1968), pp. 82ff.

# Further Reading

## *Romeo and Juliet*

Appelbaum, Robert. " 'Standing to the Wall': The Pressures of Masculinity in *Romeo and Juliet*." *Shakespeare Quarterly* 48 (1997): 251–72.

    Appelbaum discusses the "dilemma of masculinity" dramatized in Shakespeare's juxtaposition of the sovereign masculine ethos of Prince Escalus and the citizens of Verona on the one hand and the "varied, unresolved, and inadequate masculinities" of the play's father figures, sons, and sonlike servants on the other. The opening "masculinist patter" of Gregory and Sampson focuses the male subject's struggle between aggressively stirring toward masculinity and "already standing there in possession of [it]." Against the "recurring spectacle of masculine aggression," Shakespeare offers a pair of alternatives: the civil peace associated with the unchallenged authority and decrees of Prince Escalus and the civil regime of heterosexual love that Romeo and Juliet pursue. But as the drama develops, neither civil peace nor civil love supplies any genuine alternative to the masculinity "of destructive aggression . . . and . . . homosocial domination." In an effort to avoid the "pathologizing of masculinity" prevalent in current gender studies, Appelbaum reads the play's ineffectual fathers and self-destructive sons "as *failing subjects*, [who] . . . may be seen as taking part inadequately, in the perpetuation of an inadequate world": "The fathers cannot enforce their own laws; the sons can neither enforce those laws on behalf of their fathers nor discover adequate forms of self-assertion." *Romeo and*

*Juliet*'s "regime of masculinity is constituted as a system from which there is no escape, but in keeping with which there is no experience of masculine satisfaction either." As played out by Romeo, however, the romantic tragedy may "seduce us into thinking that there is both one and the other."

Boose, Lynda E. "The Father and the Bride in Shakespeare." *PMLA* 97 (1982): 325–47.

Observing that twenty-one of Shakespeare's plays and one of his narrative poems (*Lucrece*) depict the father-daughter relation, Boose focuses on its representation in the wedding ceremony. Following the analysis of this rite of passage provided by the anthropologist Arnold van Gennep, Boose divides the wedding ceremony into three phases: separation of the daughter from her father and family, transition, and reincorporation through the formation of a new family when the marriage is consummated. According to Boose's application of her wedding model to the individual Shakespeare works, *Romeo and Juliet*, with its secret wedding that excludes Juliet's father, circumvents the ritual that should release her from her father's control. Rather than proceeding through the sequence of the three phases of the rite of passage, the play presents in 3.4 the separation phase in which Capulet gives his daughter to Paris as coinciding with the reincorporation phase of 3.5 in which Romeo and Juliet consummate their marriage. The dark threat to Romeo and Juliet is dramatized by Capulet's subsequent invasion of Juliet's bridal chamber to dissolve her marriage to Romeo by informing her of her upcoming wedding with Paris. The rest of the play, on Boose's analysis, progresses through inverted and disordered rituals: the conversion to "black funeral" (4.5.91) of the festivities intended for Juliet's wedding; the Capulets' discovery that their "daughter bleeds" (5.3.210) not because of consummation of marriage but because she is newly dead in their family tomb; and Montague's and Capulet's promises richly to adorn the tombs of each other's children as if they were settling dowry and jointure negotiations prior to the solemnization of a marriage.

Brooke, Nicholas. "*Romeo and Juliet.*" In *Shakespeare's Early Tragedies*, pp. 80–106. London: Methuen, 1968.

For Brooke, *Romeo and Juliet* may be associated with the love sonnet as a "tragedy of romance, or of love," with "its romance theme, its persistently lyrical tone, and the accentuated formality of its structure and language." Until Mercutio's death in 3.1, which Brooke styles prosaic in the sense of accidental, irrelevant, and ridiculous, the tone of the play is predominantly comic (despite some intimations of the tragedy to follow), but it then changes in key to the more serious, the decisively tragic. Brooke proceeds through the play, commenting on individual scenes to capture the tone of each. For example, the opening scene begins with the "lumpish prose" of "dolts" and rises to the "crescendo" of "fully heroic verse" in the Prince's speech, before descending to "lightness" when Romeo offers to be witty about love. The Nurse's speeches set the tone for 1.3—"earthy, sentimental, warm-blooded, bawdy, repetitious"—as do Mercutio's in 1.4: "cynical and reductive of any degree of romantic pretension." In 1.5 "the opening movement of the play is recapitulated in a rapid development from bustling prose to lusty verse to the full dance and Romeo and Juliet encountering in a full-blown sonnet." In 2.1 Mercutio offers a parody of what we will witness in 2.2, but in that scene only "Romeo is . . . fair game for Mercutio's mockery," for Juliet's grandly erotic language—"My bounty is as boundless as the sea" (2.2.140)—eludes it. In 2.4 and

2.5 the comic sense is fully restored. After the turn to tragedy in 3.1, Juliet's speech opening 3.2, spoken in ignorance of Tybalt's death and Romeo's banishment, provides "a magnificently full-bodied evocation of sexual desire," and a sense of what might have been, were the lovers now not so evidently "death-marked." In Act 4 when the Capulets bewail the mock-death of Juliet, and Peter calls for a merry dump from the musicians, there is mirth in tragedy, just as there was the hint of tragedy in the play's early comic action. In the last act, the deaths of Romeo and Juliet are not "very real," but are "far more obviously the beautiful consummation of the unfulfilled love." Thus the play explores the love-death tradition of the sonnet and the superiority and inferiority of this tradition to the world of common day.

Charlton, H. B. "Experiment and Interregnum: *Romeo and Juliet, King John, Julius Caesar.*" In *Shakespearian Tragedy*, pp. 49–82. Cambridge: Cambridge University Press, 1948.

With *Romeo and Juliet*, according to Charlton, Shakespeare moves away from the well-established Renaissance practice of drawing upon history for the plots of tragedies as he did in *Titus Andronicus, Richard II*, and *Richard III*. Instead, Shakespeare takes the story of Romeo and Juliet from contemporary fiction, Arthur Brooke's *The Tragicall Historie of Romeus and Juliet* (1562). To achieve "the inevitability of tragedy," Shakespeare resuscitates "the half-barbarian, half-Roman deities of Fate and Fortune." The feud is the means by which Fate acts. The dialogue, for which Shakespeare follows suggestions in Brooke, repeatedly invokes Fortune. However, for Charlton, *Romeo and Juliet* fails as "all-compelling tragedy" because the feud lacks the required intensity, especially in the first two acts. The elder Capulet and Montague are ridiculous figures in their attempts to fight each other, and are easily subdued to peaceableness by the Prince—so much so that Capulet suppresses Tybalt's efforts to attack Romeo at the Capulets' party in 1.5. For Charlton, the success of the play lies not in its tragic structure, but in the particular local beauties of its poetry and in Shakespeare's invention of Mercutio and development of the figure of the Nurse.

Gurr, Andrew. "Intertextuality at Windsor." *Shakespeare Quarterly* 38 (1987): 189–200.

Between May 1594 and 1600, according to Gurr, there were only two companies, the Lord Chamberlain's and the Lord Admiral's, competing for the attention of London playgoers. This led the two companies to become deeply imitative of one another. *Romeo and Juliet* was a Lord Chamberlain's play, and its recorded popularity with students at the Inns of Court, London's law schools, makes it a likely candidate for competitive imitation by the Lord Admiral's. In Gurr's estimation, William Haughton's *Englishmen for my Money*, written for the Lord Admiral's, imitates *Romeo and Juliet*'s depiction of a daughter disobeying her parents and marrying for love, putting on stage three daughters trying to escape marriages arranged by their father. More specifically, Haughton gestures toward Shakespeare's play by having each of the three daughters appear above talking to her lover below, as in 2.2 of *Romeo and Juliet*. A second play that Gurr relates to *Romeo and Juliet* is Henry Porter's *The Two Angry Women of Abington* with its story of a pair of lovers divided from each other by the mutual enmity of their mothers, and with its own version of *Romeo and Juliet*'s 2.2. As Gurr notes, however, the relation of Porter's play to the Lord Admiral's Men and to *Romeo and Juliet* is far from certain. Although Porter is associated with the Lord Admiral's in the late 1590s, *The Two Angry Women* may date from a much earlier time and, whatever company staged it, may have influenced Shakespeare rather than the reverse.

Holmer, Joan Ozark. " 'Draw, if you be men': Saviolo's Significance for *Romeo and Juliet*." *Shakespeare Quarterly* 45 (1994): 163–89.

In *Vincentio Saviolo his Practise*, a fencing manual published in 1595, Holmer finds both a *terminus a quo* for *Romeo and Juliet* and an important new source for understanding the tragic complexity of the play's fatal duels. *Romeo and Juliet* is distinguished by the highest frequency of Italian fencing terms in the Shakespeare canon and is especially indebted to Saviolo's manual, the only one of its kind in the mid-1590s to present "the full corpus of Italian terms of rapier fence." In addition to fashionable Italian jargon (e.g., *passado, punto reverso, hay*, and *alla stoccata*), technical English terminology (e.g., puns on the musical and fencing terms "time," "distance," and "proportion" at 2.4.22), and duello language (e.g., "occasion," "cause," "injury," "field," and "satisfied"), Shakespeare borrowed Saviolo's code of the "truly honorable *duello*," characterized by right reason and the pursuit of truth and justice, to counterpoint the aggressive masculinity dominant in the fictive world of Verona and in Elizabethan culture at large. Holmer pays considerable attention to 3.1 in order to demonstrate how Saviolo illuminates the ethical issues and matrix of choices confronting the dueling Tybalt, Mercutio, and Romeo precisely at the point where the play turns from comedy to tragedy. In contrast to the prevailing sense of "the duello as a vengeful practice" mandated for personal injury, Saviolo's "godly definition" of the honorable duello casts

Romeo's initial refusal to duel with Tybalt "not as vile submission [Mercutio's view] but rather as courageous wisdom." Initially the least guilty of the three young duelists in the scene, Romeo soon becomes "trapped by the fury that fuels revenge as the vulgar motive for dueling."

Jackson, Russell. *Romeo and Juliet*. Shakespeare at Stratford Series. London: Arden Shakespeare, 2003.

In his examination of post–World War II Royal Shakespeare Company productions of *Romeo and Juliet*, Jackson provides a comparative analysis of directorial decisions as they relate to three production choices: the creation of Verona as a setting, the depiction of the play's main characters (Romeo, Juliet, Friar Lawrence, Mercutio, and the Nurse), and the staging of the play's conclusion. The productions covered are those of Peter Brook (1947), Glen Byam Shaw (1954, 1958), Peter Hall (1961), Karolos Koun (1967), Terry Hands (1973, 1989), Trevor Nunn and Barry Kyle (1976), Ron Daniels (1980), John Caird (1984), Michael Bogdanov (1986), David Leveaux (1991), Adrian Noble (1995), Michael Attenborough (1997), and Michael Boyd (2000). These fifteen productions "constitute an intriguing commentary on the range of the text's possibilities, and at the same time reflect the changing aims and circumstances of the organizations that produced them." The introduction provides an overview of the productions to be discussed and documents the ways that audience expectations relating to *Romeo and Juliet* since the 1940s have changed: "Verona has become more of a living city and less of a Renaissance ideal, the bawdy humour has been given freer expression, and the lovers are now measured by the standards of modern young people rather than a poetic and artistic ideal."

Kahn, Coppélia. "Coming of Age: Marriage and Manhood in *Romeo and Juliet* and *The Taming of the Shrew.*"
In *Man's Estate: Masculine Identity in Shakespeare*, pp.
82–118. Berkeley: University of California Press, 1981.

For Kahn, *Romeo and Juliet* enacts a conflict
between differing conceptions of manhood: on the one
hand, manhood as "violence on behalf of the fathers,"
and, on the other hand, "manhood as separation from
the fathers and sexual union with women." The feud,
therefore, is a deadly rite of passage that "promotes
masculinity at the price of life." There is plentiful evidence in Sampson and Gregory's opening dialogue,
with its bawdy punning on sexual arousal and fighting,
to illustrate the play's association of masculine identity
with violence. Nonetheless, in the first two acts, Romeo
and Juliet re-create their identities in their mutual love
and seem thereby to find refuge from the feud. In 3.1,
though, the shame of having allowed Mercutio to fight
Tybalt and die at the Capulet's hands turns Romeo
against his new identity founded on love and back to
the pursuit of a masculinity of violence. Almost immediately Juliet discovers that she too cannot escape
patriarchal influence, when Capulet, who has suffered
shame in Tybalt's death because the old man could not
restrain his younger kinsman's pursuit of vengeance
against Romeo, decides to enforce his power over his
family by reversing his earlier judgment that Juliet is
yet too young to marry and to give her immediately to
Paris, over her objections. Consequently, Romeo and
Juliet "are consumed and destroyed by the feud," but
they also "rise above it, united in death."

Laslett, Peter. *The World We Have Lost—Further
Explored.* London: Methuen, 1983.

Laslett, a social historian, addresses Shakespeare's
striking departure from earlier versions of the Romeo

and Juliet story in making Juliet only thirteen at the time of her marriage and having Lady Capulet claim to have been a mother at Juliet's age. Proceeding from the conviction that Shakespeare's play is powerfully influential on our current understanding of the past, Laslett seeks to correct this understanding by reference to surviving parish records of age of marriage in Shakespeare's England. Such records establish that the average age for marriage then was in the twenties. Marriages of children as young as Juliet, which were highly exceptional, seem usually to have been effected by their parents as a means of maintaining control over property. Laslett also produces records of variation in the age of sexual maturation according to class, place, and time. He demonstrates that the age of puberty has dropped sharply during the twentieth century in today's first world countries, and more sharply among the privileged than in the working class, so that we are physically ready for marriage much earlier than were our ancestors. Rather than understanding Juliet as typical of women of her time in marrying at thirteen, we might instead appreciate that Shakespeare has transformed the marriageable young woman of earlier versions of the story into an unmarriageable child in his play.

Lawlor, John. "*Romeo and Juliet.*" In *Early Shakespeare*, edited by John Russell Brown and Bernard Harris, pp. 123–44. Stratford-upon-Avon Studies 3. London: Edward Arnold, 1961.

Lawlor resists Charlton's account of *Romeo and Juliet* as a failure as tragedy by approaching the play from the perspective of medieval tragedy. Chaucer's tragic poem *Troilus and Criseyde*, Lawlor observes, concludes not merely with the destruction of Troilus on Fortune's Wheel, but with his attainment of a new understanding. At the end of both Chaucer's great poem and Shakespeare's play "out of evil comes not good merely but a greater good. What we see in the close of *Romeo and Juliet* is not simply a renewal of a pattern disturbed, but its reordering; life is not continued merely; it is regenerated. . . . Death has no final power over the lovers of *Romeo and Juliet*. . . . It is earth, the realm of Fortune, that is the loser. . . . Love is placed, fittingly, at once beyond reach and beyond change." The greater good and the regeneration inhere in the love between Romeo and Juliet, "a new thing in the world of the play" that transcends Romeo's "own conventional passion for Rosaline," "Mercutio's lighthearted sensuality," the matchmaking father Capulet, the inconstant Nurse, the manipulative Friar, and the "simple and likeable suitor, Paris." "These two children [Romeo and Juliet], as the managing adults of their world see them, are, truly, innocents abroad. But they are quick to learn; in Romeo's attempted consolation of Juliet at their final leave-taking [3.5] we see the beginning of maturity in the man, while Juliet's improvised but spirited dissimulation of her true feelings (when reproved for grief by her mother) is evidence of her purpose, growing in its turn." *Romeo and Juliet* "offers a meeting-place of the old *tragedie* of ineluctable doom and a newer thing—the plain truth that man will not willingly relinquish his transitory happiness."

Liebler, Naomi Conn. "'There is no world without Verona walls': The City in *Romeo and Juliet*." In *A Companion to Shakespeare's Works*, edited by Richard Dutton and Jean E. Howard, 1:303–18. Malden, Mass.: Blackwell, 2003.

Liebler begins her study of *Romeo and Juliet* by noting how the play's hybrid nature as "half comedy, half tragedy" leads many critics to view it as a failure in both genres. It fails as tragedy if judged by Aristotle's criterion calling for "the representation of an action that is serious, complete, and of a certain magnitude"; and as comedy, if compared to its "more satisfying apotheosis" in *A Midsummer Night's Dream*. Emphasizing the play's urban focus, Liebler argues for it as tragedy, albeit a new, non-Aristotelian kind. Central to her reading is Verona's tragic ethos: a city defined by intramural tensions and devoid of any kind of cohesive community, Verona functions as the collective protagonist of the play. Performing "an indictment of . . . civic institutions and structures of authority . . . , [*Romeo and Juliet*] shift[s] the focus off the [the young lovers] who serve as the agents for that performance, and on to the collective city for which they stand. . . . Their micro-function dissolves into the macro-structure that contains them." A dying city by the play's end—its younger generation gone, its communal culpability foregrounded throughout, and its deadly competitive drive still strong in the rival statues that will lie side by side—Verona, "like a good tragic protagonist, commits suicide, kills itself by the failure of its own immune system, here figured in the weakened hierarchical structures of authority that cannot or will not look after their own collective best interests." The walls of Verona hold within them no hope for regeneration.

Novy, Marianne. "Violence, Love, and Gender in *Romeo and Juliet* and *Troilus and Cressida*." In *Love's Argument: Gender Relations in Shakespeare*, pp. 99–124. Chapel Hill: University of North Carolina Press, 1984.

For Novy, Romeo and Juliet establish a private world in which "both are active and gender is not polarized." However, beyond their private world masculinity is characterized by violence, femininity by weakness. This external world intrudes upon them when Romeo cannot escape entanglement in the blood feud and Juliet must continue living with her parents and conceal her marriage. Novy observes Romeo's language in his descriptions of his pursuit of Rosaline as an attack reinforced, he hopes, by Cupid with his arrows. Such masculine aggression is gone from his account to Friar Lawrence of his desire for Juliet, according to which as lovers they are mutually wounded. "Romeo understands the value of reciprocity in love. He wants its ritual—'Th' exchange of thy love's faithful vow for mine' [2.2.134]—and explains to Friar Lawrence, 'She whom I love now / Doth grace for grace and love for love allow' [2.3.91–92]." According to Novy, Romeo's decision to keep his marriage secret even from his friends Benvolio and Mercutio signals that his love for Juliet is "a challenge to associations of masculinity and sexuality with violence." However, Romeo is not able finally to transcend such associations himself when he fears, just before he kills Tybalt, that his love has made him effeminate. The Friar is no help to the lovers, because he can think of the feminine only in terms of weakness when he chastises Romeo's disabling grief for the killing of his wife's kinsman as "womanish" and when he counsels Juliet to pretend obedience and death rather than actively seeking to join Romeo. "The lovers cannot negotiate recognition by the outer world except by their deaths because of their residual commitment to the outer world and its gender ideals."

Porter, Henry. *The Two Angry Women of Abington: A Critical Edition.* Edited by Marianne Brish Evett. New York: Garland, 1980.

Porter presents us with a feud between families, the Barneses and Gourseys, in rural England. In this play it is the mothers, rather than the fathers as in *Romeo and Juliet*, who are at odds. Mistress Barnes suspects an illicit relationship between her husband and Mistress Goursey, and a visit to the Barneses by the Gourseys becomes the occasion for Mistress Barnes to antagonize Mistress Goursey. Mistress Barnes then quarrels with her son Philip as well and then with her daughter Mall, who is anxious to marry. Barnes seeks to marry Mall to Frank Goursey, partly in order to reconcile the two mothers. While Goursey quickly agrees to the match, both Mistress Barnes and Mistress Goursey seek to keep Mall and Frank apart. The latter part of the play is set at night when most of the characters, moving about without torches, engage in confused conversation as they fail to find those for whom they are searching. Their disorientation is the source of much broad comedy, as is the garrulousness of their servants, one of whom has the nickname "Proverbs." When the characters finally come together, Mistress Barnes admits that she has no grounds for her suspicions about her husband and Mistress Goursey, and Barnes vows his innocence to Goursey. Once the mothers are reconciled to each other, they endorse the marriage of Mall and Frank. Porter's play shares occasional language and a "balcony scene" with *Romeo and Juliet*, but uncertainty concerning the date of composition and performance of *Two Angry Women* makes it impossible to identify the direction in which influence may have flowed from one play to the other.

Porter, Joseph A., ed. *Critical Essays on Shakespeare's Romeo and Juliet*. New York: G. K. Hall; London: Prentice Hall International, 1997.

In addition to excerpts from Porter's *Shakespeare's Mercutio: His History and Drama* (1988) (see below), this anthology reprints the following essays: Clifford Leech, "The Moral Tragedy of *Romeo and Juliet*" (1976); Gayle Whittier, "The Sonnet's Body and the Body Sonnetized in *Romeo and Juliet*" (1989) (see below); Catherine Belsey, "The Name of the Rose in *Romeo and Juliet*" (1993); Jonathan Goldberg, "*Romeo and Juliet*'s Open Rs" (1994); Amy J. Riess and George Walton Williams, "'Tragical mirth': From *Romeo* to *Dream*" (1992); and E. Pearlman, "Shakespeare at Work: *Romeo and Juliet*" (1994). The volume includes one new essay, Donald W. Foster's "The Webbing of *Romeo and Juliet*," which uses electronic scholarship to probe the workings and habits of Shakespeare's mind. In his introduction, Porter notes how the collected essays address two "front-burner topic[s]" in Shakespeare studies: (1) Shakespeare's practice of composition, specifically his revisions, and his "witting or unwitting recycling of his own and others' words," and (2) sexuality and gender. The most striking feature of *Romeo and Juliet* commentary at the end of the twentieth century is the extensive attention paid to Mercutio.

Porter, Joseph A. *Shakespeare's Mercutio: His History and Drama*. Chapel Hill: University of North Carolina Press, 1988.

In an attempt to account for Mercutio's ability to discomfit readers across four centuries, Porter traces the history of Mercutio before Shakespeare, with Shakespeare, and after Shakespeare. Porter also examines Shakespeare's representation of the conflict between male friendship and love for a woman as it is played out in the Mercutio-Romeo-Rosaline triangle. From Mercutio's allegedly classical past as the Greek Hermes and the Roman Mercury, Porter finds Shakespeare carrying forward the god's role as it appears in both Homer's *Odyssey*, where Mercury intervenes to save Odysseus from Circe's spells, and Virgil's *Aeneid*, where Mercury orders Aeneas to abandon Dido and sail for Rome. In these epics Hermes/Mercury calls for the end to infatuation with the female, just as Mercutio does in mocking Romeo's love of Rosaline. Porter also notes how Renaissance texts feature Mercury as herald and patron of eloquence, functions readily associated with Mercutio's remarkable verbal facility in his puns, rhymes, and jokes. During the Queen Mab speech, Porter suggests, it is as if Mercutio has been possessed by his namesake god. Finally, Porter traces changes to Mercutio's role in early adaptations of Shakespeare's play by Thomas Otway, Theophilus Cibber, and David Garrick; in promptbooks for chiefly nineteenth-century productions; in other records of performance well into the twentieth century; and in film. While the role in the past was often bowdlerized, the stage, across history, has also had some success, in Porter's estimation, in finding its own ways to realize Shakespeare's marvelous creation.

Shakespeare, William. *The Most Excellent and Lamentable Tragedie of Romeo and Juliet*. Edited by George Walton Williams. Durham: Duke University Press, 1964.

Williams edits *Romeo and Juliet* according to the tenets of the New Bibliography, a school of editing and textual criticism that gained ascendancy in England and North America in the latter half of the twentieth century. Its editorial procedures were laid out by W. W. Greg in his "A Rationale of Copy Text," *Studies in Bibliography* 3 (1950–51): 19–36. Following Greg, Williams devotes his introduction to his determination of which of the early printings of the play—the First Quarto of 1597 or the Second of 1599—stands in closer relation to Shakespeare's own manuscript. Selecting the 1599 text as enjoying the closer relation and judging it, for the most part, to have been printed directly from such a manuscript, Williams prints that text (except for the passage in it evidently printed directly from the First Quarto) in its original or old spelling (hence the spelling *Tragedie* in the title of his edition). Whenever he emends the Second Quarto so as to change its meaning, he explicitly records the change in a textual note, often including in the note a discussion of the issues involved. His other changes to the Second Quarto—the ones not affecting meaning—he lists as Emendations of Accidentals. By referring to the Textual Notes and the Emendations of Accidentals a reader could reconstruct the text of the Second Quarto entirely from Williams's edition. He also prints a Historical Collation in which he documents the meaningful or substantive differences between his edited text and both the early printed texts and a great many important editions of the play published in the century before his edition. Williams adds to the New Bibliographical method of editing his own innovation when he includes extensive staging notes addressing issues and problems concerning performance.

Snyder, Susan. "Beyond Comedy: *Romeo and Juliet* and *Othello*." In *The Comic Matrix of Shakespeare's Tragedies*, pp. 56–90. Princeton: Princeton University Press, 1979.

Snyder's reading of genre in *Romeo and Juliet* has become the accepted understanding of how the play is structured generically. Up until Mercutio's death in Act 3, Snyder contends, *Romeo and Juliet* is essentially a comedy. Through the use of go-betweens and intrigue, the young couple find a way around the obstacles that separate them and manage to marry. Only Tybalt takes the feud really seriously and is therefore cut out of the range of expression of the other young men in the play with their "lyric love, witty fooling, friendly conversation." The characters are the gentry and servants of comedy, and among them violence and disaster are "unrealized threats." Mercutio functions as the clown of this romantic comedy as "the best of game-players, endlessly inventive and full of quick moves and countermoves." With his death, the play reverses its comic movement and heads toward tragedy. Suddenly, Romeo takes the feud as seriously as does Tybalt, and it becomes Romeo's "personal law" that determines the tragic necessity of his future: "he *must* kill Tybalt, he *must* run away, he is Fortune's fool." However, Shakespeare is writing one play, not two, a comedy followed by a tragedy. Just as there are intimations of tragedy in the otherwise comic first two acts, in the tragic concluding acts "there is one last hope for comedy. If the lovers will not adjust to the situation, perhaps the situation can be adjusted to the lovers." Friar Lawrence attempts the adjustment by counseling Romeo to accept his exile and wait till his return can be arranged, and then, as circumstances quickly change, persuades Juliet to pretend obedience and death until Romeo can take her from the tomb. Yet "the onrushing tragic action quite literally outstrips the slower steps of accommodation before our eyes." This process of becoming rather than simply being tragic makes *Romeo and Juliet* unique among Shakespeare's tragedies.

Stone, Lawrence. *The Family, Sex and Marriage in England 1500–1800*. New York: Harper and Row, 1977.
Stone's massive study sheds interesting light on *Romeo and Juliet*'s depiction of the feud and of the marriage of the title characters in a patriarchal society. According to Stone, in Shakespeare's period there was both great suspicion towards others and a proneness to violence such as is found in the play's feud. At the same time, the state, represented by the Prince in the play,

was on the rise, and it competed for allegiance with the kinship ties of the extended or open lineage family. Even within families, interpersonal relations were remote, partly because of the probability of imminent death from epidemic disease. Children were fostered out, as Juliet is to her nurse, and parental discipline was harsh, motivated by the alleged need to break the child's sinful will—as Juliet experiences at the hands of Capulet. However, according to Stone, the ideal of a "companionate" marriage increasingly surmounted the patriarchal model of marriage in the sixteenth and seventeenth centuries. In this period the early marriage of Romeo and Juliet, though, would have been highly unusual. Marriage then was generally postponed for ten or more years after puberty to provide time for the accumulation of capital and furniture for a separate residence, as custom dictated for a married couple.

Utterback, Raymond V. "The Death of Mercutio." *Shakespeare Quarterly* 24 (1973): 105–16.
  Reading Mercutio's death as a primary motivating force for the major subsequent events, Utterback contends that the circumstances attending the death establish a pattern that runs throughout the play. "This pattern comprises, first a prevailing situation containing threats, anxieties, dangers, and risks . . . the opposition of the rival houses [of Montague and Capulet] and the threat of violent and fatal conflict. . . . Second, a provocation occurs [in Tybalt's insults to Romeo in 3.1]. The third element . . . is a passionate response to the provocation: [Mercutio's challenge to and attack on Tybalt]. Fourth, a tragic consequences follows [Mercutio's and Tybalt's deaths]. Finally, the pattern concludes in a blurring of the sense of personal responsibility for the events by a shift of . . . attention to the impersonal elements of the situation," as in Romeo's reference to

himself as "Fortune's fool" (3.1.142) after he has killed Tybalt. According to Utterback, this pattern recurs in the events surrounding the deaths of Romeo and Juliet and in the actions of Friar Lawrence.

Whittier, Gayle. "The Sonnet's Body and the Body Sonnetized in *Romeo and Juliet.*" *Shakespeare Quarterly* 40 (1989): 27–41.

Whittier describes the Petrarchan convention as it appears in *Romeo and Juliet* as one "emptied of its traditional lyric treasures," despite the fact that Petrarch's influential sonnet form operates in the play even before it appears in the dialogue that Romeo and Juliet share in their first encounter (1.5). In the sonnet that functions as the Prologue, the lyrical emotion is supplanted by public narrative. The "Petrarchan word" has some power over Romeo at the beginning of the play when he is in love with Rosaline, whom he loves apparently only because he has heard love discussed. She appears in the play simply as a name, one that invokes the rose, "the ubiquitous symbol of feminine beauty." Romeo piles up Petrarchan oxymora in his praise of her and his descriptions of his love for her. Advertising Paris to Juliet as a mate, Lady Capulet also "speaks . . . a written poem"; hers is about "the book of love." However, when Romeo sees Juliet as hanging "upon the cheek of night / As a rich jewel in an Ethiop's ear" (1.5.52–53), Shakespeare departs from Petrarchan conventions in giving him an original figure of speech. Romeo continues to celebrate Juliet in 2.2 in language that exceeds that of his literary father Petrarch. "If tradition calls the lady's eyes celestial bodies, then Romeo removes the very sun from the sky: 'It is the East, and Juliet is the sun' [2.2.3]." For him, "she is the body of the cosmos." Thereafter the sonnet form operates more as a structuring feature than a verbal one. For example, when Juliet takes the potion, she incorporates the Petrarchan scheme of antithesis—"living death." According to Whittier, Shakespeare has transformed the conventions of Petrarchan poetry so that "lyric freedom" has declined to "tragic fact."

## Shakespeare's Language

Abbott, E. A. *A Shakespearian Grammar.* New York: Haskell House, 1972.
    This compact reference book, first published in 1870, helps with many difficulties in Shakespeare's language. It systematically accounts for a host of differences between Shakespeare's usage and sentence structure, and our own.

Blake, Norman. *Shakespeare's Language: An Introduction.* New York: St. Martin's Press, 1983.
    This general introduction to Elizabethan English discusses various aspects of the language of Shakespeare and his contemporaries, offering possible meanings for hundreds of ambiguous constructions.

Dobson, E. J. *English Pronunciation, 1500–1700.* 2 vols. Oxford: Clarendon Press, 1968.
    This long and technical work includes chapters on spelling (and its reformation), phonetics, stressed vowels, and consonants in early modern English.

Hope, Jonathan. *Shakespeare's Grammar.* London: Arden Shakespeare, 2003.
    Commissioned as a replacement for Abbott's *Shakespearian Grammar,* Hope's book is organized in terms of the two basic parts of speech, the noun and the verb. After extensive analysis of the noun phrase and the

verb phrase come briefer discussions of subjects and agents, objects, complements, and adverbials.

Houston, John. *Shakespearean Sentences: A Study in Style and Syntax*. Baton Rouge: Louisiana State University Press, 1988.

Houston studies Shakespeare's stylistic choices, considering matters such as sentence length and the relative positions of subject, verb, and direct object. Examining plays throughout the canon in a roughly chronological, developmental order, he analyzes how sentence structure is used in setting tone, in characterization, and for other dramatic purposes.

Onions, C. T. *A Shakespeare Glossary*. Oxford: Clarendon Press, 1986.

This revised edition updates Onions's standard, selective glossary of words and phrases in Shakespeare's plays that are now obsolete, archaic, or obscure.

Robinson, Randal. *Unlocking Shakespeare's Language: Help for the Teacher and Student*. Urbana, Ill.: National Council of Teachers of English and the ERIC Clearinghouse on Reading and Communication Skills, 1989.

Specifically designed for the high-school and undergraduate college teacher and student, Robinson's book addresses the problems that most often hinder present-day readers of Shakespeare. Through work with his own students, Robinson found that many readers today are particularly puzzled by such stylistic characteristics as subject-verb inversion, interrupted structures, and compression. He shows how our own colloquial language contains comparable structures, and thus helps students recognize such structures when they find them in Shakespeare's plays. This book supplies worksheets—with examples from major plays—to illuminate and remedy such problems as unusual sequences of words and the separation of related parts of sentences.

Williams, Gordon. *A Dictionary of Sexual Language and Imagery in Shakespearean and Stuart Literature.* 3 vols. London: Athlone Press, 1994.
    Williams provides a comprehensive list of words to which Shakespeare, his contemporaries, and later Stuart writers gave sexual meanings. He supports his identification of these meanings by extensive quotations.

# Shakespeare's Life

Baldwin, T. W. *William Shakspere's Petty School.* Urbana: University of Illinois Press, 1943.
    Baldwin here investigates the theory and practice of the petty school, the first level of education in Elizabethan England. He focuses on that educational system primarily as it is reflected in Shakespeare's art.

Baldwin, T. W. *William Shakspere's Small Latine and Lesse Greeke.* 2 vols. Urbana: University of Illinois Press, 1944.
    Baldwin attacks the view that Shakespeare was an uneducated genius—a view that had been dominant among Shakespeareans since the eighteenth century. Instead, Baldwin shows, the educational system of Shakespeare's time would have given the playwright a strong background in the classics, and there is much in the plays that shows how Shakespeare benefited from such an education.

Beier, A. L., and Roger Finlay, eds. *London 1500–1700: The Making of the Metropolis.* New York: Longman, 1986.

Focusing on the economic and social history of early modern London, these collected essays probe aspects of metropolitan life, including "Population and Disease," "Commerce and Manufacture," and "Society and Change."

Bentley, G. E. *Shakespeare's Life: A Biographical Handbook*. New Haven: Yale University Press, 1961.
This "just-the-facts" account presents the surviving documents of Shakespeare's life against an Elizabethan background.

Chambers, E. K. *William Shakespeare: A Study of Facts and Problems*. 2 vols. Oxford: Clarendon Press, 1930.
Analyzing in great detail the scant historical data, Chambers's complex, scholarly study considers the nature of the texts in which Shakespeare's work is preserved.

Cressy, David. *Education in Tudor and Stuart England*. London: Edward Arnold, 1975.
This volume collects sixteenth-, seventeenth-, and early-eighteenth-century documents detailing aspects of formal education in England, such as the curriculum, the control and organization of education, and the education of women.

Dutton, Richard. *William Shakespeare: A Literary Life*. New York: St. Martin's Press, 1989.
Not a biography in the traditional sense, Dutton's very readable work nevertheless "follows the contours of Shakespeare's life" as he examines Shakespeare's career as playwright and poet, with consideration of his patrons, theatrical associations, and audience.

Honan, Park. *Shakespeare: A Life*. New York: Oxford University Press, 1998.

Honan's accessible biography focuses on the various contexts of Shakespeare's life—physical, social, political, and cultural—to place the dramatist within a lucidly described world. The biography includes detailed examinations of, for example, Stratford schooling, theatrical politics of 1590s London, and the careers of Shakespeare's associates. The author draws on a wealth of established knowledge and on interesting new research into local records and documents; he also engages in speculation about, for example, the possibilities that Shakespeare was a tutor in a Catholic household in the north of England in the 1580s and that he played particular roles in his own plays, areas that reflect new, but unproven and debatable, data—though Honan is usually careful to note where a particular narrative "has not been capable of proof or disproof."

Schoenbaum, S. *William Shakespeare: A Compact Documentary Life.* New York: Oxford University Press, 1977.

This standard biography economically presents the essential documents from Shakespeare's time in an accessible narrative account of the playwright's life.

## Shakespeare's Theater

Bentley, G. E. *The Profession of Player in Shakespeare's Time, 1590–1642.* Princeton: Princeton University Press, 1984.

Bentley readably sets forth a wealth of evidence about performance in Shakespeare's time, with special attention to the relations between player and company, and the business of casting, managing, and touring.

Berry, Herbert. *Shakespeare's Playhouses*. New York: AMS Press, 1987.

Berry's six essays collected here discuss (with illustrations) varying aspects of the four playhouses in which Shakespeare had a financial stake: the Theatre in Shoreditch, the Blackfriars, and the first and second Globe.

Berry, Herbert, William Ingram, and Glynne Wickham, eds. *English Professional Theatre, 1530–1660*. Cambridge: Cambridge University Press, 2000.

Wickham presents the government documents designed to control professional players, their plays, and playing places. Ingram handles the professional actors, giving as representative a life of the actor Augustine Phillips, and discussing, among other topics, patrons, acting companies, costumes, props, playbooks, provincial playing, and child actors. Berry treats the twenty-three different London playhouses from 1560 to 1660 for which there are records, including four inns.

Cook, Ann Jennalie. *The Privileged Playgoers of Shakespeare's London*. Princeton: Princeton University Press, 1981.

Cook's work argues, on the basis of sociological, economic, and documentary evidence, that Shakespeare's audience—and the audience for English Renaissance drama generally—consisted mainly of the "privileged."

Greg, W. W. *Dramatic Documents from the Elizabethan Playhouses*. 2 vols. Oxford: Clarendon Press, 1931.

Greg itemizes and briefly describes almost all the play manuscripts that survive from the period 1590 to around 1660, including, among other things, players' parts. His second volume offers facsimiles of selected manuscripts.

Gurr, Andrew. *Playgoing in Shakespeare's London.* Cambridge: Cambridge University Press, 1987.
Gurr charts how the theatrical enterprise developed from its modest beginnings in the late 1560s to become a thriving institution in the 1600s. He argues that there were important changes over the period 1567–1644 in the playhouses, the audience, and the plays.

Harbage, Alfred. *Shakespeare's Audience.* New York: Columbia University Press, 1941.
Harbage investigates the fragmentary surviving evidence to interpret the size, composition, and behavior of Shakespeare's audience.

Hattaway, Michael. *Elizabethan Popular Theatre: Plays in Performance.* London: Routledge & Kegan Paul, 1982.
Beginning with a study of the popular drama of the late Elizabethan age—a description of the stages, performance conditions, and acting of the period—this volume concludes with an analysis of five well-known plays of the 1590s, one of them (*Titus Andronicus*) by Shakespeare.

Shapiro, Michael. *Children of the Revels: The Boy Companies of Shakespeare's Time and Their Plays.* New York: Columbia University Press, 1977.
Shapiro chronicles the history of the amateur and quasi-professional child companies that flourished in London at the end of Elizabeth's reign and the beginning of James's.

# The Publication of Shakespeare's Plays

Blayney, Peter W. M. *The First Folio of Shakespeare*. Hanover, Md.: Folger, 1991.

Blayney's accessible account of the printing and later life of the First Folio—an amply illustrated catalogue to a 1991 Folger Shakespeare Library exhibition—analyzes the mechanical production of the First Folio, describing how the Folio was made, by whom and for whom, how much it cost, and its ups and downs (or, rather, downs and ups) since its printing in 1623.

Hinman, Charlton. *The Norton Facsimile: The First Folio of Shakespeare*. 2nd ed. New York: W. W. Norton, 1996.

This facsimile presents a photographic reproduction of an "ideal" copy of the First Folio of Shakespeare; Hinman attempts to represent each page in its most fully corrected state. This second edition includes an important new introduction by Peter W. M. Blayney.

Hinman, Charlton. *The Printing and Proof-Reading of the First Folio of Shakespeare*. 2 vols. Oxford: Clarendon Press, 1963.

In the most arduous study of a single book ever undertaken, Hinman attempts to reconstruct how the Shakespeare First Folio of 1623 was set into type and run off the press, sheet by sheet. He also provides almost all the known variations in readings from copy to copy.

# Key to
# Famous Lines and Phrases

A pair of star-crossed lovers . . .       [*Chorus*—Pro. 6]

. . . sad hours seem long.      [*Romeo*—1.1.166]

Alas that love, so gentle in his view,
Should be so tyrannous and rough in proof!
     [*Benvolio*—1.1.174–75]

. . . I will make thee think thy swan a crow.
     [*Benvolio*—1.2.94]

. . . Queen Mab . . . She is the fairies' midwife . . .
     [*Mercutio*—1.4.58–59]

O, she doth teach the torches to burn bright!
It seems she hangs upon the cheek of night
As a rich jewel in an Ethiop's ear . . .
     [*Romeo*—1.5.51–53]

You kiss by th' book.      [*Juliet*—1.5.122]

My only love sprung from my only hate!
Too early seen unknown, and known too late!
     [*Juliet*—1.5.152–53]

He jests at scars that never felt a wound.
But soft, what light through yonder window breaks?
     [*Romeo*—2.2.1–2]

O Romeo, Romeo, wherefore art thou Romeo?
[*Juliet*—2.2.36]


That which we call a rose
By any other word would smell as sweet.
[*Juliet*—2.2.46–47]


O, swear not by the moon, th' inconstant moon,
That monthly changes in her circled orb,
Lest that thy love prove likewise variable.
[*Juliet*—2.2.114–16]


Love goes toward love as schoolboys from their books,
But love from love, toward school with heavy looks.
[*Romeo*—2.2.166–68]


How silver-sweet sound lovers' tongues by night,
Like softest music to attending ears.
[*Romeo*—2.2.176–77]


Good night, good night. Parting is such sweet sorrow
That I shall say "Good night" till it be morrow.
[*Juliet*—2.2.199–201]


Thy head is as full of quarrels as an egg is full of
meat . . . [*Mercutio*—3.1.23–24]


. . . 'tis not so deep as a well, nor so wide as a church
door, but 'tis enough. 'Twill serve.
[*Mercutio*—3.1.100–101]


A plague o' both your houses! [*Mercutio*—3.1.111]


Gallop apace, you fiery-footed steeds . . . [*Juliet*—3.2.1]

Wilt thou be gone? It is not yet near day.
It was the nightingale, and not the lark,
That pierced the fearful hollow of thine ear.
                              [*Juliet*—3.5.1–3]

Night's candles are burnt out, and jocund day
Stands tiptoe on the misty mountain-tops.
                              [*Romeo*—3.5.9–10]

Thank me no thankings, nor proud me no prouds . . .
                              [*Capulet*—3.5.157]

. . . past hope, past care, past help.     [*Juliet*—4.1.46]

Not stepping o'er the bounds of modesty.
                              [*Juliet*—4.2.28]

Death, that hath sucked the honey of thy breath,
Hath had no power yet upon thy beauty.
                              [*Romeo*—5.3.92–93]

. . . never was a story of more woe
Than this of Juliet and her Romeo.
                              [*Prince*—5.3.320–21]